THE KNIGHT
WHO SAVED
ENGLAND

PUBLISHING

THE
KNIGHT
WHO SAVED
ENGLAND

William Marshal and the
French Invasion, 1217

R I C H A R D   B R O O K S

First published in Great Britain in 2014 by Osprey Publishing,
PO Box 883, Oxford, OX1 9PL, UK
PO Box 3985, New York, NY 10185-3985, USA

E-mail: info@ospreypublishing.com

Osprey Publishing is part of the Osprey Group

A CIP catalogue record for this book is available from the British Library

Richard Brooks has asserted his right under the Copyright, Designs and Patents Act, 1988, to be identified as the Author of this Work.

Print ISBN: 978 1 84908 550 2
ePub ISBN: 978 1 4728 0836 3
Pdf ISBN: 978 1 4728 0835 6

Index by Zoe Ross
Typeset in Adobe Caslon Pro
Maps by Bounford.com
Originated by PDQ Media, Bungay, UK
Printed in China through Worldprint Ltd.
Front cover: A twelfth century replica helm with a faceplate. (© Board of the Trustees of the Armouries, object no. Di 2014-1812.)

14 15 16 17 18   10 9 8 7 6 5 4 3 2 1

Osprey Publishing is supporting the Woodland Trust, the UK's leading woodland conservation charity, by funding the dedication of trees.

www.ospreypublishing.com

CONTENTS

LIST OF ILLUSTRATIONS

PLATE SECTION

Closely formed *conrois* of knights pursue fleeing opponents with lances couched for maximum impact. *(M.736 f7v – Life of St Edmund, twelfth century. New York, The Pierpont Morgan Library ©2013. Photo Pierpont Morgan Library/Art Resource/Scala, Florence)*

The Young King's effigy at Rouen cathedral. The inscription reads:
> *Whose brother was called the Lion Heart*
> *Henry the Younger sought a place in Normandy by right of arms*
> *In the year 1183 cruel death took him hence*
> *(Author's photo)*

Effigy of Richard I in Rouen cathedral: only Richard's heart is at Rouen; his body was buried at Fontevraud beside his parents. *(Author's photo)*

The keep and ruined inner ward of King Richard's 'saucy castle' at Château Gaillard, perched high above the River Seine. *(Author's photo)*

One of King John's favourite objects, a *denier* or silver penny. *(Author's photo; original coin courtesy of Mark Wingham)*

The overgrown ruins of Tancarville Castle where William lived as a squire. *(Photo courtesy of Marcel Barbotte and Les Amis du Château de Tancarville)*

A nineteenth-century impression of a Crusader's first sight of Jerusalem. *(Postcard in author's collection)*

Chepstow Castle on the River Wye in the early twentieth century. *(Postcard in author's collection)*

The Marshal's Tower at Chepstow Castle, seen from the barbican. *(Author's photo)*

William's castle at Kilkenny converted into an eighteenth-century Irish Ascendancy mansion. *(Postcard in author's collection)*

The murder of Thomas Becket in 1170, after a thirteenth century image. *(Author's collection)*

Twelfth-century blacksmiths forging the tools of war, including a rare representation of horse armour. *(MS 0.9.34 f24r, by kind permission of the Master and Fellows of Trinity College Cambridge)*

No longbowmen are recorded fighting at either battle of Lincoln, but one appears amidst the decoration of the cathedral's western porch, a reminder of their ubiquity in English society. *(Author's photo)*

Rochester Castle from the side attacked by King John, engraved in the eighteenth century. *(Postcard in author's collection)*

Dover Castle from the east showing the depth of the fortified area: the French attacked from right to left. *(Postcard in author's collection)*

King Saul's battle with the Amalekites from a French Old Testament c.1250: knights and sergeants lead off bound prisoners, driving sheep and cattle before them. *(M638 f24v – New York, The Pierpont Morgan Library. ©2013. Photo Pierpont Morgan Library/Art Resource/Scala, Florence)*

Newark Castle, the scene of King John's death and the Marshal's last military enterprise. *(Author's photo)*

Goodrich Castle was in the front line of the Welsh uprising of 1215–17. *(Author's photo)*

Joshua's Conquest of Ai showing all the horrors of a medieval siege. *(M638 f10v – New York, The Pierpont Morgan Library. ©2013. Photo Pierpont Morgan Library/Art Resource/Scala, Florence)*

The Bishop of Winchester's Wolvesey Castle. Both the structures seen here were built during the reign of King Stephen. *(Author's photo)*

Lincoln from the south-west in the eighteenth century, hardly altered since the Middle Ages. *(Image courtesy of The Collection: Art and Archaeology in Lincolnshire (Usher Gallery, Lincoln))*

One of the fine medieval townhouses attributed to Lincoln's thirteenth-century Jewish community perched on the aptly named Steep Hill. *(Author's photo)*

Lincoln Castle and Cathedral in the twelfth century, showing the former's West Gate entered by Peter des Roches and Fawkes of Bréauté during the battle's opening moves. *(Drawing by David Vale; courtesy of the Society for Lincolnshire History and Archaeology and the Usher Gallery)*

Lincoln's northern gate at Newport Arch, the last Roman gate in England still in use for traffic. *(Author's photo)*

The West Gate of Lincoln Castle retains its original box-like structure, beyond the modern bridge. *(Author's photo)*

The exterior of the Lucy Tower after an eighteenth-century sketch made before housing blocked the view. *(Original watercolour courtesy of Eileen Brooks)*

Lincoln Castle's East Gate through which Fawkes attacked the Franco-rebel knights on Castle Hill. *(Author's photo)*

Castle Hill, the scene of the main action viewed from the castle walls: Fawkes sortied bottom left, to be joined by William from Bailgate. *(Author's photo)*

The Siege of Lincoln as imagined by Matthew Paris: a crossbowman directs a parting shot at fleeing rebels, while the Angevin leopards fly over an expiring Count de la Perche. *(MS 16 55v, by kind permission of the Master and Fellows of Corpus Christi College Cambridge)*

The probable site of the rebels' attempt to rally at the junction of Steep Hill and Christ's Hospital Terrace. *(Author's photo)*

A modern impression of the East Bargate after an eighteenth-century sketch. *(Original watercolour courtesy of Eileen Brooks)*

The quay at Sandwich was still in commercial use at the turn of the twentieth century. This would have been the nearest point for William to have observed the progress of the battle. *(Courtesy of Sandwich Museum)*

The River Stour's winding course today, looking back towards Sandwich: in the Middle Ages these reed beds were open sea. *(Author's photo)*

A medieval boarding action pictured by Matthew Paris, resulting in wholesale slaughter of the losers: missile weapons include a staff-sling and longbow projecting a jar of some unspecified substance. *(MS 16 56v, by kind permission of the Master and Fellows of Corpus Christi College Cambridge)*

An early twentieth-century reconstruction of the capture of a French vessel by Henry III's great ship the *Queen* in the Bay of Biscay in 1225. *(Author's collection)*

The chapel at St Bartholomew's Hospital: material evidence for the battle's location off Sandwich. *(Author's photo)*

The circular nave of the Temple Church was inspired by the Church of the Holy Sepulchre in Jerusalem that William visited in the 1180s. Henry III added the Gothic chancel in the 1240s. *(Author's photo)*

Inside the Temple Church: William's effigy lies nearest the font accompanied by his sons William and Gilbert on his left and at his feet respectively. *(Photo by Christopher Christodoulou; courtesy of the Temple Church)*

William's sorely damaged effigy suffered worse injuries during the Blitz than the Marshal ever did in his lifetime. *(Author's photo)*

The Flower of Chivalry: part of a modern tapestry celebrating the Marshal's part in the foundation of New Ross in Leinster. *(Reproduced by kind permission of The Ros Tapestry Project Ltd. © The Ros Tapestry Project Ltd)*

PREFACE

illiam Marshal, Earl of Pembroke and Striguil, was a survivor. Born in the 1140s, he witnessed the loss of Normandy under King John, and set his seal to Magna Carta in 1215. Having served four kings, he became regent on the death of King John, and ruled England until his own death in 1219. At an age when most men of his day were long dead, he won two of the most important battles of the Middle Ages to confirm England's separation from Europe and preserve Magna Carta's revolutionary guarantees of personal freedom. Younger son of a minor baron distinguished chiefly for his brutal opportunism, William had gained celebrity on the tournament field, coming to symbolise the knightly qualities of prowess, loyalty, and wisdom. Time has laid his memory waste, but traces remain: ruined castles either side of the Channel; references in chronicles and government records; the Statute Book's most ancient clauses; a battered effigy in the City of London. Most illuminating of all, the epic *History of William Marshal* survived six centuries of oblivion to provide an unparalleled portrait of the life of a feudal magnate. Its survival is typical of the Marshal's good fortune. Without it none of the modern studies of William's life could have been written; our understanding of his contribution to a crucial period of English history would be sadly diminished.

CURRENCY, MEASURES, AND NAMING CONVENTIONS

Medieval money was specified in three units, rather than the modern two:

Pounds (£)

Shillings (s) at twenty to the pound, worth 5 new pence each.

Pence (d) at twelve to the shilling, worth 0.42 new pence each.

Amounts were expressed using one or more of these as appropriate, e.g. £5 3s 7d (£5.18), or 2s 6d (12.5p), or 8d. All financial settlements required the physical transfer of hard cash. There was no paper money. The only coins were silver pennies, or *deniers* as the *History* calls them. Pounds and shillings were for accounting purposes only. Many transactions were denominated in marks, worth 13s 4d each (67p). The superior silver content of English pennies resulted in the one-to-four exchange rate between English money and the Angevin currency that the *History* often used.

For linear measurements I have used miles, yards, and feet, giving metric equivalents in parentheses. There are 1,760 yards to a mile (1.6km), and 3 feet to the yard (30.48cm and 0.9144m respectively).

English was not a written language during William's lifetime. Most personal names have come down to us in Latin or French forms. King John's contemporaries knew him as *Jean Sans Terre*, but it seems pedantic to call his father Henri II (*sic*). Cultural and political affiliations were fluid, compromising efforts to assign names according to their owner's modern nationality. Many Normans and

Poitevins were anglicised after the loss of Normandy in 1205, but still spoke French. I have, therefore, rendered personal names into their English forms throughout, hence Baldwin of Béthune and King Philip Augustus of France. Few people, other than William Marshal – named after his father's occupation – had fixed surnames. Most were known from their place of origin, attached to their Christian names by 'de'. I have generally rendered this as 'of'. Complex forms such as 'des' I have left, as in William des Roches, while Hubert de Burgh is too well known to alter.

The political complexities of the First Barons' War defy simple labelling of opposing sides. 'Rebels' is a fair description of the baronial opposition to King John until French intervention in the autumn of 1215, after which 'Franco-rebel' is more appropriate. Many sources speak of English (i.e. royalist) and French (i.e. rebel), in order to discredit the latter. The fleets at the battle of Sandwich were, however, unequivocally national. The Welsh referred to their English enemies throughout as French or Flemings.

I have, with one exception, avoided footnotes, identifying the sources of quotations in parentheses or in the text. Modern commentators are named with brief introductions, their works listed in the Select Bibliography. This has two sections. The first lists medieval sources by the English name under which they are commonly known, followed by the title under which they have been published. The second lists modern works by author, in the conventional manner. Translations are mine, which has allowed me to present quotations from the *History* as blank verse or prose as appropriate. Dr Gregory's translation for the Anglo-Norman Text Society is of course definitive. Interpolations within quotes are shown by square brackets '[e.g.]'.

ACKNOWLEDGEMENTS

The author would like to thank the following for their invaluable assistance: Marcel Barbotte of the Amis de Tancarville; Ken Brooks; David Carson; John Curry; Kate Moore, Marcus Cowper and Laura Callaghan at Osprey; Dr Geoff Denton of the Winchester Museums Service; Ian Drury; Nigel Drury; Jo Fletcher; Ray Harlow of Sandwich Museum; Colin Harris; Jeff James; Matthew Little; Peter and Wendy Smith; Mark Wingham; the staff at the Portsmouth History Centre and the British Library.

INTRODUCTION

DEATH AT THE CATHEDRAL

The English rode to battle gaily, as if to a tournament. The morning sunshine of the first Saturday after Pentecost shone on the white crosses stitched to their surcoats, for these men were Crusaders, newly shriven and assured of heaven if they fell in action. Before them lay the sprawling mass of Lincoln Castle, much battered by hostile siege engines, for the blockading army in the city beyond included French knights and engineers, the best in Europe. But where were the French, usually so forward in a tourney? Perhaps they had miscounted the strength of the approaching host, less than a thousand all told, misled by the spare shields and banners flying from the wagons that followed the fighting men.

Scouts rode to and fro, speaking with the castle's loyal defenders, probing the ancient town walls for a way in. Crossbowmen infiltrated the castle's outer gate, but that was too narrow a path for knights.

The Earl of Chester's vanguard veered off to the north gate, while the main body of the relieving army rode straight on towards the west wall. There the warlike Bishop of Winchester had found an undefended gate, carelessly walled up, too near the castle for the besiegers to watch closely. When the leading sergeants, professional men-at-arms serving for pay, dismounted to pull away the loose stones stacked against the timbers of the old West Gate, there were no hostile eyes to see them.

The attackers burst through so suddenly that their own leader had still to put on his helmet. William Marshal, Earl of Pembroke, 'The Marshal', was seventy years old but vigorous enough to have been chosen guardian of the realm and its boy king, Henry III. 'Wait for me,' he called out, 'while I get my helm.' William's men did not stop, however. They pressed on into the city, killing the besiegers' chief engineer as he placed a fresh stone in the sling of his machine. Not to be left behind, the Marshal spurred on his horse, carving a path three lances deep in the enemy ranks, driving all before him. Surging past the castle, the English turned right into the open space before the cathedral, to find a great mass of French and rebel English knights. One of the latter broke his lance upon William Longsword, Earl of Salisbury, but the Marshal dealt him such a blow that he slid off his horse, and slunk away to hide. Crossbowmen appeared on the castle walls and roof tops, picking off the horses of the enemy knights below like so many slaughtered pigs. The Earl of Chester's men, having smashed their way through another gate, threw their weight into the battle. Unhorsed riders were dragged away in chains. Sparks flew as swords clashed on swords, or glanced off helmets.

As the opposing knights recoiled, William seized the bridle of their commander, Thomas, Count de la Perche, 'a man strenuous in arms and drawn from royal blood, who had not yet reached the age of thirty' (*Waverley Annals*). Called on to surrender, he refused to do so, swearing great oaths. Provoked beyond endurance, Sir Reginald

Croc, a valiant knight, lost patience and ran his sword point through the count's helmet eye-holes. In a last spasm, Thomas smote the Marshal three double-handed blows over the head, denting his helmet, and fell down dead. This was an unexpected departure from the script: leading knights were rarely slain out of hand; William and the count were first cousins, and everyone grieved to see him killed.

The loss of their commander was a fatal blow for the besiegers, who retreated down the steep slope towards the River Witham. They rallied halfway, only to break again as the Marshal's men emerged from between the castle and cathedral, and the Earl of Chester appeared on their right flank. The broken army fled south down the High Street to the Bargate, fortuitously blocked by a stray cow. Over 300 French and rebel knights were captured, though only three men of note were killed in the fighting. Two hundred panic-stricken knights escaped to London, seeing Marshals in every bush. The single most decisive battle of medieval English history, after Hastings, had been won at less cost in human life than many tournaments.

FOR GOD AND THE MARSHAL

William Marshal's helter-skelter victory at Lincoln on Saturday 20 May 1217 was the final exploit of one of the most remarkable men of an age filled with larger than life figures: Henry II, King of England, his consort Eleanor of Aquitaine, and their sons: Henry 'The Young King', Richard 'Coeur de Lion' and John 'Softsword'. More dubious characters included John's mercenary leader Fawkes of Bréauté, named from the scythe he allegedly used to kill his first man, or the French master pirate and necromancer Eustace the Monk, whose ability to make himself invisible did not save him from summary decapitation in the bowels of his flagship.

William began life during the so-called Anarchy of the mid-twelfth century, the penniless younger son of a Wiltshire landowner: a robber baron described by a local bishop as 'a limb of hell and root of all evil'. William had to make his own way, combining a strong arm with a calculating eye and cool head. We know about his ascent from an epic poem: *l'Histoire de Guillaume le Maréchal*, referred to below as the *History*. Composed soon after its subject's death in 1219, this is the first surviving vernacular biography of medieval times to feature a non-royal layman. Written by a professional poet or *trovère* named John, probably from Touraine, its sources were recollections of the Marshal's own tales of his early days, the eyewitness testimony of his intimate followers, and long lost documents. Together these make the *History* a unique record of the life of a knight errant and great feudal magnate.

Narrowly escaping death as a hostage when aged five, William was apprenticed to arms in Normandy, making his fortune on the international tournament circuit, where he earned a reputation as 'the finest knight in the world'. Such praise from a French observer is remarkable: jousting was a French-dominated sport. England was considered a poor country for breeding knights. William's career took off with his entry into royal service. He was wounded defending Queen Eleanor against Poitevin renegades, ransomed, and appointed military tutor to Henry II's heir, known as the 'Young King', acting as his tournament manager. After the Young King's premature death, William wore his Crusader's cloak to the Holy Land. When the future Richard I rebelled in 1189, William was one of the few to stand by the 'Old King' to the bitter end.

Despite this, William became a key figure at Richard's court, marrying the heiress to vast estates in Wales and Ireland, and acting as royal justiciar during the king's absence on Crusade and as military adviser in the never-ending war with King Philip Augustus of France. On Richard's death, William played a leading role in the accession of his brother John, being rewarded with the Earldom of Pembroke. His reputation and restraint helped him survive accusations of treachery following the loss of Normandy. Despite John's enmity, William remained faithful throughout the disturbances that brought the unwilling king to make the unprecedented concessions enshrined in Magna Carta.

It was William's fidelity, as well as his prowess and longevity, that persuaded the loyal barons of England to entrust him with the regency on John's death. It was no common emergency. John had driven his barons beyond revolt, to the point of offering the crown to Louis the Dauphin, eldest son of Philip Augustus. By the spring of 1217, French and rebel troops held most of south-east England including London, Windsor, and Winchester. Dover and Lincoln were besieged. The crisis represented the gravest threat to England's independence between the Norman Conquest and the Spanish Armada. Had Louis succeeded, England might have become a French province, much as Languedoc had done following the battle of Muret in 1213. Seizing his moment, however, William smashed the Dauphin's northern army at Lincoln, jousting down streets too steep for modern traffic. Panic-stricken, Louis withdrew from Dover, and summoned reinforcements from France. Two months later these were intercepted at sea and destroyed, forcing Louis to withdraw. Never again would foreign invaders thrust so deep into English territory.

WILLIAM'S LEGACY

William's victory was more than just a military success. He had already reissued Magna Carta, within a month of John's death, undermining the rebels' political platform. He confirmed it again after Lincoln, permanently subjecting the arbitrary power of the king to the rule of law. Without Magna Carta, parliamentary government and English common law would not have developed as they did. American and French revolutionaries of the eighteenth century would have had no constitutional example to inspire them. There might have been no Gettysburg Address or European Declaration of Human Rights. At the time of the battle, England's rulers spoke French, as they had since 1066. A French victory at Lincoln might have delayed the emergence of a distinctive English cultural identity for another century. Without the patronage of an Anglophone nobility there might conceivably have been no Chaucer and, hence, no Shakespeare.

William's charge at Lincoln elevates him from the status of an international sporting champion, or another self-seeking magnate, to that of saviour of his country. If his early career made him a super-star in his own time, its dramatic conclusion, with its long-term significance for England and the world, should make him a national hero today. William's victories, however, are morally ambivalent. Like those of Oliver Cromwell, they occurred during a civil war between Englishmen, subverting traditional narratives of English history as a glorious pageant. Henry III was a peaceful king who preferred paintings to jousting. He came to resent and disparage the tournament champion who had preserved his throne. The Marshal clan fell into disfavour, and, lacking male heirs, historical oblivion.

Lincoln is a rare example of a medieval battle with long-lasting consequences. Most wars in the Middle Ages were won by raids and sieges. In the only major battle of his career, William showed a remarkable grasp of the military principles of mobility, concentration, and surprise, striking at Lincoln while the Dauphin's forces were divided; gaining access to the city through an old gate the enemy had overlooked. Once inside, he successfully combined missile action by crossbowmen on roof tops with shock action in the streets below. Lincoln is more indicative of how English soldiers fought in the high Middle Ages than the ultimately pointless victories of the Hundred Years War which attract so much attention.

Existing studies of the Marshal pay insufficient attention to the military aspects of his life. Sidney Painter's *William Marshal: Knight Errant, Baron and Regent of England* presents a romanticised view of the Marshal's career: his chivalry was calculating and sometimes brutal. Georges Duby's *Guillaume le Marechal ou le meilleure chevalier du monde* (translated as *The Flower of Chivalry*) treats the Marshal as a muscular simpleton. David Crouch's *William the Marshal: Knighthood, War and Chivalry* focusses on the political and administrative aspects of William's career, treating battles and campaigns as incidental.

None of these makes use of the *History*'s extensive detail of real and sham fights to set William's career in the military context of his day, or looks beyond the Marshal family narrative to evaluate his contribution to the interminable Anglo-French wars of the 1190s and 1200s. What were the relations of the 'finest knight' with those devious monarchs John and Philip Augustus? How did he resolve the contradiction between the individualism of the knight errant and the prudence demanded of the royal counsellor? The baronial class has often been depicted as consisting of obtuse reactionaries. The *History*'s lucky survival provides a unique opportunity to challenge this caricature. Previously available only in Middle French, or in a nineteenth-century précis, it has recently appeared in modern English verse with every scholarly facility. As Lincoln's 800th anniversary approaches, the time seems right to reconsider the reputation of England's forgotten champion.

Chronology

1141	Rout of Winchester: burning of Wherwell Abbey
	William Marshal probably born at Marlborough
1152	Siege of Newbury: William held hostage
1159	William leaves home to become squire in Normandy
1166	Knighted before battle of Drincourt; scores first tournament successes
1168	Wounded and captured defending Queen Eleanor
1170	Coronation of Young King; William appointed tutor-in-arms
1173	Young King's Revolt
1176	Begins seven-year tournament career
1182	William loses Young King's favour and leaves court
1183	Returns to witness Young King's death; takes Cross
1184	Pilgrimage to Jerusalem
1185	Joins Henry II's household
1188	Angevin-Capetian war; William masterminds Henry II's raiding strategy
1189	Defence of Le Mans; William stands by Henry II in final illness
	Accession of Richard I; William marries Isabel of Clare
1190	Richard departs on Third Crusade; William appointed justiciar
1194	Richard returns; William becomes Marshal of England
	Accompanies Richard to Normandy; commands rearguard at Fréteval
1197	Milli raid and siege of Arras
	Death of Richard; William supports John's accession
1202	Renewed Capetian aggression; sieges of Arques and Mirebeau
1203	Murder of Arthur of Brittany and loss of Normandy
1205	William loses royal favour after refusing to serve overseas
1207	William withdraws to Ireland

1208	William's knights fight proxy war against John's Irish justiciar
1210	John's Irish expedition
1211	John's Welsh expeditions (x2)
1212	Plot to murder John; William rallies Irish barons to king
1213	William restored to favour
1214	Battle of Bouvines confirms Angevin loss of Normandy
1215	Baronial revolt; John issues Magna Carta
	Civil war and siege of Rochester
1216	French invasion overruns south-east England
	Death of John and accession of Henry III
	William elected regent; reissues Magna Carta
1217	Battle of Lincoln: William destroys Franco-rebel army
	Battle of Sandwich: French reinforcements intercepted at sea
	Treaty of Kingston: French withdraw
	Magna Carta: second reissue
1218	Restoration of order; siege of Newark
1219	William's illness and death

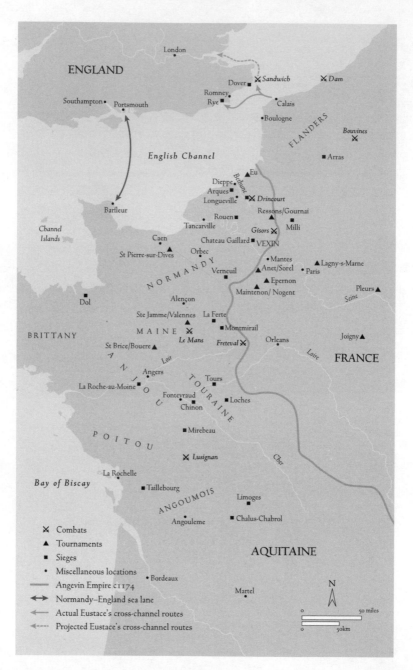

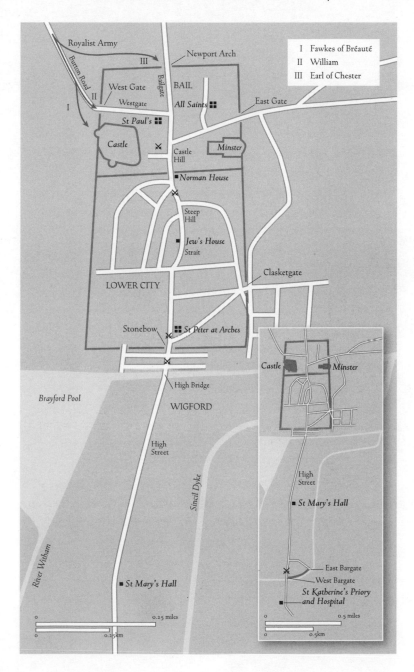

Royalist Army

III   Newport Arch

Burton Road

II

I

West Gate

Baligate

BAIL

Westgate   All Saints ▦   East Gate

St Paul's ▦

Castle ✕ Castle Hill   Minster

■ Norman House

✕

Steep Hill

■ Jew's House
Strait

Clasketgate

LOWER CITY

Stonebow ✕ ▦ St Peter at Arches

✕

High Bridge

Brayford Pool   WIGFORD

High Street

Sincil Dyke

River Witham

■ St Mary's Hall

	I	Fawkes of Bréauté
	II	William
	III	Earl of Chester

0   0.25 miles

0   0.25km

Castle   Minster

High Street

■ St Mary's Hall

✕   East Bargate
     West Bargate
St Katherine's Priory and Hospital
■

0   0.5 miles

0   0.5km

I

ANGEVIN INHERITANCE

he battle of Lincoln was only the latest in a series of dramatic shifts in England's political fortunes. Over the preceding 150 years, the country had endured foreign occupation and a near-collapse of central government. For a while, it emerged as the financial powerhouse of an empire stretching from the Cheviots to the Pyrenees, only to fall victim once more to civil war and foreign aggression.

AFTER DOMESDAY

William the Conqueror's victory at Hastings in 1066 brought an unsought attachment to the Duchy of Normandy and a wholesale political and cultural realignment. Anglo-Saxon England had looked northwards. Hastings was the last leg of a three-cornered contest for the throne between an Englishman, a Norwegian, and a Norman Frenchman. Scandinavian intrusions into English affairs did not cease for another three decades, when Magnus Barelegs of Norway shot a Norman Earl of Shrewsbury dead on an Anglesey beach in 1098, before sailing away for ever. Norman England would look south. Five of her seven kings between 1066 and 1216 were born overseas in modern France, and four died there. The English Channel was an internal waterway for over a century. William Marshal crossed it repeatedly, first as a young squire in 1159, finally as an elder statesman in April 1216. The mobility of twelfth-century elites reflected the fluidity of Western European politics. Borders were porous, governments migratory, lordship discontinuous.

The chief beneficiaries of England's new arrangements were the Conqueror's Norman followers. Their duke became a king, equal in status to his suzerain, the King of France. French-speaking Normans displaced Anglo-Saxon landholders. Latinate ecclesiastics imposed a new liturgy, extinguished the Old English literary tradition, and rebuilt Anglo-Saxon churches in the Romanesque style that the English still call Norman. In the courts, trial by combat, blinding, and castration replaced oath-taking and fines.

The most concrete symbols of subjection were the defensive structures known as castles that sprang up at strategic points across the country. Usually they took the form of a conical mound or motte, topped with a wooden blockhouse, as illustrated in the Bayeux Tapestry. Sometimes mottes were associated with earth ringworks or baileys. Sometimes they reinforced existing enclosures like the Anglo-Saxon *burgh* at Wallingford, or the Roman walls at Lincoln and Chichester. Earlier English fortifications were refuges for the population. The new structures were small, a quarter of an acre (0.1ha) at the base, safe deposits for wives and other valuables, easily held by a few against the many. The most important, like the Tower of London or those at Rochester and Colchester, were great square-faced stone slabs, with entrances on the first floor. The 'bones of the kingdom', they were the largest secular buildings of their day, 90 feet (27m) high, with walls 15 feet (4.5m) thick. Known in modern English as 'keeps', their French name *donjon* relates linguistically to dungeon, domination, and danger. They were uncompromising, vertical expressions of dominance. William Marshal held several, notably at Chepstow and Goodrich. Cheap and easy to construct, the simpler motte and bailey spread quickly. Domesday Book, the inventory that William I made of his conquests in 1086, named forty-nine. Robert of Torigny, writing in the late twelfth century, counted 1,115 at the accession of Henry II, few subject to any central authority.

The spread of castles across north-west Europe in the eleventh century was a physical manifestation of the extreme fragmentation of political power characterised as feudalism. A term invented much later and taken up by Karl Marx, 'feudal' has become a byword for the archaic. In the medieval context it relates to a system of holding land in return for military service that developed around the turn of the first millennium. A would-be tenant did homage to a landholder, becoming his man or vassal, and receiving a piece of land, a *feodum* or fief, complete with its agriculturalists, on whose produce they all lived. For this the vassal undertook to serve his lord or *seigneur* with horse and arms, and mount guard in his castle. In return the lord provided many of the services of the modern state: physical and legal protection, even a measure of social security. It was a practical response to the collapse of central authority following the Viking attacks of the tenth century, the breakdown of communications and urban life, and the disappearance of money.

Feudal society at its height consisted of three broad classes of person: men of prayer, men of the sword, and men of the countryside. Women were of little political account. Few feature in the *History*, except as close relations or props for some exploit. The clergy enjoyed a self-conscious moral superiority as representing the only social hierarchy to survive the break-up of the Roman Empire. Unable to bear arms, they monopolised learning and the mysteries of the sacraments. Their views shape modern perceptions of the Middle Ages, as the Church's institutional continuity favoured the preservation of ecclesiastical records. William Marshal's life coincided with the great age of chronicles, making it possible to verify many of his biographer's statements. Originally written by cloistered monks, later chronicles were often produced by secular clergy, who might be very worldly indeed. Roger, Vicar of Howden in Yorkshire, travelled to France, Scotland, and Palestine in the king's service. A royal judge, spy, and diplomat, Roger's works include unique copies of official correspondence, such as Richard I's reports of his victories at Arsuf and Courcelles. Even monkish chroniclers were not necessarily cut off from the world, as they gathered news from travellers taking advantage of monastic hospitality. Ralph of Coggeshall's account of Richard I's death probably came from the dying king's chaplain. Ralph was a Cistercian, an order whose network of monasteries was particularly effective at collecting and disseminating information. King John's alienation of the white brothers was not his least mistake. Clerics in royal households lay behind the twelfth-century explosion of documentary evidence – legal writs and accounting records – hard evidence to back up or refute chroniclers and poets. In the 1170s William Marshal employed a clerk of the royal kitchens to track his tournament winnings, a reminder of the mass of domestic records that have been lost.

The men of the sword contested clerical pre-eminence, asserting their own moral worth as the hands of the body politic, carrying out the directions of justly constituted authority. Their leaders were the barons or magnates, who in Norman England held their lands directly from the Crown, hence the expression tenants-in-chief.

Senior ecclesiastical figures, bishops, and abbots were also tenants-in-chief, expected to maintain their own military following. The Archbishop of York sent sixty knights to fight in the battle of the Standard in 1138. While William Marshal was learning his trade in the 1160s, Henry II's inquest into knight service in England identified 270 lay tenants-in-chief. Another survey in 1199 listed 165, among them William Marshal, Earl of Pembroke. A fluid class varying widely in wealth and influence, barons enjoyed broad judicial and fiscal powers and controlled most of the nation's material assets. Often misrepresented as ignorant reactionaries and inveterate opponents of royal government, they were the king's natural advisers and companions, sharing similar economic and cultural interests.

The physical exercise of royal and baronial power depended on a broader class of armed followers, known as knights from the Old English *cniht*. Of ambiguous social origins, by the eleventh century their possession of such expensive items as armour and horses clearly differentiated them from the peasantry. Chroniclers described them as soldiers, *milites* in Latin. The 1166 survey identified some 6,278 knights' fees – the territorial units owing a mounted warrior's service – in England. Allowing for wastage this represented some 5,000 actual knights. Some were *vavassours* or landed knights, married men who lived on their estates, but were still available for military duties. Younger men or *bacheliers*, who had yet to settle down, formed the military households or *familia* of kings and magnates. Sleeping together on the floor of their lord's hall, they lived a roistering life. Often the bastard or younger sons of good families, unable to marry unless an elder brother died or an heiress came along, they were ripe for trouble. Well fed, physically fit, and boiling over with repressed sexual energy, they swarmed out of their castles in times of unrest like angry wasps, to pillage and burn. Unsympathetic clerics punningly labelled them *malitia*, malice not soldiery. The *Anglo-Saxon Chronicle* saw little difference between the destructive passage of Henry I's royal household, and the ravages of an invader. William Marshal spent twenty-two years as a household knight before leaping into the upper reaches of the nobility by his marriage to Isabel of Clare, bypassing the *vavassours'* staid ranks in one bound.

The great mass of the labouring population, society's feet in contemporary social analysis, lived outside the polite world of the *History*. Total English numbers are uncertain, perhaps two million at the Conquest, doubling by the early thirteenth century. Bound to the soil, they played no part in early medieval politics, except as victims. Magna Carta's famous guarantee of due legal process applied only to free men, entitled to bear arms. The rejoicing in France after the nation-defining victory of Bouvines in 1214 was confined to the court and towns.

The twelfth-century economic revival created a new class of burgesses or townsmen, who had escaped the bonds of serfdom to supply goods and services that the countryside could not provide. Magnates like William Marshal took advantage of this new urban wealth. Fresh in London to marry his heiress, he borrowed from his alderman host to finance the festivities. Towns were small. Domesday Book suggests that London's population was just 12,000 in 1086. Winchester was next at 6,000. Towns would increasingly assert their independence, as their numbers and prosperity increased. The *History* records burgesses joining hesitantly in the defence of their town during William's first battle at Drincourt, emboldened by his example. Fifty years later, London was the mainspring of the opposition to John, inserting commercial clauses into Magna Carta, and resisting the regent to the very end. William was more than a passive consumer of urban wealth. He founded new towns in Ireland, notably at New Ross, secured trading privileges for Pembroke, and reduced feudal reliefs at Haverfordwest and Kilkenny.

The Anglo-Norman social model did not apply throughout the British Isles. As today, England shared the British mainland with two other entities: Scotland and Wales. When William was born, the former was fast becoming a unitary kingdom, the Scottish kings performing a balancing act between their powerful southern neighbour and an inflammable mixture of English-speaking Lowlanders and Gaelic or Norse speakers in Galloway and the Highlands. An elastic border that sometimes reached as far south as the Rivers Tees and Ribble provoked sporadic conflict throughout William's life. The *History* reflects the new southern orientation, however. It records just one encounter with Scottish knights, at a tournament near Le Mans.

The Marshal's dealings with Wales were more extensive, following his marriage into one of the great Marcher families. Unlike Scotland, Wales remained a patchwork of mutually hostile chiefdoms. Welsh annalists styled their warlords *Dux* or leader, not prince. Divided by geography, united only by culture, the principal Welsh political units were Gwynedd in the north, Powys in the centre, and Dyfed in the south. Inheritance practices ensured deadly family rivalries. Six members of Powys' ruling dynasty between 1100 and 1125 were killed, blinded, or castrated by relatives, one every four years. Political disunity and economic backwardness made Wales a tempting prize for land-hungry Normans, who pushed up to the foot of the mountains and along the southern Welsh coast. When William Marshal appeared in the 1190s, the frontier had stabilised along the Welsh Marches, a military border running from Chester down to Hereford, and around by Monmouth into Pembrokeshire. Violence was endemic. William of Braose massacred his Welsh dinner guests at Abergavenny in 1176, as revenge for his uncle's killing the year before. Such vendettas demanded constant military preparedness.

Beyond Wales lay Ireland, 80 miles (120km) across the sea from the great land-locked harbour of Milford Haven. Unconquered by the Romans, Ireland was an unknown quantity before 1169. Then Norman adventurers sailed from Pembrokeshire to exploit the internecine wars that, in the Irish chronicler's expressive phrase, made all Ireland 'a trembling sod'. Four decades later, Ireland would provide William with a refuge from King John's disfavour, and an alternative power base.

Historians dislike the omnibus expression 'Celtic Fringe', with its spurious implication of cultural uniformity. From an English perspective, however, these areas represented a hostile 'other', with several common features. The author of *Gesta Stephani*, the Deeds of King Stephen, contrasted England's settled society with the barbaric world beyond: 'a country of woodland and pasture ... [which] breeds men of an animal type, naturally swift footed, accustomed to war, volatile always in breaking their word as in changing their abode'. Richard of Hexham described the Scots king at the battle of the Standard surrounded by his knights, 'the rest of the barbarian host roaring around them'. Except in southern Scotland, social structures were heroically pre-feudal, marital customs unspeakable, and speech incomprehensible. Populations were smaller outside England: perhaps a million in Scotland and 300,000 in Wales, with half a million Irish. Their potential for mischief was by no means negligible, as William's final years would show.

A TIME OF WAR

The feudal combination of weak government and a militarised ruling class ensured chronic political instability. The most notorious English example occurred during Stephen's reign (1135–54) when the *Anglo-Saxon Chronicle* claimed with gloomy hyperbole that Christ and his angels slept for nineteen winters. The expression 'Anarchy' exaggerates the breakdown of government, but it shared much with the conflicts of John's reign: a disputed succession, an inadequate king, and overwhelming military challenges.

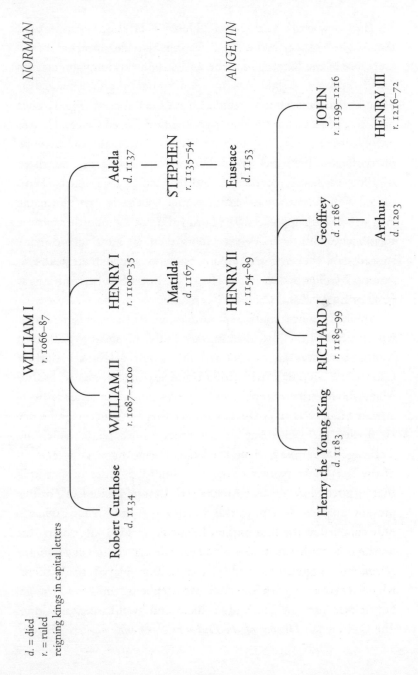

NORMAN

ANGEVIN

WILLIAM I
r. 1066–87

Robert Curthose
d. 1134

WILLIAM II
r. 1087–1100

HENRY I
r. 1100–35

Adela
d. 1137

STEPHEN
r. 1135–54

Matilda
d. 1167

Eustace
d. 1153

HENRY II
r. 1154–89

Henry the Young King
d. 1183

RICHARD I
r. 1189–99

Geoffrey
d. 1186

JOHN
r. 1199–1216

Arthur
d. 1203

HENRY III
r. 1216–72

d. = died
r. = ruled
reigning kings in capital letters

The Conqueror's youngest son, Henry I (1100–35), consolidated the Anglo-Norman realm by defeating his elder brother Robert Curthose in the battle of Tinchebrai (1106), and imprisoning him for life in Bristol Castle. A man against whom the Welsh annalists thought that 'none could contend except God himself', Henry once made his point by throwing an opponent off Rouen Castle. He was less effective at providing an heir. His only legitimate son drowned off Barfleur in the wreck of the White Ship, leaving an elder sister. Matilda was female, vindictive, and married to a foreigner, Count Geoffrey of Anjou, whose Latin name Andegavia gave the name Angevin to her supporters. The family did not acquire the surname Plantagenet until later. When Henry died, after eating too many stewed eels, the Anglo-Norman magnates broke their oaths to support Matilda, and accepted Henry's nephew, Stephen of Blois, as King of England and Duke of Normandy.

Stephen's unfortunate reputation derives from his enemies, who controlled the historical narrative after his death. William of Malmesbury was an unashamed panegyrist of Robert Earl of Gloucester, Matilda's half-brother and leading supporter. Walter Map, who described Stephen as 'a fine knight but in other respects almost a fool', was an Angevin courtier. Stephen's successor, Henry II, denied the legitimacy of his predecessor's reign, which he disparaged as *tempus guerrae*, the time of war. Angevin denigration of the last Anglo-Norman king resembles the Tudor propaganda that inspired Shakespeare's Richard III. Less prejudiced authorities present Stephen as a powerful warrior – *bellator robustissimus* – only subdued at the first battle of Lincoln in 1141 after being hit on the head with a rock. *Gesta Stephani* described him as *munificus et affabilis* – generous and pleasant. That played to William Marshal's advantage when he fell into Stephen's hands as a hostage, but it was not the stuff of a successful twelfth-century king. The Old French *History of the Dukes of Normandy and the Kings of*

England agreed. Stephen was *debonaire et moult piteus*, admirable qualities, but unlikely to ensure firm government.

Stephen's ineffectual image was well established by the 1220s when the *History of William Marshal* was written: 'in his time was England in great sorrow and strife, and the kingdom in great discord, for no peace nor truce nor agreement was kept nor justice done'. It was not only Angevin propagandists, like William of Malmesbury, who recalled 'a land embittered by the horrors of war', when freebooters flocked to England for plunder. William of Newburgh reckoned there were 'as many kings or rather tyrants as ... lords of castles'. Their methods resembled those practised in King John's time: pillage of churchyards where people placed their property under ecclesiastical protection, torture of anyone suspected of possessing hidden wealth, systematic blackmail of religious and local communities.

Like John, Stephen faced a coalition of powerful enemies, making it difficult to concentrate against any of them. Magnates, including some bishops, resisted royal attempts to constrain their castle-building, 'each defending, or more properly speaking, laying waste their neighbourhood' (William of Malmesbury). Stephen defended himself well enough at first, but never crushed his opponents, a precocious illustration of Clausewitz's principle that while the defensive is the stronger form of war, it is unlikely to achieve a decision. Stephen's defeat and capture at Lincoln in February 1141 was disastrous. The *History* saw it as a major blow to the king's prestige, leaving him nothing but the crown.

The Angevin Rout of Stockbridge in September saved Stephen from death in captivity, but he remained a lame duck, suffering major territorial losses in Normandy and northern England. Magnates, including William's father, defected, seeking protection from lords better able to provide it. Royal revenue collapsed preventing the king hiring mercenaries to replace disaffected knights. When rival armies met, the leading men refused to fight. The stalemate lasted a dozen years, before the Church brokered a compromise peace, allowing Matilda's son Henry to succeed on Stephen's death. Just as John's baronial opponents rallied to his successor, so Stephen's supporters accepted Henry II in 1154.

DEVIL'S BROOD

Notorious for his deadly quarrel with Thomas Becket, Henry II better deserves to be remembered for his restoration of order following the Anarchy. Flemish mercenaries were sent home, unauthorised castles demolished, and the King of Scots evicted from England's three northern counties. A series of great Assizes or edicts laid the enduring foundations of English judicial practice. His contemporaries saw Henry as the Alexander of the West, though Jordan of Fantôme said he preferred craft to war. The Victorian constitutional historian Bishop Stubbs rated him alongside Alfred the Great and William the Conqueror. Such was Henry's speed of movement that Louis VII of France thought he must fly rather than travel by horse or ship. Henry's energetic expansion of his inheritance made him the most powerful ruler in Western Europe by the 1180s, eclipsing his lacklustre French suzerain.

The core of Henry's possessions were England and Normandy, which he inherited from his mother, Matilda. The paternal County of Anjou and its associated territories on the Loire, Henry inherited after a brother's lucky death. Brittany, a longstanding target of Norman acquisitiveness, he gained by marrying his third son Geoffrey to its heiress in 1166. Ireland he was given by the Pope. South of the Loire, from Poitou to Gascony, stretched the Duchy of Aquitaine, the patrimony of Henry's wife Eleanor, whom he married following her divorce from Louis VII in 1152. The latter, she said, was more of a monk than a king. *Molt vaillante et courteise*, gallant and courtly, she would play a key role in William Marshal's rise.

Labelled the Angevin Empire for modern convenience, this personal union of lordships comprised three strategic areas: England and Normandy were richest and best governed; Aquitaine the poorest and most unruly, its quarrelsome Poitevin lords a byword for treachery – William Marshal suffered his most serious wound at their hands. Anjou was richer than the south but less docile than the north. Communications were assured by sea to the west and by Roman roads running up through Poitiers and Chinon to the commercial and ecclesiastical centres at Tours and Angers, bypassing the future French heartland between Orleans and Paris. Nationalist-minded historians have emphasised the Empire's linguistic and legal disunity, and taken its collapse for granted.

The attractions of French administration and culture were less apparent in the mid-twelfth century. The Capetian kings who claimed to rule *Francia*, the northern French lands settled by the Franks, took their name from Hugh Capet, who usurped Charlemagne's mantle in 987. They struggled even to control their demesne lands in the Ile-de-France; their resources were dwarfed by the great feudal principalities of Normandy, Champagne, and Flanders. Eleventh-century Paris with a population of 3,000 was half the size of Winchester. Its rise to political and cultural significance only began after Louis VI, known as the Fat, made it his capital in the 1120s.

There was no compelling reason in 1170 why government from London or Rouen should have appeared less inviting than from Paris. Nevertheless, the Angevin Empire's components were vulnerable. Dispersed around the French periphery, they lay open to attack down the Seine and Loire Valleys, unable and unwilling to come to one another's help. Two days' march from Paris, Normandy was especially exposed. Brittany and England's

Celtic neighbours were a constant liability. Only England provided support in depth. The chief weakness of the Angevins was their inability to sink personal differences in the family interest. Henry's marriage broke down in the late 1160s, his four sons becoming weapons in the parental battle.

The king's initial plan seems to have been to divide his empire among them, under overall direction of the eldest, another Henry. In earnest of this, the king had the latter crowned in 1170, aged fifteen, imitating contemporary French practice. Feudal custom sought to ensure that lands inherited from the father's lineage remained intact. Younger sons were compensated elsewhere. The Young King would receive all his patrimonial inheritance: England, Normandy, and Anjou. Richard the second son would have his mother's Aquitanian inheritance, as Count of Poitiers, while Geoffrey was settled with his Breton heiress. Only John, the youngest, was unprovided for, his father dubbing him *Jean Sans Terre* or Lackland.

Young Henry stood to gain most in the long run, but meanwhile had less real authority than his brothers. An annual allowance of £3,500 a year, the earnings of 2,300 foot soldiers, gave him wealth without responsibility. It was a morally corrosive combination. Robert de Torigny, Abbot of Mont St Michel, commented that it was insufficient for the greatness of his heart; the *History* said he could deny no-one. Feckless and feather-brained, the Young King became a rallying point for Henry II's enemies: a wife embittered by royal infidelities; a French king nervous of Angevin power; dissident barons smarting from years of firm government. All looked towards the rising star.

Shortly before Easter 1173, the Young King left court and fled to Paris, the first Angevin to seek a kingdom by dismembering his inheritance. With French support and wild promises, he conjured up a four-front war against his father: French and Flemish in northern Normandy, Scots in northern England, mutinous barons in Brittany and East Anglia. Henry II with his loyal knights and 10,000 Brabançon *routiers* – paid infantrymen – saw them all off. The Count of Flanders went home after an archer shot his brother; Louis VII withdrew, having burnt Verneuil and abducted its citizens; the Scots invested Carlisle but were scared off by rumours of a relief force; Henry's Brabançons chased the Breton lords into Dol, killing over a thousand of their supporters, and forcing eighty of their leaders to surrender. Meanwhile the English rebels were beaten outside Bury St Edmunds at Fornham, and their army of unemployed Flemish weavers annihilated. Jordan de Fantôme wrote in his eyewitness verse history:

> *The wool of England they gathered very late*
> *Upon their bodies descend crows and buzzards*

The following year brought the Young King no better luck. While contrary winds stopped him joining his English supporters from Gravelines, his father sailed from Barfleur to do penance at Becket's new shrine at Canterbury. Spiritual absolution brought immediate military reward. Angevin loyalists marching the same night from Newcastle captured William the Lion, King of Scotland, as he ate breakfast outside Alnwick Castle. Within a month Henry kicked away his son's last prop by raising the French siege of Rouen, the demoralised besiegers destroying their siege engines as they left.

Abandoned by Louis VII, his followers reduced to selling their horses and armour, the Young King sought peace. His father blamed his son's evil counsellors, particularly Queen Eleanor, whom he placed in internal exile at Winchester. Nearly a thousand rebel prisoners were released without ransom, although castles were confiscated and woodlands cut down to pay for wartime devastation. The Old King appeared stronger than ever, but the substantive issues between him and his impatient brood remained unresolved.

For nearly ten years, the Young King diverted himself on the tournament circuit, while his brother Richard engaged in more serious hostilities against his Poitevin vassals. Tensions boiled over during a family Christmas at Caen in 1182. The Old King asked Richard to do homage for Aquitaine to his brother, as future head of the family. This was offered with such bad grace that the latter refused it, riding south to join Richard's Poitevin dissidents. When Henry II went to Limoges to mediate, the Young King's men shot at him from the castle, their arrows piercing his surcoat and hitting one of his household knights in the eye. Parricidal violence was not unprecedented. William the Conqueror was injured fighting his son Robert Curthose at Gerberoy in 1079, and his horse killed beneath him. While the Young King simulated reconciliation, his brother Geoffrey ravaged their father's estates, carrying off church ornaments, devoting towns and villages to the flames, depopulating fields and byres, sparing none, in the chronicler's cliché, on grounds of age, sex, status, or religion.

The Young King broke out again, doing his best to justify Walter Map's description of him as 'a prodigy of untruth, a lovely palace of sin', standing by while his knights beat his father's envoys with swords, and threw them off bridges. Unable to pay his *routiers*, the Young King plundered Poitou's sacred places, including the great shrine of St Martial, proto-evangeliser of Aquitaine, at Limoges. Pressing south, he fell sick at Uzerche in Lot. Roger of Howden thought he developed dysentery out of pique at his inability to do his father any further harm, an acute fever followed by *fluxis ventris cum excoratione intestinorum* – the bloody flux. A fortnight later, on the evening of 11 June 1183, Young Henry died at Martel in the Dordogne, the picture of penitence, lying on a bed of ashes, wearing a hair shirt and a noose around his neck.

The Old King refused to visit his dying son, fearing further treachery, and hid his grief as princes were supposed to do. The *History* echoes the lamentations of the Young King's tournament companions. Chivalry was reduced to idleness, largesse orphaned, and the world cast into darkness. Transported northwards, the well-salted remains inspired such popular hysteria at Le Mans that they were buried temporarily, pending transfer to Rouen. Despite his plundering, the Young King left nothing but debts. His chaplain stole the collection at Le Mans. One of his *routiers* took William Marshal hostage as surety for his men's wages. The Count of Flanders described the dead prince as the flower of Christian men and the fountain of largesse, but his end was as futile and self-seeking as his life.

The Young King's death threw Henry II's plans into confusion, intensified by Geoffrey of Brittany's death three years later, when he was trampled by his horse during a tournament at Paris. Reduced to two sons, Henry faced a wholesale management reshuffle. Ingrained mistrust following the disastrous experiment of the Young King's coronation prevented him from recognising Richard, Eleanor's favourite, as his primary heir. Richard, in turn, would not surrender Aquitaine to John, his father's favourite, as the first step in a general redistribution of territory. This irreconcilable dispute would bring Henry II to his grave.

The one constant factor behind the diplomatic twists of these years was the slow-burning malice of the new French king, Philip II, and his unremitting pursuit of the destruction of the Angevin Empire. At every turn, he backed a competing claimant against the Angevin incumbent, first Richard against his father, then John against Richard, then Geoffrey's posthumous son Arthur against John, and finally his own son Louis against John's heir Henry III. The *History* describes Philip as more cunning than a fox, and blamed him personally for the deaths of the Old King and all his sons. There is no doubt that Philip dominated Western European international relations after 1200. Tripling the size of the Capetian royal demesne, he well deserved the title 'Augustus' awarded him by Rigord, the official French historian.

The spark that lit the final conflagration of Henry's reign came from the Middle East. Frankish Crusaders from Western Europe exploited Muslim disunity in the last years of the eleventh century to carve out a number of Christian principalities in Syria and Palestine. Reunited under the great Saladin, Arab and Turkish forces annihilated the Crusading states' armies at Hattin near Lake Tiberias on 4 July 1187. The shock killed Pope Urban III outright, and inspired a wave of Crusading fervour across Europe. The *History* thought that no man of worth had not abandoned wife and children to take the Cross and avenge God's disgrace. Defaulters were handed a distaff and wool in the same way that women distributed white feathers during the First World War. Count Richard was among the first to take the Cross. Even cautious politicians like Henry and Philip felt compelled to do likewise. When Henry returned to England in January 1188 to prepare his departure, however, Philip attacked the town of Châteauroux north-east of Poitiers, menacing the Angevins' south-eastern flank. This, remarked the *History*, was the start of the great war whose effects were still felt. King Henry was at a disadvantage, reduced against his will to fighting fellow Crusaders who continually urged departure, while doing everything they could to prevent it.

At first Richard and Henry made common cause. Henry's obstinate refusal to confirm Richard as his heir, however, allowed Philip, the Angevins' feudal lord, to undercut the Old King by offering Richard the counties of Touraine, Anjou, and Maine. *Une vileine enprise*, a vile undertaking, commented the *History*, by which Philip would rob Henry's heirs of their lands. Soon Richard and Philip were sharing the same plate and even bed, a reflection of primitive domestic arrangements rather than mutual passion. In November, they arrived together for a conference at Bonmoulins in lower Normandy. Convinced his father meant to disinherit him in John's favour, Richard knelt in homage to Philip, and rode away to prepare for war.

That winter Henry fell ill. Richard and Philip raided his territory as baronial support faltered. Henry fortified Le Mans, his birth place and a communications hub between Normandy and Anjou. Ditches were cleared, and houses pulled down around the gates to clear fields of fire. After Whitsun both sides went armed to a conference between Ferté-Bernard and Nogent-le-Rotrou sponsored by a pope anxious to expedite the Crusade. Richard lined up with the French, who denied the Pope's authority to interfere in a domestic dispute. Henry withdrew to Le Mans, like a fox to his earth. On 12 July his enemies dug him out, provoking the nearest thing to a battle in the whole war. Arrangements had been made to burn down the suburbs in case of attack, and the flames spread to the city. Smoked out of his lair, Henry fled south by a circuitous route to Chinon.

Henry was on his last legs militarily and medically. The Norman magnates had led their forces as far as Alençon, 30 miles (50km) north of Le Mans, but withdrew when Henry retreated away from them. Most of his Welsh infantry were killed retiring from Le Mans. Henry's health worsened, the ulcers on his heels spreading to his feet, legs, and body, giving him no rest. William Marshal, one of the few to stand by the king to the bitter end, recalled his going first red then a leaden hue, suggesting gangrene. Richard and Philip treated Henry's illness as a ruse, and pressed their advantage. On 3 July, they captured Tours by escalade, the River Loire being particularly low. Next day, hardly able to sit his horse, Henry submitted to their demands at Ballan-Miré, south of the Loire between Azay-le-Rideau and Tours. Even Philip was embarrassed, spreading a cloak on the grass for the dying king, who preferred to be held in the saddle.

Thunderstorms rumbled as Henry surrendered his continental lands to Philip, receiving them back for 20,000 marks and a binding commitment to make his vassals swear fealty to Richard. Giving the latter the kiss of peace, he is supposed to have hissed in his son's ear the hope that he would live to be avenged. The *History* has a similar tale of Henry promising to give his enemies their fill of war, if only William got him through his current fix. Returning to Chinon, Henry took to his bed, dark blue and feverish, unable to see, hear, or speak coherently. He died before the chapel altar three days later, blood streaming from nose and mouth. Richard had won. He soon recovered his territorial losses, but not the money, roughly a third of Philip's ordinary annual revenue, nor the independence he had sworn away. Dukes of Normandy historically avoided oaths of fealty, regarding themselves as subject to nobody but God. Richard's empire was physically intact, but legally and morally compromised.

LIONHEART

Richard I spent his whole reign fighting, except for thirteen months as a prisoner in Germany. Apart from his captivity and exorbitant ransom, Richard is best remembered for his role in the Third Crusade, ending the siege of Acre and winning an exemplary battle against Saladin at Arsuf. He never saw Jerusalem, but ensured that a residual Christian foothold survived in Palestine for another century. The twenty-six months between Richard's embarkation at Marseilles in August 1190 and his departure from the Holy Land in October 1192 were not the costly diversion from responsibilities nearer home that his critics allege. The Crusading experience was an essential item in the medieval grandee's *curriculum vitae*. Three kings of France campaigned in Palestine. Richard's great-grandfather Fulk V of Anjou had become King of Jerusalem in the 1130s. Henry II never visited the Holy Places, but he funded 200 knights to defend them. Richard's expedition honoured a long-standing Angevin commitment.

His situation was less secure than that of his predecessors, however. He left behind his brother John, whose name headed the list of traitors handed to the Old King after Ballan-Miré. Richard treated John with mingled generosity and caution, granting him swathes of land in the West Country and Midlands, but keeping the castles under royal control. He further limited John's scope for mischief by exiling him to Normandy, appointing a team of justiciars to rule England, and recognising his nephew Arthur as his heir. Once Richard departed, however, no power on earth could keep John overseas. By the autumn of 1192 divisions among the justiciars, nervous of alienating Richard's most obvious heir, allowed John to assert his claim to be *rector totius regni*, ruler of the whole kingdom, a title not dissimilar to that which William Marshal used twenty-five years later.

Philip's early return from Acre in the summer of 1191 leaving Richard behind ensured a prompt resumption of the three-cornered Capetian-Angevin game of beggar-my-neighbour. Defying the traditional immunity of Crusaders' property and his personal oath not to attack Richard until at least forty days after the latter's return, Philip invaded Normandy early in 1193, immediately he knew of Richard's capture near Vienna in December 1192 while travelling home from Palestine. Philip captured Gisors and the border castles along the River Epte, but took fright at Rouen when the citizens derisively opened the gates before him. John joined in, gaining control of the royal castles at Nottingham, Tickhill, Wallingford, Windsor, and Marlborough. Shiploads of Flemish mercenaries gathered in Channel ports, as they had in the Young King's time. The justiciars stood firm, however, guarding the coast and besieging John's garrisons. He fled abroad in November to join Philip, ceding him most of Normandy, the worst example yet of the Angevin capacity for self-harm.

Richard was not always much wiser. He had struck a deal with Philip on the way to Palestine that simultaneously gave the French king cause for resentment and a weapon. The agreement terminated

Richard's long-standing betrothal to Philip's half-sister Alice, in return for 10,000 marks. It also provided that Richard's hypothetical heirs by his new fiancée, Berengaria of Navarre, should hold their continental inheritance as tenants-in-chief of the King of France by *parage*, that is sharing their patrimony between them. If Richard died without legitimate issue, these provisions gave Philip the legal excuse to drive a wedge between John and his nephew Arthur.

Richard had also alienated Duke Leopold of Austria, casting down his banner at Acre and denying him a share in the plunder. Leopold took his revenge for this slight by capturing Richard on his way home, and selling him on to Henry VI, Emperor of Germany. Richard was related to Henry's Saxon rivals, giving the emperor good reason to accept Philip Augustus' bribes to detain Richard indefinitely. Queen Eleanor's ransom proposal of 150,000 silver marks was an offer Henry could not refuse, however. A freshly released Richard landed at Sandwich on 13 March 1194, to complete his justiciars' work by compelling John's garrison at Nottingham Castle to surrender. Before escaping the emperor's grasp, he was forced to recognise Henry as his liege lord, paying him £5,000 a year. The whole Angevin Empire was now subject to foreign overlords: England to the emperor; its continental lands to Philip Augustus. The only consolation was that Leopold, excommunicated for violating Crusader immunity, had developed gangrene after a riding accident, and perished horribly after amputating his own foot with an axe.

Richard transferred operations to Normandy, hoping to recover the losses suffered during his absence. The ensuing conflict was one of skirmishes, sieges, and mutual devastation. Contradictory sources and a lack of obvious turning points obscure the chronology, different authorities sometimes assigning the same event to different years. English sources and the war's conclusion suggest Richard had the upper hand. More than once Philip ran away to avoid confronting his rival: at Fréteval in July 1194 when the French treasury and archives were lost, and outside Gisors in September 1198, when the bridge broke and, as King Richard wrote in his battle report, Philip drank of the River Epte. When Philip attacked his Flemish vassals for supporting Richard, they destroyed the bridges behind him and flooded the low-lying countryside so that he was lucky to escape drowning or starving.

Both sides raided relentlessly. Only highlights are recorded: Philip's destruction of Evreux, when he desecrated the churches and carried off the holy relics, or the capture of Philip's cousin, the Bishop of Beauvais. Roger of Howden reckoned that Philip burnt twenty-five Norman towns in 1198, besides Evreux for a second time. Mercadier, 'chief of the accursed race of Brabançons' and Richard's favourite *routier*, plundered Abbeville fair, killing numerous French merchants and carrying off more for ransom. The *History* thought Philip had had enough by summer 1198. Richard hemmed him in so tightly he did not know which way to turn. Anglo-Norman self-confidence was such that thirty of their men did not hesitate to attack forty French, an inversion of the traditional pecking order.

Militarily beaten and morally discredited by his bigamous marriage and cynical breaches of Crusader immunity, Philip Augustus offered to return all his wartime gains, with the exception of Gisors and the Vexin border area. Negotiations were fraught. Such was Richard's hatred for Philip, he had abstained from Communion for seven years, rather than forgive him. When the kings met between Les Andelys and Vernon at Le Goulet on the Seine to agree a five-year truce, Richard spoke from a boat. The imprisoned Bishop of Beauvais, was a particular problem. Taken in arms, helmet laced on like any knight, he was objectionable to Richard for seeking to prolong his imprisonment in Germany and as a notorious incendiary of Angevin lands, a false Christian let alone bishop. When a papal intermediary suggested letting him go, the king's rage was so frightful that the luckless Italian fled fearing imminent castration.

The long rivalry ended off stage, almost by accident. Richard went south early in 1199 to confront the incorrigibly rebellious Viscount of Limoges during the military closed season of Lent. Besieging the insignificant tower of Chalus-Chabrol in Haute Vienne, he was hit in the left shoulder with a crossbow bolt, *envenimé* according to the *History*. It was after dinner, in the evening. Richard was slow in seeking medical attention and too quick in breaking off the arrow shaft. Extracting a 4-inch (10cm) bolt head from rolls of fatty neck tissue by flickering torchlight was a hopeless task for Mercadier's luckless surgeon. Within a fortnight, Richard was dead of gangrene on 6 April 1199. The *History* thought that Fortune, which casts down the good and exalts the wicked, had struck down the best prince in the world. William the Breton, Philip's chaplain, thought Richard's death a visitation from God. It was the luckiest stroke of Philip's career. His only credible opponent was eliminated at a stroke, leaving a succession disputed between the double-dealing John and the twelve-year-old Arthur of Brittany.

SOFTSWORD

John's reputation remains contentious. Unlike his French contemporaries he had no official chronicler to polish the royal image. The St Albans historians, Roger of Wendover and his copyist Matthew Paris, pursued a virulently anti-royal line, endorsed by moralistic Victorians. More recent historians, impressed by the written evidence for the reign, have lauded John's administrative achievements. Even his military record has attracted favourable reviews, belying contemporary opinion. Gervase of Canterbury styled him *Johannem mollegladium* – John Softsword – a softness transmuted into unprecedented cruelty. The sober *Barnwell Chronicle* took a mixed view:

> *a great prince, but less* [than] *happy, and like Marius* enjoying both kinds of fortune. Generous and open-handed towards foreigners, but a robber of his own people, trusting more in aliens than his own. Hence he was abandoned by his people before the end, and ultimately mourned by few.*

William of Newburgh described John as nature's enemy. A papal legate thought him more William the Bastard than Edward the Confessor. On his deathbed, able to say what he thought, William Marshal is supposed to have cautioned Henry III against his *felon ancestre*. At best John was unlucky, his elaborate schemes outrunning his means. He left an empty treasury, a diminished patrimony, a ruined economy, and a country wracked by civil war.

When Richard died John seized the treasury at Chinon, and took control of Anjou and Poitou with Queen Eleanor's help. Richard's servants, alerted by the dying king, swiftly asserted John's claims to Normandy and England. Anglo-Norman custom favoured brothers over nephews, and Arthur was rejected as proud and difficult. He disliked 'those of the land', and was subject to *felon conseil* – bad advice from his Breton mother. The accession crisis was soon resolved, but John's insecurity persisted, nourishing fears of treachery that undermined relations with his magnates, and undercut his attempts to defend his patrimony. Back at Le Goulet in May 1200, John restored the truce Philip had agreed with Richard. The terms looked favourable, but John recognised Philip's jurisdiction in Anjou, paying a stiff 20,000 marks as a feudal relief. He dropped the Flemish allies who controlled access to Normandy's north-eastern

---

* A Roman general who died in 86 BC, having been exiled then restored to the consulate.

frontier, and accepted a marriage alliance between Philip's son Louis and his own niece, Blanche of Castile. John had weakened his own hand, while presenting Philip with a card that in time he could play against the throne of England itself.

Three months later, on 24 August 1200, John married Isabel, heiress to the County of Angoulême on the River Charente, a strategic area dominating the main road from Poitiers to Bordeaux. With luck, the gambit might resolve John's lack of a legitimate heir and stabilise the Angevin Empire's southern flank. He was married already, and his new queen hardly of age, but time and the Church could resolve those difficulties. More seriously, Isabel was promised to Hugh the Brown, Count of la Marche, and one of the Lusignan clan, the Angevins' deadliest enemies south of the Loire. Not only did John abduct and marry his enemy's wife, he offered him crooked justice, hiring professional champions to resolve the issue by judicial combat.

John's sharp practice converted a brilliant coup into a *casus belli*. The *History* viewed it as the occasion of the shameful war in which John lost his lands. The Lusignans appealed to their feudal overlord, the King of France. When John refused to plead, Philip's court pronounced him contumacious. On 28 April 1202 John forfeited all his continental lands, not just south of the Loire but in Normandy too. Outright dispossession rarely followed such sentences, but Philip was a new type of ruler. Intent on subordinating his great feudatories, in particular the Angevins, he would fight a total war.

The Angevins' strategic position had deteriorated since hostilities began in 1188. Philip's revenues had almost doubled, partly through his inheriting the County of Vermandois in northern France, partly through fiscal reform. Historians argue about the two sides' relative financial advantage, but Philip could now maintain a sizeable standing force on the Norman frontier: 257 knights, 245 mounted sergeants and 1608 foot, besides 300 *routiers*. Normandy's devastation in the 1190s had alienated the Norman Church and magnates. Their disinclination to fight forced John to employ more *routiers*, whose depredations, as if in an enemy's country, did nothing to encourage Norman support. The Duchy was a strategic liability, dependent on outside help. This could only come from England, John's southern possessions being poor and disaffected. As for Richard's ally, Baldwin Count of Flanders, he was away on Crusade, soon to perish in a Bulgarian dungeon.

John might have held out, despite his moral and financial handicaps, by resolutely exploiting the defensive resources of the country until Philip ran out of money or luck. He nearly did so in July 1202. Philip had been keeping John's nephew Arthur safe at the French court as a card to be played when his claim to the Angevin dominions might prove most embarassing to his uncle. Now sixteen years old and freshly knighted, Arthur invaded Anjou with 200 choice knights and besieged his grandmother, Queen Eleanor, in the castle at Mirebeau or Mirabel, 16 miles (25km) north of Poitiers. John was at Le Mans and reacted with Angevin vigour. The enemy had got inside Mirebeau's town walls, and blocked all the gates except one. Cheerfully awaiting John's arrival, they were confident in their own numbers and courage. John marched 80 miles (120km) in two days, and broke into the town with an all-out onslaught early on 1 August, to catch the French eating breakfast. All his enemies fell into his hands, including Arthur and the Lusignans. The blow might have ended the war at a stroke, except, commented the *History*, for the evil destiny and pride which always brought him down.

Much of the credit for Mirebeau was due to William des Roches, Seneschal of Anjou. Like William he had been one of Henry II's last-ditch loyalists. Instrumental in the decision to march on Mirebeau, he lost three horses killed beneath him fighting at the town gate. Careless of this debt of honour, John broke promises not to take his prisoners north of the Loire, carting twenty-two of them off in chains to starve to death at Corfe Castle in Dorset. Even his closest followers were embarrassed. Inconsistent as always, he released others, including the Lusignans, who promptly revolted. Such, commented the *History*, is their way. Arthur was held at Falaise, menaced with blinding and castration, triple rings of iron round his feet. Taken to Rouen, he disappeared from the record about Easter 1203, probably stabbed by his uncle after dinner, and dumped in the Seine. Once more John had converted success into disaster. Supplanted as seneschal, William des Roches joined the rebels, who now included the outraged Bretons. Norman tax yields fell away as John's moral authority disintegrated. Exploiting the universal outrage, Philip Augustus swore he would never abandon his attempts to bring John down.

Military collapse soon followed. The medieval aversion to confrontation in the open was reinforced in John's case by fears of treachery. The *History* recalled his taking indirect roads for fear of ambush, and sleeping in castles rather than hostelries. He may not have been altogether wrong. Count Robert of Alençon gave John dinner and kissed him on the mouth, before transferring homage to Philip the same day. Gervase of Canterbury thought John was rendered an ineffectual coward by traitors who surrendered his castles to the King of France. Philip exploited such people, but despised them, telling William Marshal they were soiled rags to be thrown into the latrine after use. The most shocking betrayal came from English turncoats. Philip advanced down the Seine to Vaudreuil, an outlying bastion of the Norman capital, just 15 miles (24km) from Rouen. As soon as Philip deployed his siege engines, the castle's commanders, Robert fitz Walter and Saer of Quincy, surrendered with all their knights and military equipment, making no attempt at resistance. Ralph of Coggeshall suggests that they doubted John's willingness to come to their aid. Even so, they disappointed contemporary expectations. The population mocked them in satirical songs, and Philip threw them in jail.

Philip encircled the vital cliff-top castle of Château Gaillard above Les Andelys on the Seine in September 1203. Richard had built his 'saucy castle' at the immense cost of £11,500 as the springboard for his intended reconquest of the Vexin. Bristling with defensive features of royal devising, Château Gaillard was reputed impregnable. With Vaudreuil gone it was isolated, but the garrison held on until March 1204, surrendering for want of provisions. By then John had left Normandy for ever:

> *... failing to lend any assistance to the besieged, because he always feared treachery from his people, he sailed away to England in December, the depth of winter, abandoning all the Normans in great distress and fear.*
>
> *(Coggeshall)*

Philip besieged and took Falaise, abjectly surrendered by its *routier* commander, then swept through western Normandy to take Caen, Domfront, and Barfleur, the Angevin embarkation point for England. Philip arrived outside Rouen in May, the citizens purchasing a fifty-day respite to seek their duke's assistance. Coggeshall says that John refused, suspecting treachery. The *History* claims that a host was summoned belatedly to Portsmouth, commenting that while the dog was doing its business behind, the wolf got away. And so, lamented Coggeshall, the illustrious city of Rouen, hitherto unconquered, surrendered. Merlin's prophecy that the sword should be separated from the sceptre was fulfilled after 139 years. Normandy and England were once more divided.

John's continental possessions all fell by autumn 1204, except the castles of Chinon and Loches, the seaport of La Rochelle, the Channel Islands, and far off Aquitaine. The strategic revolution was as complete as that of the 1150s. Philip kept his Norman conquests as royal demesne, consolidating his financial lead over his Angevin rival, who was driven to ever more radical steps to fill his war-chest. The Channel was now the front line, a potential invasion route. Where Henry II had menaced Paris from Gisors, French fleets now threatened the English coast from Cherbourg and Boulogne. At Christmas 1216 a French prince would hold court in London. As Stephen found in the 1140s, defeat in Normandy presaged civil strife in England.

ROAD TO RUNNYMEDE

John devoted a decade to recovering his overseas patrimony. The protracted time scale is explained partly by the difficulty of the task, partly by his enemies' diversionary tactics. He first tried just twelve months after Rouen fell, assembling the largest fleet yet seen at Portsmouth, 1,500 ships with innumerable knights, to invade Normandy and Poitou. As so often with John's plans the enterprise foundered in a miasma of contradictory advice and mutual recrimination. The last Angevin stronghold at Chinon fell a week after the expedition broke up, following horrendous portents, including an ass-headed monster struck by lightning near Maidstone. A smaller expedition to Poitou enjoyed some success, but John had missed his best chance of counter-attacking while the Normans were still unreconciled to French rule.

John was distracted by problems nearer home for the next seven years. His quarrel with Pope Innocent III over the election of a new Archbishop of Canterbury began in 1207. The dispute escalated into a formal Interdict which suspended ecclesiastical services throughout England and Wales until John recognised the papal candidate Stephen Langton. A brilliant scholar who organised the Bible into its current chapters, Langton was tainted by French connections unacceptable in the king's leading adviser. In the short run the Interdict was advantageous to John, who confiscated £50,000 of Church revenues. In the longer term it undermined his legitimacy, and invited foreign intervention.

John's presence on English soil created other strains, sharpened by his predatory financial policies. Previously the English could benefit from Henry II's legal reforms, while blaming royal officials for any miscarriage of injustice. John's personal role in government after 1204, which so excites the admiration of administrative historians, made the king himself the focus of resentment. This was especially so among the magnates, whose cases the king reserved for himself. These often entailed cash payments for the king's good will, which exceeded the litigant's ability to pay. It is not surprising that Magna Carta has been described as a rebellion of the king's debtors, or that one of its most enduring clauses prohibited the sale of justice.

Besides inflating the profits of justice, John sought new or increased sources of revenue. Traditional feudal incidents, such as fines on marriage, trebled in scale. Henry II had levied scutage, a payment in lieu of personal military service, seven times in thirty-two years. John did so eleven times in sixteen years, while almost trebling the rate to 3 marks in 1214. He invented taxes on moveable goods and customs dues, and stockpiled huge quantities of coin in barrels at royal castles ready for the great counter-offensive. Some thirty million silver pennies were withdrawn from circulation, half the national stock, depressing prices and choking economic activity.

Baronial indebtedness consolidated political and financial grievances, as John exploited baronial debts to enforce political discipline, even upon his closest associates. One of John's leading supporters during the accession crisis, William of Braose had captured Arthur at Mirebeau. In the winter of 1207–08, however, he lost royal favour. The *History* professed not to know why; the issue remained sensitive. The official reason was non-repayment of debts incurred for new Irish estates. John's extreme actions suggest a darker cause. When he demanded hostages to ensure his magnates' loyalty against the Pope, William's wife Matilda defied John and her husband, refusing to surrender her children to someone who had murdered his own nephew. Clearly the Braose household knew too much about Arthur's death, the fullest account of which comes from Margam Abbey in South Wales, a religious establishment to which they had suspiciously close ties. The family fled to Ireland, after an ineffectual rebellion, pursued by John and a large army. William escaped to France disguised as a beggar, but Matilda and her eldest son were shipwrecked in Galloway, handed back to John by their rescuers, and starved to death in a dungeon at Windsor Castle. The moral for potential victims of the king's malice was clear.

Pending hostilities with Philip Augustus, John launched expeditions against Scotland in 1209, Ireland in 1210, and Gwynedd in 1211. The apparent success of John's activities on England's Celtic flanks is sometimes contrasted with his failure elsewhere, but his insatiable demands for tribute and hostages poisoned relations, and created common grievances with English dissidents. Strands of opposition coalesced in 1212. Llewelyn ap Iorwerth of Gwynedd had surrendered hostages and paid tribute of hawks, dogs, steeds, and cattle two years before. Now he revolted, with other Welsh leaders, exterminating castle garrisons and causing great slaughter of the English in Powys. Possible motives include John's provocative new castle at Aberconwy, papal attempts to destabilise John's throne, and Llewelyn's treasonable relations with Philip Augustus. John abandoned plans to attack the latter, turning on the Welsh instead. He hired 8,330 pioneers to clear the road, twice the number his grandson Edward I would use. Suddenly the king cancelled the whole exercise, hanged his hostages, and barricaded himself inside Nottingham Castle, surrounded by foreign crossbowmen.

John's own magnates were plotting, either to kill him outright, or to deliver him to the Welsh. Among those implicated were Robert fitz Walter, lately of Vaudreuil, and Eustace of Vesci whose wife John was rumoured to have seduced.

Pressure mounted the next year, as a papal legate incited Philip to invade England. A popular preacher, Peter of Pontefract, prophesied that John would not be king after Ascension Day, without specifying which one. While Philip gathered ships at Boulogne and threatened to exterminate the English, John massed forces along the coast from Ipswich to Portsmouth. By the end of May, the crisis had passed. The papal legate double-crossed Philip, and cut a deal with John to end the Interdict. John went a step further. He did homage to the Pope, making England a feudal dependency of the Holy See. A fortnight later, on 30 May, English ships fell upon Philip's fleet in the River Zwyn at Dam near Brugge, capturing 300–400 vessels and destroying more on the beach. Not since Adam's day, judged the *History*, had such a fleet come to grief. Philip watched it blaze, as if the sea was on fire. The year's other big loser was Peter of Pontefract, hanged at Wareham in November.

John was now ready to counter-attack. His treasury was stuffed with 200,000 marks and domestic opposition silenced by his submission to the Pope. A Flemish-German army led by John's nephew Otto of Brunswick, the German emperor, hovered on Philip's northern border. John sailed for La Rochelle on 9 February 1214, accompanied by few earls but many knights of inferior fortune. The plan was to divide French forces or retake Normandy while they fought Otto. The scheme was over-complicated and fatally dependent on Poitevin support. In any case, Philip Augustus could now afford two armies, fielding over 2,000 knights between them. John manoeuvred skilfully to draw away the southern French army, but his Poitevin allies refused to engage inferior numbers at La Roche-au-Moine eight miles (12km) down the Loire from

Angers at Savennières. Roger of Wendover avers that both sides ran away. While John retreated to La Rochelle, the main French army under Philip crushed Otto at Bouvines, between Lille and Tournai. One of the great battles of the century, Bouvines left France predominant in Western Europe. It sealed the loss of Normandy, and fixed John's course for the rest of his reign.

I I

FINEST KNIGHT

illiam Marshal had more experience of the ups and downs of Angevin politics than most. He had known five English kings by 1214. As he spent his life in royal company, it is fitting that his deeds, like theirs, should be recorded for posterity, a rare distinction in an age unmindful of laymen.

The *History's* 19,214 lines of rhyming couplets were lost for six centuries, until the single known copy, written on twenty-seven parchment sheets, surfaced at Sotheby's in 1861. First published in the original Middle French in the 1890s, the poem took another century to appear in English. A pioneering example of French literature, it was probably written at Chepstow in South Wales. Its author acknowledges two sponsors: William Marshal the Younger and John of Earley. William's successor had filial and personal reasons to refurbish his father's memory, which was under assault in Henry III's faction-ridden court. While the heir bore the financial costs, the moral impetus behind the work came from the old Marshal's devoted squire, John of Earley. John also provided much of the raw material, blending eyewitness testimony from 1187 onwards with recollections of William's reminiscences.

Episodic and chronologically confused at first, the *History* assumes increasing authority from the late 1180s when John of Earley entered the Marshal's service. Isolated anecdotes make way for coherent political and military narrative, sometimes confirming existing sources, sometimes providing new insights. This extended portrait of the whole life and career of a layman was unusual for the thirteenth century. It paints a colourful and realistic picture of the period, from the perspective of the dominant knightly class, packed with insights into medieval warfare, undistorted by the chivalric stereotypes of later authors. It deserves to be better known.

The author of this remarkable work, another John, was no monkish chronicler. A layman, he wrote in the aristocracy's own language, preferring earthy proverbs to clerical homily. Modern historians disagree over his age, some accepting his claims to have witnessed events in the 1180s. His frequent protestations of truthfulness may be a rhetorical device: Geoffrey of Villehardouin, Marshal of Champagne, made similar claims for his self-justifying account of the Fourth Crusade of 1205. John's attempts to reconcile contradictory accounts of the battle of Lincoln, however, suggest an underlying honesty. His inaccuracies are predictable and forgivable: an understandable discretion when writing of sensitive matters, and narrative distortions that reflect William's flickering memory of days long past.

HOSTAGE TO FORTUNE

Like most medieval people, William had little idea of his age. Outside royal circles, births were rarely recorded. The end of life, with its passage to a better world, was more important. William

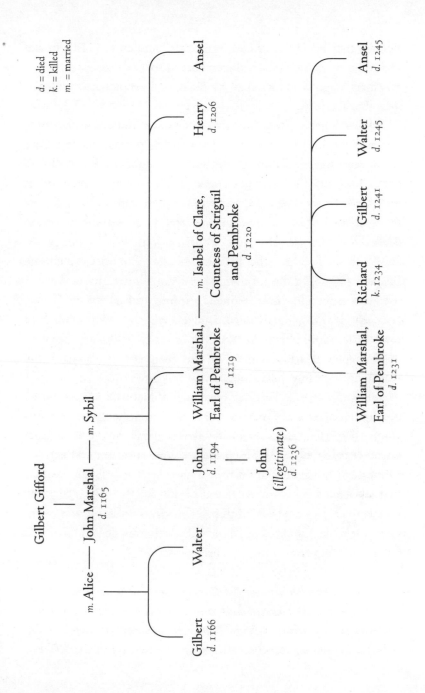

claimed that he was over eighty in 1216, placing his birth in the 1130s. The Marshal family's documented role in the disturbances of Stephen's reign suggests that William exaggerated his longevity for political effect.

William's grandfather Gilbert Gifford was Marshal at the court of Henry I. A mid-ranking official responsible for maintaining order and supervising the stables, he bequeathed his function to William's father, John fitz Gilbert, who served Stephen in that role until at least 1136. Soon afterwards the title transferred from the office to the man, for in 1141 we find him referred to as *Johannes agnomine Marescallus*, Marshal by name. By then John was no longer in Stephen's service, and the Marshal family never performed the everyday physical duties of that office again. John may have broken with the king following Stephen's capture at Lincoln, or before. As early as 1137 he fortified Ludgershall and Marlborough, a royal castle dominating the Kennet Valley in Wiltshire. Stephen was besieging Marlborough when the opening convulsions of the Angevin revolt drew him away.

John's ambiguous loyalties bear out William of Malmesbury's description of him as 'a man of surprising subtlety'. *Gesta Stephani*, another West Country source, saw him as 'artful and ready for great acts of treachery'. The *History* presented him as valiant and faithful, neither earl nor baron, but astonishing everyone with the largesse that attracted a *mesnie* or warband of 300 knights. *Gesta Stephani* reveals the economic basis of that generosity, associating John with freebooters like Geoffrey of Mandeville, who was denied Christian burial and hung from a tree in a lead shroud:

> John ... *who commanded Marlborough Castle, ceaselessly disturbed the peace of the kingdom; built castles with amazing skill in places agreeable to himself, brought under his own control the lands of the Church, having chased out the tenants ... And when he was struck*

with the sword of the Church's power [i.e. excommunicated], *he was not cowed, but more and more obdurate.*

The demise of Robert fitz Hubert illustrates John Marshal's methods. A renegade Angevin with a penchant for smearing his victims' bodies with honey and exposing them to wasps, Robert seized Devizes Castle by a night assault using rope ladders. Seeking to infiltrate Marlborough Castle under cover of peace negotiations, he was himself betrayed. John's men slammed the gates behind him, and chased his confederates back to Devizes. Robert was fettered, starved, tortured, and finally returned to Robert of Gloucester, who hanged him outside Devizes to the chroniclers' applause.

John Marshal had joined the Angevin camp by August 1141, appearing second in a list of Matilda's supporters at the siege of Winchester. The siege's end and the panic-stricken *dispersio Wintoniensis*, or Rout of Winchester, form one of the most dramatic episodes of his career. Superior numbers of royalists hemmed in the Angevins, themselves besieging the bishop's castle at Wolvesey. Short of food, the Angevins broke out westwards. John was trapped at Wherwell Abbey, where the Andover road crosses the River Test. His men were dragged off in chains, while armed bands rampaged through the sacred precincts, and nuns fled screaming through the flames. John stood fast in the tower, while molten lead dripped off the burning roof, threatening his last companion with instant death if he tried to surrender. Scorched and blinded in one eye, John finally escaped, walking the 11 miles home.

The *History* presents this dramatic episode as a rearguard action, in which John Marshal covered Matilda's escape. It also claims that he advised her to sit astride her horse, instead of sideways as ladies usually did, in order to outpace her royalist pursuers. Two of the three contemporary sources, however, put the storming of Wherwell Abbey before Matilda's withdrawal. Several hundred Angevin knights had fortified the convent, to protect their communications westwards, when overwhelming numbers of royalists stormed it, early on 14 September. This cut Winchester off from the north-west, and precipitated the Angevin retreat later the same day. The chronicler John of Worcester is sometimes quoted in support of the *History*'s account. However, he specified *Stolibricge* or Stockbridge, the next crossing downstream from Wherwell, as the place where the Angevin rearguard under Robert of Gloucester, not John Marshal, came to grief. Local tradition places the fighting just east of Stockbridge at *Le Strete*, a paved ford of Roman origin. Today, this is a roundabout, where the Winchester road crosses the Andover–Romsey road.

Covered by Robert's last stand, Matilda escaped, riding astride like a man, escorted by her lifelong friend Brian fitz Count. Once past Stockbridge, she could head north over the downs for Ludgershall, giving Wherwell a wide berth. In this crisis Matilda seems more likely to have entrusted her safety to faithful supporters like Robert and Brian than to the weathercock Marshal. No contemporary account says who advised Matilda on equitation. John Marshal does seem an appropriate commander at Wherwell, on his own route home. John of Worcester mentioned an unspecified John there, while William is unlikely to have invented his father's disfigurement. The *History* appears to have conflated the most dramatic elements of a story that was a very distant memory by the 1220s, giving John Marshal the lead role. What actually happened mattered less than what William and his contemporaries believed. Such ancestral devotion to the Angevin cause constituted a compelling claim upon the dynasty's gratitude.

William's birth occurred some years after the Rout of Winchester. Wiltshire had become the civil war's front line, as John Marshal fought Stephen's sheriff for local supremacy. Stephen's defeat at Wilton in 1143, however, portended a strategic shift. The sheriff changed sides, becoming the Angevin Earl of Salisbury. The Middle Ages were a very physical age, so peace was made flesh by John Marshal marrying the new earl's sister, Sybil. John was already married with two sons, but the Church's generous definition of consanguinity made it easy to dispose of a wife who had served her political turn. Allowing for such manoeuvres and the birth of an elder brother, William was probably born at Marlborough in 1147. His Christian name was the most popular of the day. Over 100 Williams attended the Young King's court at Christmas 1171. It was also a compliment to his mother's kin, being her uncle's name. William was attached from birth to a lineage more powerful than his own.

Younger sons were minor pieces on the feudal chessboard. Like pawns they might be risked to protect more important pieces. The earliest lines of the *History* derived from William's memories rather than hearsay concern such an occasion. Pushing eastwards down the Kennet, John Marshal built one of his unofficial castles at Newbury. It cut the road between royalist castles at Winchester and Oxford, and threatened Stephen's strategic heartland in the Thames Valley. Our only contemporary informant is Henry of Huntingdon. He says that Stephen besieged Newbury in 1152, took it, and moved on to Wallingford. The *History's* fuller account sheds light on the conduct of sieges, the character of Stephen, and the precarious existence of younger sons.

Sieges followed a set pattern: summons, defiance, and ritual show of resistance, followed by a pause while the garrison appealed to their lord for help. John Marshal played for time, claiming he also had to consult his superiors. Knowing his man, Stephen demanded a hostage and was given the five-year-old William. John promptly broke the truce by provisioning the castle. William, as the *History* put it, was *en aventure*. When Stephen threatened the child with hanging, John feigned indifference, saying he still had the anvils and hammers to make more and better sons.

Taking hostages was a common medieval way of reinforcing contracts. Stephen's exchange for Robert of Gloucester after the Rout of Winchester was guaranteed by an elaborate rotation of high-status hostages. Matters did not always end so happily, however. King John hanged twenty-eight Welsh hostages in 1212, including a seven-year-old. The chivalric King William the Lion of Scotland castrated the son of Earl Harald of Maddadson when the latter invaded Caithness. Fortunately for William, Wiltshire was not Wales or Scotland, and Stephen, as John Marshal may have calculated, was not King John.

A deadly charade followed, featuring a gallows, a stone-thrower, and a siege gallery to which William was attached as a human shield. Each time, William's naïve chatter saved him from being catapulted into the castle, or crushed by a millstone dropped off the wall. Finally, he became a household pet, playing around Stephen's flower-strewn tent. He claimed to have beaten the king at jackstraws, a jousting game played with the spear-like heads of the plantain, *plantago lanceolata*, a suitable exploit for a future tournament champion. Newbury also marks the first appearance of the backbiting flatterers that the *History* styled *losengiers*, whose jealousy plagued William's career. The poet knew better than to accuse Stephen of threatening his subject's life. It was the king's courtiers who loaded William into the stone-thrower, and the king who rescued him.

The image of a hard-pressed king playing jackstraws is a reminder of how medieval households swarmed with young people, from wellborn squires to unwashed turn-spits. William would soon join the throng. Only eldest sons expected a significant inheritance. Younger sons of good family left home to pursue one of two permissible *métiers*, or occupations: chivalry or the Church. Late in the 1150s, William rode off with a single companion to become a knight, his belongings rolled up in his cloak. In those unaffected times even the sons of a king might have done the same.

William's destination was the Seine Valley, where his distant cousin and namesake was hereditary Chamberlain of Normandy, and a well-known maker of knights. His castle's overgrown remains still stand at the northern end of the great Tancarville bridge, 10 miles (16km) east of Le Havre, including a twelfth-century square tower that William might recognise. It was usual for great English families, remarked Gervase of Tilbury, to send their sons to France, 'to be trained in arms, and have the barbarity of their native tongue removed'. William would have spoken English at home. He would speak French in future, like a gentleman. Some knightly skills are self-evident: handling the shield, swordplay, gripping the lance, and sitting straight in the saddle. Brutal mock combats instilled the toughness that carried John Marshal home from Wherwell. Henry II's sons all learnt to be thrown to the ground, to see their blood flowing, and feel their teeth cracking under an opponent's blow. A twelfth-century educational theorist thought aspirant knights should learn riding, swimming, shooting the bow, boxing, bird baiting, and versifying. He omitted serving at table, an essential skill for maintaining the bonds of conviviality that bound feudal society together. Even a king's son might carve his lord's meat, as the Young King did during Philip Augustus's coronation feast.

The *History* glosses over William's time at Tancarville. Perhaps he was homesick like Ordericus Vitalis, the early twelfth-century chronicler sent away from his English provincial home at much the same age as William. There were those who resented William's presence, *losengiers* who complained that he ate, drank, and slept too much. They called him *gaste-viande*, greedy-guts, but the chamberlain defended his young cousin with the obscure prediction that he would yet pull the bean out of the stew, rather like Little Jack Horner pulling the plum out of his Christmas pie. One thing William did not do was learn to read. When he received letters he employed a clerk to read them properly. Perhaps John Marshal, the hard man of

Wiltshire politics, shared the proverbial view that anyone at school till twelve before learning to ride a horse was only fit for priesthood.

William's tournament successes suggest that he profited by the chamberlain's instruction. His physique was well adapted to his *métier*. An eyewitness, probably John of Earley, thought that 'there might be no better made body in the whole world'. This is conventional praise, along with the height and broad hips essential for any cavalryman. We are on firmer ground with William's unfashionable brown colouring and well-attested strength. During one tournament, he dashed out from lunch, his mouth full of fresh herring, to carry off an injured knight in full armour, to pay the bill. After eight years at Tancarville, aged nearly twenty, William was ready for knighthood.

KNIGHT ERRANT

Knighthood was a high point in the existence of every young man of good family, marking the start of adult life. The *History* tells us that in William's case the chamberlain simply belted on his sword, although it becomes apparent that William received all the standard knightly accoutrements: warhorse or destrier, cloak, and hauberk. The whole outfit cost the approximate annual output of a village. The ceremony descended from Germanic traditions of equipping every freeborn youth with the arms of manhood. In the twelfth century's more stratified society, it bestowed access to the new class of mounted warriors. Known as *chevaliers* in French, they have left us the word chivalry. This was both an activity and a set of values. At one level it was the practice of mounted warfare. The Angevin knights at Winchester rode out daily *por faire chevalerie* – to do chivalry.

Chivalry was also the ethical framework governing that activity. It evolved from the need of knightly households to reduce the physical risks of continual warfare, and mitigate the social consequences of individual acts of violence. The success of such efforts to moderate conflict was limited, given the nature of medieval society. Unarmed knights remained fair game. Attacks from behind were not unknown. Common combatants, sergeants and *routiers*, were outside the system. Uneven in its application, chivalry represented the first secular steps towards today's laws of war. Its moral basis, a fusion of Christian and martial values, was represented by three essential qualities: prowess or skill at arms, loyalty to one's lord, and largesse or generosity to equals and inferiors. The *History* presents William as their living embodiment. It places less emphasis on a fourth element, the service of one's lady, but both William and his father gained much through the service of women, and profited greatly by their marriages.

The occasion of William's knighting is controversial. The location was Drincourt, a market town in northern Normandy. Now called Neufchâtel-en-Bray, Drincourt occupies a central point on the River Béthune which flows north-west to Dieppe. King John attacked it in 1201, as did the Young King in 1173. Alexander of Parma besieged it in 1592 during the French Wars of Religion. The Luftwaffe destroyed it in 1940 with incendiary bombs. The *History* describes a cruel war also, castles garrisoned from Mortagne in the west to Arques near Dieppe.

The *History*'s first editor, Paul Meyer, identified the conflict in which William was engaged at the time of his knighting with the Young King's Revolt of 1173, when Drincourt was indeed besieged. This wrecks the poem's chronology, and jumbles up the sides. The *History*'s account of a fluid mounted action is impossible to reconcile with a static siege. A more satisfactory date is 1166, when the Counts of Flanders, Boulogne, and Ponthieu revolted against Henry II, as the text reports. This also fits the *History*'s sequence of events, which places Drincourt before William's first tournament later that year, and puts him safely on the Angevin side. The date's uncertainty is a reminder of William's obscurity. Nobody remembered the undistinguished ceremony, rushed through on the eve of battle, perhaps for a whole troop of Tancarville graduates.

Neither Drincourt nor Lincoln fit the stereotype of a medieval pitched battle fought in the open, as both occurred in built-up areas. Medieval Drincourt was built east of the River Béthune. Since diverted westwards to prevent flooding, the twelfth-century Béthune then flowed along the foot of the steep incline up which runs the main street, the Grande Rue Saint-Jacques, past the church. Henry I's castle, which gave Drincourt its modern name, lay at the far northern corner of the medieval town. Long demolished, the probable site of William's knighting is marked only by a ring of trees and a deep ditch on the north side. A suburb known as St Vincent lay north-west of the main town on the Eu road, now the D1314, beyond a ditch crossed by the *History*'s 'master bridge'. The fighting seems to have revolved about the latter, the counts' raiding party having broken into the suburb, the defending Normans trying to expel it.

The forces quoted display the usual medieval contradiction between small precise numbers, like the chamberlain's twenty-eight knights, and the 2,000 that the *History* attributes to the enemy. Eighty knights dined at the chamberlain's expense after the battle, a reasonable figure if supplemented by two or three sergeants each. Despite Drincourt lying 16 miles (25km) from the border, the Normans were surprised, and rushed about shouting, 'To arms, to arms', hastily pulling on their armour. The Constable of Normandy, who should have taken command, rode off *vilainement* – like a cowardly peasant – leaving the chamberlain to save the town.

Neufchâtel's repeated destruction complicates attempts to reconstruct the battle. Sidney Painter, William's American biographer, places the chamberlain south-west of the Béthune, outside the town, an odd place to defend it against an attack from the north, one that would have required the defenders to charge up the steep main street. It seems more likely that the chamberlain's party formed up within the castle, and rode out along the Rue du Vieux Château to turn right across the master bridge. As they went, the chamberlain rebuked William for pushing into the front rank among the more experienced knights.

The enemy were already inside the town. Seizing shields and gripping lances, the opposing squadrons put their horses to a gallop, and crashed together, shattering lances and smashing shields into fragments. Such was the noise of sword blows on helmets, a thunderclap might not have been heard. The defenders gained the advantage, and chased the raiders across the back bridge that carried the Eu road across the outer ditch into the countryside. Here fresh troops in good order reinforced the attackers, driving the tired and disorganised Normans back to the master bridge. Four times the battle swayed to and fro, before the townspeople joined in with axes and clubs to clear the street.

The *History* makes much of William's prowess, describing him laying out swathes of the enemy, giving and receiving great blows, and rallying the shaken Normans, cheered on by an admiring chorus of townspeople. Near the end of the battle, thirteen Flemish sergeants set upon him while he was drawing breath in a sheep-fold, snagging him with an iron hook kept for pulling down burning houses. William broke away by clinging to his horse's *peitral* or breast strap, but they ripped off thirteen links of mail, and left an enduring scar on his shoulder. More seriously, his precious destrier was killed. Everyone, even the French, agreed that the honours of the day were William's, but he had failed in the knight's duty to profit from his prowess. Teased by an older knight while celebrating the town's delivery, he did not even have an old horse collar to show for the day's fighting. Unable to replace his destrier, he sold his cloak to buy a broken down rouncey, a better animal for a robber than a knight.

Marooned at Tancarville, William was rescued by a tournament at Sainte-Jamme-sur-Sarthe, near Le Mans. The chamberlain needed forty knights, and he grudgingly gave William a new destrier: an unmanageable brute, but swift as a hawk. Called 'Blancart', its name lingered in William's memory for half a century. He had learned his lesson from Drincourt, and captured three knights, their ransoms buying him all the horses he wanted. He attended another event on his own, winning the prize. Still in Tancarville colours, a mark of quality, William embarked on his first tour, from the lower Rhine, through Flanders and Normandy, down to Anjou. He was not always successful. Years later he refused to return a horse to a knight who had treated him similarly when an unknown. But William was learning the business, not just the physical arts of jousting, but the bargaining and horse trading that went with it. At length, rich enough to appear before his family in style, he bid his mentor farewell, and sailed for England.

William appears not to have seen his family since he left home, and his trip was undertaken for practical reasons. His father and half-brothers had died, leaving the Marshal patrimony to his elder brother John. There is no sign that William expected anything from him. Instead he sought out his maternal uncle Patrick, Earl of Salisbury. This was a shrewd career move. Representing a more prestigious lineage, Earl Patrick had greater influence at court, where the elder John Marshal had lost favour after spreading seditious prophecies. A sister's son was a useful addition to any household, closely related but without inconvenient patrimonial claims. A knight of proven valour, William was a welcome recruit to the *mesnie* Earl Patrick was about to lead overseas.

There was always trouble in Poitou – 'wolf skin' or *peil de loup*, as the *History* called it – as local lords resisted the centralising activities of their Angevin overlords. While Henry II hunted Poitevin dissidents, Earl Patrick guarded Queen Eleanor at Lusignan. Shortly after Easter 1168, the queen was ambushed while out riding. She was hurried away to safety, but Earl Patrick, still unarmed, received a lance thrust from behind while mounting his destrier. The *History* presents this as typical Poitevin treachery. It even uses the expression 'assassin', from the Middle Eastern sect of that name, rather like invoking Al-Quaida today. Unarmed knights were fair game, however. Twenty years later William himself charged Richard Coeur de Lion in his *pourpoint* or padded linen jacket, and claimed that he would have been within his rights to kill him.

Enraged by his uncle's underhand killing, William charged into the melee, bringing one Poitevin down before the others killed his horse. Backed against a hedge, he stood at bay like a wild boar, defying them to come on, until somebody climbed through the hedge and speared him from behind, thrusting up beneath the hauberk. William was lucky to escape death, the lance passing through both thighs, projecting 3 feet (nearly 1m) beyond. Blood gushed out when the weapon was withdrawn, leaving a trail on the ground. John, Lord of Joinville, a veteran of St Louis's Crusade in 1249, describes blood pouring from a similar wound, as if from the bung-hole of a barrel. Fearing Henry II's vengeance, William's captors dragged him from one obscure refuge to another, while he bandaged his wounds with his legging ties. Surprisingly, he recovered, to be ransomed by the queen.

This violent episode was the decisive moment of William's career. Terribly injured in the queen's defence, in an echo of John Marshal's stand at Wherwell, William had forged a bond with the house of Anjou that survived fifty years and more than one contretemps. His instinctive gallantry earned him the gratitude of Europe's most powerful woman, whose name the *History* reminds us meant 'pure and gold'. She gave William almost everything a young knight might want: horses, arms, money, fine clothes, and promotion. Following the Young King's coronation, William was chosen as the fifteen-year-old prince's tutor-in-arms, responsible for his security and military education. This was astonishing progress for a twenty-three-year-old *bachelier* of obscure origin. Together the two travelled much and spent much, William acting as what the eighteenth century would call the Young King's bear-leader. The Young King's charters confirm William's pre-eminent position, listing him first among the lay witnesses, preceding other household knights.

The *History* maintains a prudent silence over William's involvement in the Young King's Revolt, except for one episode. Pursued by Henry II's forces, the Young King's household decided to knight the prince immediately. Naturally the Young King chose his tutor to perform the ceremony as the best knight present. Unfortunately a reliable eyewitness recorded Henry II knighting his son before his coronation in 1170. As with Wherwell Abbey and the jackstraws, the incident's literal truth matters less than its affirmation of lifelong royal favour. We must assume that William participated in both the sieges of Drincourt and Rouen, his name appearing in government lists of rebels at the close of hostilities. Forgiven if not chastened, the Young King returned to England for a year of hunting, never to William's taste, and the insipid variety of jousting known as *plaids*. Life began again in April 1176, as the Young King and his tutor sailed from Portchester to rejoin the international tournament circuit.

The twelfth-century tournament craze was at its height. Competitive jousting had developed in France in the late eleventh century, as knights learned to grip a lance tightly underarm, and charge full tilt at an opponent to knock them clean out of the saddle. It was at once a pastime and a vocational exercise. Known in England as *conflicti Gallicani* – French fights – tournaments were also called *nundinae* or fairs from the swarms of hangers-on. The Church condemned them as a distraction from fighting the infidel and an incitement to the more pleasurable sins. Governments feared them as a threat to public order. Neither ecclesiastical nor administrative disapproval affected the sport's popularity. Its sponsors were great feudatories like the Counts of Champagne or Flanders. Enriched by the twelfth-century expansion of trade and industry, they found tournaments an effective way of asserting their power and prestige, as the parallel recovery of royal power menaced their political independence. The Young King's addiction to the pursuit was a continuation of rebellion by other means. The *History* describes sixteen tournaments in which William took part:

WILLIAM'S TOURNAMENT RECORD

Year	Location (Department)	Exploits
1166	Ste Jamme/Valennes (Sarthe)	Takes three knights
1166	St Brice/Bouere (Mayenne)	Wins prize: a Lombard horse
1176	Ressons/Gournai (Oise)*	Copies Flemish tactics
1176	Unlocated ('Normandie')*	'Sire et mestre' of own lord
1176	Anet/Sorel (Eure-et-Loir)*	Team tactics defeat French
1177	Pleurs (Marne)	Wins prize
1177	Eu (Seine-Maritime)*	Takes ten knights and twelve horses
1178/79 (exact date unknown)	Joigny (Yonne)	
1179	Maintenon/Nogent (Eure-et-Loir)*	
1179	Anet/Sorel (Eure-et-Loir)	Leads Young King's *mesnie*
1179	Épernon (Eure-et-Loir)	
1179–80	Lagny-sur-Marne (Seine-et-Marne)*	Flies own banneret
1180	Épernon (Eure-et-Loir)	

1182	Ressons/Gournai (Oise)*	Defends estranged lord
1183	Ressons/Gournai (Oise)	
1183	St Pierre-sur-Dives (Calvados)	

* Tournaments at which the Young King was present

Tournaments had a specific geographical range, like rugby or bull-fighting. The baker's dozen of locations in the *History* occupy a rough quadrilateral from Eu on the Channel, south-east towards Troyes, then west past Le Mans, before turning north towards the Channel near Caen. Events avoided royal strongholds, sponsors preferring the debatable locations chosen for real battles. The central cluster of tournament venues listed above all lay in Eure-et-Loir, on the Angevin-Capetian border. Participants came from further afield: 'Avalterre to Montjoux' says the *History* – the Lower Rhine to the St Bernard Pass. William's first victim was a Scotsman. Individual *mesnies* formed local teams, grouped into national sides: Anglo-Norman, Flemish, or French, never Spanish or Italian. At the height of the season, there might be a tournament every other week. Sponsors avoided wet weather, bad for horses and equipment, but respites were shorter than in real wars: Advent to Epiphany, Easter, Whit, and All Saints. Twelfth-century tournaments were not the regulated individual jousts of the later Middle Ages. More a free-for-all scrimmage, they were conducted in the hope of gain, a form of gambling, in which knights wagered their bodies and equipment against their strength and skill at arms.

There were no lists in the sense of a fenced-off fighting area. Fighting ranged across a loosely defined area of open countryside, taking in barns, old mottes, vineyards, and even villages. There were a few conventions: *commençailles* beforehand when young knights showed off; truces between bouts; *recets* or safe refuges surrounded by a palisade; release of prisoners and settling up accounts at the end; a prize awarded by the sponsors. Otherwise, tournaments resembled real battles, with sharp swords and realistic tactics, but no lethal intent. That would have been counter-productive. Horses were not targeted for the same reason. Tournaments were not without fatalities, however. The knight credited with inventing them died in one. William's third son, Gilbert, was killed when his destrier's reins broke. The brave were to be found amongst the horses' hooves, for cowards would not hazard their lives in the press (*History*).

William survived his eighteen-year tournament career unscathed, though perhaps a little dazed. It was standard practice to beat a knight around the head until he was sufficiently disoriented to be dragged away. William was found after the Pleurs tournament with his head on an anvil, having his helmet knocked back into shape, so he could take it off. The *History* describes sixteen tournaments in which William took part, and implies many others. He reckoned at the end of his life that he had taken over 500 knights, with their horses and equipment. His top recorded score for one event was at Eu, where he captured ten knights and twelve horses, one of them twice. Captures came so easily that he made a joke of them. Before Joigny, he responded to a minstrel singing 'Marshal give me a good horse', a popular song of the day, by joining the *commençailles* to get one. Occasionally the *History* claims that William fought for honour, or gave his winnings to Crusaders. Usually he operated on commercial lines. He formed a partnership or *compagnonnage* with another of the Young King's household, a Flemish knight called Roger of Gaugi or Jouy, and took 103 knights between Whitsun 1177 and the following Lent. The Young King's clerk of the kitchen, Wigain, kept a list, which John the *trovère* consulted half a century later.

Besides consolidating his reputation, William was responsible for managing Team Angevin. The Young King was very much the underdog when he landed at Barfleur in April 1176. Henry II had banned tournaments in England, which, as William de Tancarville had warned William, was a fine country for *vavassours* but not for knights errant. The Young King had a choice *mesnie*, anxious to do well, but little luck. French knights laughed when the English appeared, having already divided the spoils. Philip of Alsace, Count of Flanders and doyen of the tournament scene, welcomed the Young King in great style, but showed him no favours on the field. The inexperienced English lacked discipline, and quickly lost formation. They suffered many defeats at the hands of Philip's knights, losing many prisoners. William's initial role in these débâcles was to save the Young King, laying about him with the great sword blows that became his trademark. Over time he observed Philip's tactics, and persuaded the Young King to imitate them. Following William's directions the English learned to stick together, keep a reserve, and counter-attack, driving their disordered opponents before them, Flemish banners trailing in the mud, riderless horses galloping about. Success was self-reinforcing, as the spoils bought more and better players, assisted by the Young King's extravagance. By 1180 he was paying his knights 20 shillings a day (Angevin), seven and a half times the wages Henry II paid his stipendiary knights. No wonder the one was always insolvent, or that the other resented his son's extravagance.

William's highest point as player-manager was the great tournament at Lagny-sur-Marne, held soon after Philip Augustus's coronation in November 1179. The field was covered in combatants, allegedly 3,000 of them, the horses unable to charge for broken lances. The Young King attended with over 200 knights, their names inscribed in the *History*. Other magnates included nineteen counts and the Duke of Burgundy. William flew his own banner, commanding a troop of fifteen knights. As usual, attackers mobbed the Young King, eager to seize so prestigious a prize. Again William rescued him, though Henry lost his helmet. The *History* had styled William *Sire et mestre de son seignor* – lord and master of his lord –

but Lagny was the end of the glory days. William's ascendancy had excited the *losengiers*, Norman members of the royal household who resented the English parvenu.

William's enemies attacked him on two fronts, accusing him of diverting celebrity and spoils due to the Young King to himself. Darker rumours alleged that he had seduced Henry's twenty-five-year-old wife Queen Margaret, the daughter of Louis VII. Twelfth-century domestic arrangements favoured adultery, combining temptation and opportunity. Unmarried *bacheliers* vied for the favour of their lord's wife as a way of gaining his love. Accommodation was ill-lit and insecure; couples married for politics not affection. Discovery, however, incurred dreadful penalties. Philip of Alsace, William's chivalric exemplar, murdered his wife's alleged seducer, hanging him upside down in a sewer. There is no evidence that William ever succumbed to his passions. Indeed, his amicable relations with Margaret's half-brother, Philip Augustus, suggest otherwise.

Rumour was enough. Deprived of the Young King's friendship, William left court, returning late in 1182 for a last outing as manager and bodyguard at Ressons/Gournai, just before Advent stopped jousting for the year. Like an Arthurian hero, William arrived at the last minute fully armed, made great inroads upon the enemy, then rode away without speaking. The tournament reflected the impasse in William's private life, and ended in stalemate, the sides separating by common accord. William made one attempt to clear his name, challenging his traducers to trial by combat at Henry II's Christmas court 1182. William would make similar appeals at later crises in his career. As on subsequent occasions, nobody was fool enough to take him on, even when he offered to cut off a finger. William's biographers sometimes treat his challenges as a joke, but they were not. His father and grandfather had each justified their claim to the Marshal's office by offering to fight for it. Duels often produced fatal outcomes, or worse. Accused of treason after fleeing a Welsh ambush, Henry II's standard bearer Henry of Essex was beaten in the ensuing duel, left for dead, and compelled to live out his days as a monk on an island in the Thames.

Denied justice, William withdrew, jostled and abused by his enemies. For the first time in his career he had nowhere to go. Cast adrift at mid-winter, his situation was desolate but not desperate. After retail therapy at the Lagny horse fair, he made for the first tournament of the New Year at Ressons/Gournai. Invited to lead the Count of St Pol's thirty-strong *mesnie*, he obliged his new patron with the loan of a fine destrier, and had a splendid time. The great patrons of the sport besieged him with extravagant offers. None of them were kings, however, and he must have nursed hopes of rehabilitation. William made his successes known at court, and went on a pilgrimage. Cologne had recently acquired the relics of the Three Kings, also victims of royal disfavour, and the Rhineland was near enough to keep in touch. The trip would bring spiritual merit, and provide a cooling-off period.

If that was William's calculation, it paid off. Besieged in Limoges by his father in March 1183, the Young King needed all his supporters. Even Geoffrey of Lusignan, one of the Poitevin lords involved in the murder of William's uncle Patrick in 1168, urged William's recall, offering to fight anyone who disagreed. Reputation and favour restored, William reached the prince's side just in time to see him die. Once more his future was in doubt. He conveyed the remains back to Henry II, but the Old King owed William nothing, seeing him as an associate of his spendthrift son, and protégé of his disaffected wife. William rejoined the tournament circuit, though not for long. One of the Young King's final pranks had been to take the Cross, an obligation he bequeathed to William. It provided an opportunity for a strategic withdrawal to gain time, a technique William would adopt in later crises.

A passage in arms to the Holy Land was the supreme spiritual moment of every knightly career, combining hopes of salvation with glittering material prospects. More than one Western adventurer had gained a crown overseas since Godfrey of Bouillon became King of Jerusalem in 1099. We cannot tell what ambitions William entertained when he left for Palestine in the autumn of 1183. Recent events may have focussed his mind on the more spiritual aspects of his journey. Pilgrims usually placed more emphasis on the expiatory than the military aspects of their journey. Fighting was incidental to seeing the Holy Places. Safer than a full-scale Crusade with its battles, plagues, and sieges, individual pilgrimages remained hazardous. Pirates and water spouts, scorpions, crocodiles, and dysentery threatened every traveller. An English visitor to Jerusalem in 1102 remembered corpses floating in Jaffa harbour and strewing the road to Jerusalem. William visited his married sisters before leaving, a rare enough attention to suggest the seriousness of his adventure. He also initiated a détente with Henry II, leaving two fine horses with him against a £25 advance for expenses.

We may assume that William travelled by sea in one of the regular pilgrim fleets, probably via Marseilles as Richard I did seven years later. As a man of consequence, he could avoid the horrors of sleeping with several hundred others a few feet above the bilges, of which a fifteenth-century pilgrim sang:

> *A man were as good as to be dede*
> *As smell thereof the stynk.*

The *History* says that William stayed away two years, doing more fine deeds than others did in seven. This is unlikely. The Crusader states of Outremer afforded little opportunity for prowess in the 1180s. The King of Jerusalem, Baldwin IV, was dying of leprosy, and hopelessly at odds with his Poitevin brother-in-law Guy, brother of

Geoffrey of Lusignan, and still more deeply implicated in Earl Patrick's murder. Saladin was still consolidating his dominance of the Muslim world. In 1185 he accepted 60,000 golden bezants, £6,000 sterling, for a truce. William probably had leisure to view the sights: the Temple and Mount of Olives, the room of the Last Supper, Calvary, and the Church of the Holy Sepulchre. The sombre itinerary, following the Young King's untimely death, clearly turned William's mind towards his own mortality. He surprised everyone on his deathbed by producing the silken pall he had bought years earlier in Palestine. He also formed a lifelong attachment to the Templars, the knightly religious order that patrolled the roads to Jerusalem. William's unaccustomed silence about his pilgrimage not only obeyed the Templar Rule that forbade boasting; it deprived John the *trovère* of his best source. The scenes of Christ's Life and Passion were too serious a matter for after-dinner reminiscences.

ROYAL COUNSELLOR

William's return to Europe in the spring of 1186 opened a more sober chapter in his life: no more tournaments. The king whose *malveillance* he once feared now welcomed him into his household. William would, with one interruption, be party to royal counsels for over thirty years. Henry also provided the means for William to support his new position: an estate at Cartmel north of Morecambe Bay and custody of Heloise of Lancaster, a royal ward whose father had died without male heirs. Marriage to her would give William similar baronial status to his brother. The lady was under-age, however, her inheritance a single knight's fee. William treated her honourably, as some might not have done, but he did not marry her either.

William's return from Outremer before the coronation of his enemy Guy of Lusignan as King of Jerusalem, ensured that he missed the battle of Hattin, where hundreds of his Templar acquaintances perished. He himself did rather well out of the opening stages of the great Angevin-Capetian war that began in the summer of 1188. William was in his element at Gisors in August, stage-managing a mock chivalric response to Philip Augustus's insincere proposal of a duel between champions to settle Capetian-Angevin differences. When Philip Augustus withdrew in a huff, his men cut down the elm tree that traditionally sheltered Franco-Norman conferences: there would be no more parleys. William's advice to Henry II was less whimsical. Henry should disband his troops, then secretly reunite them at a pre-set rendezvous. Crossing the border unopposed, they ravaged the Seine Valley as far as Mantes, destroying an orchard Philip Augustus had planted: fair exchange for Henry's elm.

A similar lightning raid followed against Montmirail, 30 miles (45km) east of Le Mans. William reverted to knight errantry, charging over the castle's unwalled bridge to attack another knight surrounded by ten foot sergeants. Only his horse's sure-footedness saved William from falling into the 60-foot (18m) deep ditch below, when their spears drove him back. The action marks John of Earley's first appearance, aged fifteen or sixteen, handing William his spear, and treating his destrier's wounds. As the war and Henry II's health went downhill, William's importance increased. When Richard left his father to join Philip Augustus, William was among those sent to bring him back. He failed, as did his first diplomatic mission to the French court in the winter of 1188–89. Over the next twenty-five years, William never once shifted Philip Augustus from his chosen path. As other followers fell away, Henry promised William a far richer heiress, Isabel of Clare, Countess of Pembroke and Striguil.

Henry's defeat at Le Mans on 12 June was the decisive engagement of the war. After the futile meeting at Ferté-Bernard, his enemies ranged east and north of Le Mans, mopping up Angevin castles. On the 10th, they were 10 miles (15km) away at Montfort, simulating a lunge towards Tours. William patrolled south down the Le Mans–Tours road next morning. Meeting enemy scouts, he displayed a new tactical maturity, and avoided contact. Hidden by mist, William went close enough to make sure he had found the French army, resisted pressure to return early or waste horseflesh in needless skirmishing, and rode back to report.

Le Mans lies at the confluence of the Rivers Sarthe and Huisne, which flow south and west respectively, joining south-west of the city. They form significant obstacles, passable only at fords and bridges. The city's artificial defences included recently cleared ditches, walls, and a castle. Henry had Welsh infantry and 700 mounted troops, but was unwilling to fight. He broke down the Huisne bridge, south of the city, and obstructed known fords with stakes. At least two fords, the Gués de Mauny and Bernisson, existed in the 1870s, either side of the bridge. Preparations were made to fire the suburbs between the city walls and the river. Apparently frustrated, the enemy stopped a bow-shot south of the Huisne, and pitched camp.

Henry rode down to the Pontlieue bridgehead next morning to observe the enemy. Not expecting a battle, he went unarmed, insisting that his household did likewise. William refused, saying that his armour was no trouble, and was left behind in some disfavour. To everyone's surprise, French knights were sounding an unknown ford with their lances, preparatory to crossing. Henry's unarmed escort launched a sacrificial charge to cover his escape, soon fulfilling William's prophecy that they would regret removing their armour.

Roger of Howden describes a panic-stricken retreat into the city, which the attackers promptly followed up. The *History*, however, suggests that William and his fifty-strong *mesnie* disputed the south gate for some time. There was no time for the customary exchange of insults as fighting ranged up and down the suburban street between moat and bridge, where railway tracks now cross the N138. William took four prisoners, although three escaped, leaving John of Earley with just the bridles as evidence. Whether the attackers chased William's men back through the gate or found another entry is unclear. Broken lance fragments lamed his horse, while one of his men ended up in the ditch. Howden's reference to attackers crossing an anonymous stone bridge have been applied to the Pont Perrin, west of the city, begging the question of how they crossed the combined streams below Le Mans to get there. Besides, such a turning movement would have prevented Henry's subsequent escape, his castles to the north-east having already fallen into enemy hands.

Still unarmed and violently angry, Henry insisted on firing the suburbs, too late to stop the enemy advance. As flames spread into the city, he fled north to Fresnay-sur-Sarthe. Howden says the French pursued him for 3 miles (4.5km), stopping at a steep banked ford, perhaps at Maule. The *History* attributes Henry's escape to William, another echo of John Marshal's stand at Wherwell. Stripped to his *pourpoint* for speed, William was skirmishing with some other knights, when Count Richard appeared similarly equipped. As William ran him down, fresh lance in hand, Richard protested he was unarmed: 'Nay, let the Devil kill you', replied the Marshal, 'for I will not!', and thrust his lance into Richard's horse, allowing Henry and many others to escape. Not since the Roman soldier slew Christ, declared the *History*, had a single lance blow achieved such a wholesale deliverance.

Henry II limped away to Chinon via Fresnay and Ste-Suzanne, while William went north to rally fugitives, but the king had lost all hope. He recalled William to stand by him at Ballan-Miré, and witness his terrible end. It was the Marshal who rallied the demoralised household, organised a vigil, and summoned Chinon's seneschal to distribute alms to the poor. Alas, there was no money.

Henry's death, like that of his son, showed how Fortune could ruin even so rich and honoured a king. A dead man, commented the *trovère*, has no friends. Once more William's last-ditch loyalty had placed his career and perhaps his life in jeopardy.

Richard I terrified his contemporaries. News of his return from Germany in 1194 caused a rebel in far-away Cornwall to die of fright. His accession gave William a major problem. He had lost Heloise, without gaining possession of Isabel. Less than a month before he had almost killed the new king. The *History* plays up the drama: the anxiety of the Old King's *mesnie* awaiting Richard at Fontevraud where they had taken Henry for burial; William's quiet confidence; the Count's impassive viewing of the corpse. When Richard taxed William with attempting to kill him, the latter took this as a slur upon his prowess. Instead of apologising, he insisted that he could easily have killed Richard, had he wanted. Plain speaking paid off. Reminded about Isabel, the new king confirmed his predecessor's promises. A man who bet everything on loyalty deserved reward.

William's haste to secure his prize was in proportion to her value. Deviating only to pay his respects to Queen Eleanor, his oldest royal patron, he proceeded directly to deliver the maid of Striguil from the Tower of London. England's second richest heiress, Isabel was daughter of Richard fitz Gilbert of Clare, lord of Nethergwent, titular Earl of Pembroke and Striguil, nicknamed Strongbow. Leader of the Anglo-Norman freebooters in Ireland, he married the daughter of Dermot MacMurrough, last Irish King of Leinster. Strongbow's early death left Isabel to inherit his titles and lands, on both sides of the Irish Sea. Granddaughter of kings, she was a potent symbol of William's success. Like his father, William married upwards. Confiding Isabel to his Irish vassals' safekeeping in 1207, he acknowledged that he owned nothing, except through her. Her infrequent appearances in the *History* reveal her as a strong character and counsellor in times of crisis. Together, they had ten children: 'from a good tree comes good fruit'.

The couple's twenty-five-year age gap was common in the Middle Ages. Women were the physical embodiment of property rights, to be snapped up by the older men who dominated feudal society. Isabel's inheritance spanned the Anglo-Norman world. Its core was the baronial honour of Striguil in South Wales, its name a contraction of the Welsh Ystrad Gwy, meaning the Wye Valley. It included Chepstow Castle and sixty-five and a half knights' fees. Her Irish lands extended over five and a half counties of Leinster in south-east Ireland. Centred on Kilkenny, they represented another 100 knights' fees. In Normandy, Isabel possessed castles near Lisieux and at Longueville, near Dieppe, country William knew well. Not all Isabel's inheritance was at William's disposal. His Irish mother-in-law occupied Striguil's choicest manors, and Richard's brother John had encroached on Leinster. Nevertheless, William's new wealth far surpassed his Cartmel estate and the money fief the Count of Flanders had given him in 1183. Duly grateful, he dedicated an Augustinian priory at Cartmel to the memory of his first lord, the Young King, using his own lands to do so.

Richard I's coronation in September 1189 demonstrated William's favoured position, the Marshal appearing third among the laity, carrying the sceptre. His surviving brothers also profited from his success: John, who carried the royal spurs as hereditary Marshal, became Sheriff of Yorkshire; Henry became Dean of York, rising to Bishop of Exeter in 1193. William himself was among the magnates appointed as justiciars to monitor William Longchamps, Richard's chancellor, entrusted with governing England during the king's absence on Crusade. Sidney Painter doubted William's qualifications for this quasi-judicial role, but knights were adept in feudal custom and frequently acted as judges. The justiciarship was another step in William's rise from adventurer to elder statesman, an ascent that might have ended abruptly had he followed Richard to Palestine. Many of William's early associates perished there, including William of Tancarville and Philip of Alsace. James of Avesnes, William's travelling companion to Cologne, met a hero's death at Arsuf.

William's marriage made him a great figure in the Marches, but Welsh affairs feature little in the *History*. It says nothing of Rhys ap Gruffydd's revolt after Henry II's death, which must have affected William's vassals in South Wales. Welsh annals describe castles taken by treachery and even a battle at Llanwhaden in Pembrokeshire. William's part in the relief of Swansea in 1192, following a ten-week siege, is only revealed by administrative evidence. Perhaps frontier warfare against a barbaric enemy who took heads not prisoners lacked the cachet of more sporting conflicts. Perhaps William was distracted by the three-cornered struggle between the justiciars, Prince John, and William Longchamps.

Gerald of Wales described the chancellor as a many-headed monster. Bishop of Ely and papal legate, Longchamps monopolised secular and ecclesiastical power. Son of a Norman official, he loathed the Marshals as Englishmen, competitors, and supporters of Henry II. He exploited the massacre of York's Jews in 1190 to confiscate John Marshal's shrievalty, besieged William's shrieval castle at Gloucester, and denounced the latter's disloyalty to Richard in Palestine. The Marshal won the round, however, collaborating with Walter of Coutances, Archbishop of Rouen, to overthrow the chancellor in October 1192. Forced to flee England dressed as a woman, Longchamps named William fourth amongst the subsequent excommunications.

William's relationship with Prince John was more ambiguous. The *History* treats John with unfaltering hostility. William, however, adopted a more pragmatic attitude. Longchamps notoriously accused him of 'planting vines', hedging his bets against John's succession. Nevertheless, William backed the other justiciars when

John revolted in 1193. Perhaps it helped that Queen Eleanor was on their side. William led 500 mercenary sergeants from the Marches to besiege John's men in Windsor, leaving as many more to hold Bristol and Gloucester. Invited to swear an oath, in the medieval fashion, to see the siege through, he suggested a more flexible approach. Some of the justiciars' men should besiege Windsor, while others pursued John's raiding parties to prevent their pillaging the countryside, undermining the besiegers' economic base. William's actions show a well-developed appreciation of warfare's financial foundations. The measures he adopted to pay his troops in the 1190s provide a foretaste of the regency's fiscal inventiveness: foreclosure of royal debts, loans from Jews and monasteries, and advances from his own pocket.

John Marshal had a less happy war, dying at Marlborough in March 1194, after a short siege conducted by the Archbishop of Canterbury. The coincidence suggests that the elder Marshal died in rebellion against Richard's justiciars while asserting the family's claim to the castle. Such a perspective lends a touch of irony to the *History*'s protestation that William never suffered such sorrow as when he heard of his brother's death. It was an implausible reaction to the death of a brother he hardly knew, by which he stood to profit. News of Richard's simultaneous return from captivity sharpened William's emotional turmoil. Reconciling fraternal and royal duty, William sent his knights to escort John Marshal to the family mausoleum at Bradenstoke Abbey. He himself rejoined the king at a speed sometimes interpreted as evidence of a guilty conscience. Thanked by Richard for defending his interests during his absence, William sailed from Portsmouth on 24 April to help recover Richard's overseas lands. Defying Longchamps's malice and Count John's treachery, William had navigated the political shoals of the justiciarship, suggesting luck if not skill. Thanks to his brother's death, he was also head of the family, inheriting John Marshal's lands and ceremonial office.

William witnessed Richard's ecstatic welcome to Normandy, its inhabitants greeting their duke with dancing, bell-ringing, and processions. Prince John abandoned his French ally, to be welcomed back as a child led astray by others. Turning south to the Loir (*sic*), Richard drew Philip Augustus after him. On 3 July, Angevin and Capetian forces encamped 10 miles (15km) apart at Vendôme and Fréteval on the borders of Maine and the Orléannais. Richard was desperate to bring Philip to battle, hoping, as Roger of Howden put it, that 'he might deliver him over to death or take him alive'. Philip was less enthusiastic. Under cover of a bold exchange of challenges he prepared for flight, without, as the *History* notes, telling his troops.

Next day was a fine panic. Many French were killed or taken, with their tents, silken draperies, riding and pack horses, fine wine, and viands. The capture of Philip's archives, which still hampers French administrative historians, also showed Richard which of his magnates had sworn to support the King of France. Philip escaped with his usual luck, turning aside to hear Mass while a Flemish mercenary directed Richard the wrong way. William displayed his customary professionalism. Placed in command of the reserve, he kept his men in hand despite every temptation, remaining out until the scattered looters returned. That evening, when everyone was bragging in the hostelry, the king announced that the Marshal had contributed more to the day's success than anyone: 'Whoever has a good rearguard, has no fear of his enemies.'

Following this unmedieval exhibition of disciplined restraint, the *History* leaps three years to present two contrasting episodes: John and Mercadier's raid in the Beauvaisis in 1197 and an obscure campaign in Flanders. While Richard's favourite *routier* captain captured the Bishop of Beauvais and slaughtered his followers, William assaulted the castle of Milli-sur-Thérain, 6 miles (9km) north-west of Beauvais, his last recorded feat of arms before Lincoln. As the attackers escaladed the walls, the defenders fought back with forks and flails, tipping a ladder-load of knights and sergeants into the ditch, with much snapping of arms and legs. The attackers recoiled, leaving a Flemish knight stuck up another ladder on a fork. Unable to restrain himself, William leapt into the ditch fully armed, and climbed the ladder to clear the parapet with great sword strokes right and left. Climbing over, he flattened the castle's commander with a blow to the head, cutting through helmet and mail coif to the flesh. Feeling he had done enough, William sat down on the prostrate constable, while gleeful Angevins poured in to sack the castle.

The other episode illustrates another side of William's military talents. Despatched to inflame the Count of Flanders against Philip Augustus, he features as tactical sage rather than storm-trooper. The count besieging an unknown town, perhaps Arras, Philip Augustus came up to relieve the garrison. The Flemish lords suggested leaving their infantry in a wagon laager while the knights skirmished outside, but William would have none of it. He thought wagons and infantry should maintain the siege while the knights massed in ordered squadrons, ready for battle. Professor Duby interprets this as chivalric obsession with offensive action. More likely, William remembered Fréteval. He knew Philip Augustus would never risk a battle. Sure enough, the latter withdrew, 'like a wise man'.

William missed Richard's last victory at Gisors, when Philip Augustus drank of the River Epte. The *History*'s account appears to derive from a third John Marshal, William's nephew, an illegitimate son of William's brother John. Bastards were a useful by-product of delaying knightly marriages. Excluded from inheritance, they depended utterly upon their legitimate kinsmen. Except for one short period, the youngest John Marshal would be a loyal member of the Marshal affinity. The *History* confirms Howden's official narrative, adding that Philip escaped by giving the royal arms to another knight, who was then captured. Richard's own account lists the man named among the prisoners, confirmation of the *History*'s reliability. William was now more than a knight or magnate. He was a *prud'homme*, a reliable source of good counsel, regardless of its acceptability or royal mood. After Richard threatened to emasculate a papal legate for suggesting he might release the Bishop of Beauvais, it was William who braved the king's fury to persuade him to resume negotiations. The Angevin sun, however, was about to set. A new reign would provide less scope for honest advice, or acts of prowess.

GREAT SURVIVOR

News of Richard's fatal wound found William hearing a legal case at Vaudreuil. Ordered to Rouen to secure its castle and treasury, he received confirmation of the king's death three days later, at bedtime. Pulling on his leggings, the Marshal went to consult the Archbishop of Canterbury staying nearby. The latter proposed Arthur as successor, advocating the direct patrilinear succession that would prevail later. William preferred the Norman tradition. He argued that John was closer, having a claim from both his father and brother. Baffled by the worst blunder of its hero's life, the *History* makes the archbishop prophesy that William would never repent so much of anything he might do. In the short term, however, William did very well from his attitude, being formally invested Earl of Pembroke in May 1199.

Renewed hostilities with France in 1202 found William defending his wife's Longueville inheritance in north-east Normandy. Philip Augustus besieged Arques Castle, in the Béthune Valley like Drincourt. Henry of Navarre fought the Spanish Army of the Netherlands there in 1592, hence the modern name of Arques-la-Bataille. The Marshal was more circumspect. Observing the siege with two other Williams, the Earls of Salisbury and Warenne, the Marshal encouraged the French to withdraw by promptly forwarding news of Arthur's capture at Mirebeau. After Philip's departure, William returned to Rouen, announcing that he had come to defend the city. In exchange the anxious citizens regaled him and his companions with their choicest vintages. Opportunities for such agreeable episodes dwindled following Arthur's disappearance. Luckily William was not at Rouen again until late in August 1203, clearing him of complicity in John's most fatal crime. As a *prud'homme* should, William warned the friendless king that his own actions had undermined his position, leaving John speechless with rage, as if transfixed by a lance.

The official French chronicler hints at a more active role for William in the ensuing débâcle. William the Breton's epic poem about Philip Augustus describes an amphibious attempt to raise the siege of Château Gaillard, led by the Marshal. The Breton's earlier prose account mentions an anonymous night operation by a few *routiers*, while English sources deny that any such effort was made. Norman accounting records contain no entries for the necessary flotilla, despite showing expenditure on cross-Channel transportation. The *History's* silence in the face of failure is unsurprising but inconclusive. It is more informative about John's final departure from Normandy: the baggage sent on ahead, the early morning start announced only to John's closest confidants, the long stages, and precautions against treachery. On 5 December 1203, William accompanied John on board ship at Barfleur, leaving behind the scenes of his youthful exploits and mature successes: 'And many well knew, there was no going back.'

William undertook diplomatic missions to Philip Augustus throughout the ensuing cold war. Politically fruitless, these proved personally embarrassing, as William struggled to preserve his wife's continental inheritance. In April 1204, Philip Augustus made clear his intention of forcing Anglo-Norman landholders to do homage to him, or lose their Norman lands. William and his fellow envoy Robert Earl of Leicester paid 500 marks each for a year's respite. Robert avoided further difficulties by dying. Before William returned next year, he obtained John's leave, so he claimed, to do homage rather than forfeit Isabel's patrimony. William now owed allegiance to two lords. It was a common feudal dilemma, but times were changing. John and Philip disliked ambiguity, and meant to make their magnates choose one lord or the other.

The issue became critical a month later at Portsmouth, when William refused to follow John to Poitou to fight Philip Augustus. Accused of treachery, William denied wrong-doing, and offered to prove his innocence in arms. He doubled John's fury by warning the magnates gathered on the seashore that what the king meant to do to him, he would do to them if he got the chance. When one of John's household knights proposed the guilty verdict that William's peers refused, he was speedily silenced. Baldwin of Béthune was the Marshal's oldest companion-in-arms. He had shared his exploits in the Young King's time, and stood beside William when he lost royal favour. Now he defended him against King John's catspaw, a landless knight, devoid of consequence. Neither of them, he said, were fit to judge so fine a knight as the Marshal. Whatever William's failings, his connections and reputation remained a bastion against John's malice.

The dispute formed part of a wider policy breakdown. While the *History* presents William at odds with the Archbishop of Canterbury, Ralph of Coggeshall describes them both arguing against the expedition, on good strategic grounds. There was no secure overseas base; the French were too strong now that they controlled Normandy; the Poitevins were incorrigible traitors; the Flemish, Philip's allies, would attack England in the absence of its defenders; John had no heir. Following emotional scenes and mutual threats, John gave way. The Archbishop, who was blamed for the fiasco, died soon after, leaving William to face John's displeasure alone.

Medieval kings had various ways of expressing annoyance. Henry II had billeted men and horses upon the recalcitrant Becket, and inspired the first John Marshal to engage the archbishop in vexatious litigation. The Young King had sent William to Coventry. King John took William's eldest son hostage. We may imagine how he felt about that, given his own experience at Newbury. We do know that when advised to take hostages from his own vassals, William refused. In 1206, he asked leave to withdraw to his Irish estates. Ireland was the edge of the known world, remote from the English political scene. Henry II went there in 1171 to escape the fallout from Becket's murder. Royal control was limited to Dublin, Wexford, and Waterford, while descendants of Strongbow's companions contested the hinterland with the native Irish. Already conscious of their separate Anglo-Irish identity, the former were a hard-boiled frontier aristocracy, addicted to Celtic harpists and headhunting, contemptuous of effete intruders like William. The native Irish lived a nomadic pastoral life that made them easy to dispossess but hard to subdue. Lacking armour they pursued hit and run tactics, taking refuge in bogs and thickets. The *History* ignores them. Compared with England, Ireland was poor, violent, and isolated.

John tried to prevent William's departure, apparently demanding his second son Richard as a supplementary hostage. The countess demurred, but William agreed. Having permission to leave, he would go, for good or ill. Even the *History* admits that not everyone in Leinster was pleased to see him. Meilyr fitz Henry, Justiciar of Ireland and one of the original invaders, was particularly hostile. He persuaded John to recall them both, precipitating William's most dangerous hour, caught between a suspicious king and a hostile Anglo-Irish nobility. William relied in this emergency upon his household knights, especially John of Earley, whom King John disparaged as *rogneux* or mangy. Towards Michaelmas 1207 (29 September), William summoned his vassals to Kilkenny, and presented them with his countess, once more with child. Taking her hand, he reminded them how her father had enfeoffed them when he conquered the land, and made them swear to guard her faithfully. No sooner had William sailed for England than Meilyr's men fired his grain-filled barns, and sacked the Marshal's 'new town', probably New Ross (Co. Wexford), killing twenty of his men.

William must have found the ensuing winter endless. The king frowned on him, and plotted with Meilyr and other unloveable associates, while easterly gales cut off all news from Ireland. John pretended at one point that William's men had been defeated with heavy loss and his countess besieged. William played his strongest suit, the dignified restraint with which he had confronted his enemies at Tancarville and Count Richard at Fontevraud. He could also trust his men. When Meilyr made the westbound passage with letters recalling William's knights, he found Ireland other than he expected. Several of the justiciar's men were already in the earl's dungeon, while William's colluded in ignoring John's summons. Instead, they allied with Hugh de Lacy, Earl of Ulster, and pillaged Meilyr's lands. The justiciar was captured and forced to surrender his son as a hostage. None of this was known in England until the first eastbound ships early in 1208. John had to admit that his schemes had miscarried, while William feigned ignorance of the proxy war's outcome. Outward peace was restored, William returning to his victorious countess in the summer. He forgave his disloyal vassals against her wishes, but not Meilyr, whose lands, castles, and offspring remained at the Marshal's disposal.

The Braose affair shattered this détente. When the fugitive Braose family washed up on the Wicklow coast in the winter of 1209–10 following their ill-fated rebellion, William took them in, a gesture of Marcher solidarity that provoked the first royal expedition to Ireland for twenty-five years. With 800 knights and 1,000 foot, it was the largest army ever seen west of St George's Channel. Landing at Waterford in late June, John punished

William by quartering his army on Kilkenny. Then he marched north to crush the de Lacys and take Carrickfergus Castle, whence Matilda Braose took ship for Galloway. Returning to Dublin in August, John accused William of harbouring the king's enemies. Once more, William denied any disloyalty, and offered to justify himself in arms. As before, none of his peers moved to help the king. In frustration, John demanded yet more hostages, this time from William's household and tenants, including John of Earley.

The king's chastisement of his Irish barons went too far in the face of an unruly native population. While English sources praised John's successes in Ireland, the Gaelic *Annals of Loch Cé* report otherwise. The Irish King of Connacht took his wife's advice and refused to give hostages. John's new justiciar, the Bishop of Norwich, raided deep into County Mayo, and North-West Ireland exploded. Anglo-Norman castles at Clones and Belleek were destroyed with much slaughter. One Cormac O'Melachlin twice defeated the bishop in the field, captured his treasure, and killed a 'multitude of foreigners' in County Offaly. The *History* says nothing of William's part in all this, its best informant, John of Earley, being locked up in Nottingham Castle.

When Cormac closed his career by burning Ballyboy Castle in 1214, William was back in England. Real traitors had sought to sell John to the Welsh in 1212, and William rallied the Irish magnates in the king's support. Castles and hostages were returned, the younger William entrusted to John of Earley. Next year, as French shipping massed in the Seine estuary, the Marshal was recalled. He hurried to the king's side, as every *prud'homme* should, 'for he always loved loyalty'. On 15 August William joined John outside Dover with 500 knights, the whole Irish establishment. Too late to witness the ending of the Interdict, he shared in the decision to send his old comrade William of Salisbury to destroy the French fleet at Dam. When John sailed for Poitou the next year, there were no quibbles about homage. The Marshal stayed behind to co-ordinate home defence.

William had regained royal confidence after eight years in the political and geographical wilderness. He never lost it again. It is hard to judge how close the Marshals came to suffering the fate of the Braose family. One of William's knights died in custody, while John of Earley, a particular object of John's hostility, suffered great hardship at Nottingham. The saving factor seems to have been William's instinctive discretion. Unlike William of Braose, he had learned to be a courtier before he became a Marcher.

III

BEFORE THE
LONGBOW

The Marshal's career spanned the peak of knightly warfare. Born amidst the chivalric free-for-all of the 1140s, he witnessed the revival of royal government that began the knightly caste's slow transformation from sinister freebooters, like Robert fitz Hubert, into Jane Austen's county gentlemen. More than once the *History* laments the passing of chivalry, its opportunities for mayhem and plunder supplanted by the anodyne pursuit of hawk and hounds. Long before William's translation from *bachelier* to earl, knights had lost the monopoly of mounted service, as non-noble sergeants and crossbowmen elbowed their way onto the battlefield. Nevertheless, knights would continue to dominate European warfare for another 300 years. Natural leaders, they provided an elite multi-purpose cavalry: complete warriors, inured to wounds and hardship, as useful for reconnaissance and dismounted action as for the charge.

Fortified by their armoured protection and class solidarity, knights constituted the most potent military force of their day. Securing Christendom's borders from Outremer to the Baltic, they stood guard over the economic and cultural developments of the twelfth century.

Historians and public have not always taken so positive a view. Just as 'medieval' is a cliché for social backwardness, 'feudal' is synonymous with military incompetence. Early students of the medieval art of war, such as Sir Charles Oman, depicted chivalric armies as an inchoate mass of individual warriors, their ill-formed lines of battle dissolving into a maelstrom of unrelated duels. Knightly commanders are dismissed as possessing neither strategic vision nor tactical insight, medieval warfare seen as a lamentable hiatus between the professionalism of antiquity and today, from which the soldier's art was only rescued by a happy succession of military revolutions. English writers in particular focus on the invincible bowmen of Crécy and Agincourt, whose arrow storms stopped dim-witted knightly armies in their tracks, adding the myth of the yeoman archer to that of the effete *chevalier*.

Such views are doubly misleading. They discount the peculiar difficulties confronting medieval commanders: their limited resources in men and money; the disproportionate power of the strategic defensive; the absence of formal command structures; the fluidity of mounted warfare. Secondly, they ignore the contemporary evidence of sound practice provided by vernacular sources such as the *History*. Mined for its chivalric and social insights, the latter's military content has been neglected, although nearly half its lines describe knightly warfare, nearly three times the number dealing with tournaments. Written for an expert audience, its revelations of what knights thought about war are as important as what it says actually happened. This chapter will consider the *History*'s account of William's military career from three points of view: the modalities of knightly conflict, the means available to early medieval commanders, and how they used those means.

Modes of Conflict

A commander can pursue military victory in one of three ways. He may seek a decision by either combat or manoeuvre, or by a combination of both. Alternatively, he may use non-military means to achieve his aim. The table below is intended to underline the argument that battles, sieges and raids are complementary ways of fighting, something many discussions fail to make clear. Modern academics tend to deny that battles mattered at all. More traditional historians tended to neglect everything else. The table puts all three on a level footing.

MODES OF WAR

Manoeuvre?	Combat?	
	Yes	No
Yes	Battle	Raid
No	Siege	Other means

Battles entail both movement and combat; sieges are violent but static; raids exploit mobility to inflict harm while avoiding battle. Other means cover various non-military activities, such as bribery, diplomacy, or subversion. These four basic options exist across all periods, although their popularity and utility vary. It is unfortunate for the reputation of medieval commanders that serious study of their activities began in the nineteenth century, when historians attributed an inflated significance to battles. Understandable in the Napoleonic afterglow, a battle-centred perspective is unhelpful when applied to the Middle Ages, a period notable for its dearth of such events. The *History* refers to twelve actions, of which half might be described as battles.

BATTLES

Action	Year	Description	Context
Wherwell Abbey	1141	Skirmish	Siege
Test Valley	c.1141	Ambush	
Drincourt*	1166	Battle/skirmish	Urban+
Lusignan*	1168	Ambush	
Gisors*	1188	Skirmish	Urban
Le Mans*	1189	Battle	Urban
Frétéval*	1194	Running fight	
Gisors	1198	Running fight	
Dam	1213	Sea battle	Siege
Bouvines	1214	Battle	
Lincoln*	1217	Battle	Siege/urban
Sandwich*	1217	Sea battle	

* Battles at which William was present

William witnessed just four battles in over five decades of active service, if one overstates the significance of Drincourt, and distinguishes the opening defence of Le Mans from the subsequent siege of its castle. Richard I fought only three battles: Barbezieux (1176), Arsuf (1191), and Jaffa (1192). No King of France risked a battle between Brémule (1119) and Bouvines (1214).

The low number of battles fought by such committed warriors as Richard I and the Marshal is suggestive. It compares with the *History*'s twenty-nine sieges, including a fictional siege of Kilkenny that King John invented to tease the Marshal in the winter of 1207–08. William assisted at twelve of these. He also attended Drincourt and Rouen with the Young King in 1173–74, stormed Cilgerran in Cardiganshire in 1204, and presided at Newark in 1218. William opened and closed his career, not with battles, but with two obscure sieges.

SIEGES

Location	Year
Winchester	1141
Newbury†	1152
Drincourt*†	1173
Rouen*†	1174
Limoges	1183
Montmirail†	1188
La Ferté	1189
Le Mans Castle	1189
Windsor†	1194
Marlborough	1194
Nottingham†	1194
Vaudreuil†	1194
Verneuil†	1194
Vierzon	1196
Arras (?)†	1197
Milli†	1197
Chalus-Chabrol	1199
Arques†	1202
Mirebeau	1202
Cilgerran*†	1204
Kilkenny (fictional)	1207/8
Carrickfergus	1210
Rochester	1215
Hertford	1216
Berkhamstead	1216
Winchelsea	1217
Farnham†	1217
Winchester†	1217
Southampton	1217
Marlborough	1217

Mountsorrel	1217
Lincoln†	1217
Newark*†	1218

* Additional to the *History*

† Sieges at which William was present. At Newbury, he was aged only five.

There were good reasons for the infrequency of battles. Knightly commanders could easily reckon the odds, and small mounted armies readily avoided fighting superior numbers. The Norman baronage failed to support Henry II at Le Mans, fearing the great numbers of the French. They were no bolder in' 1194, when Richard I was campaigning on the Loire and Philip Augustus besieged Fontaine, just outside Rouen. Philip Augustus commonly avoided battle, despite the negative consequences of running away at Fréteval and Gisors. He only fought at Bouvines because his enemies overtook him. Rational calculation was not confined to cowardly foreigners. King Stephen's siege of Oxford (1142) collapsed when his men refused to await an Angevin relief column gathering at Cirencester.

Caution was entirely rational. Battles were uncertain, often ending with the leading protagonists' death or capture. Harold's demise at Hastings is the most celebrated example, but Henry I's brother Robert Curthose spent twenty-eight years in captivity after Tinchebrai. King Stephen might have done the same after the first battle of Lincoln. Renaud of Boulogne, who fought beside William at Le Mans, died in a French dungeon thirteen years after his capture at Bouvines. William's leading opponents at Second Lincoln and Sandwich, the Count de la Perche and Eustace the Monk, were both killed. Devoted followers might assume their lord's coat of arms, but anonymity was no guarantee of safety. Peter II of Aragon was cut down at Muret in 1213 posing as a simple *bachelier*, a shocking waste of a king's ransom. Richard I's £100,000 ransom set a twelfth-century record, but less distinguished captives faced equally ruinous demands. King John paid 5,000 marks to recover Vaudreuil's treacherous commanders in 1203. The *History* does not say how much Queen Eleanor paid the Lusignans for William in 1167, but he was lucky to have so generous a patron. One of the *History's* recurrent themes is the role of Fortune in life and war, foreshadowing Clausewitz's belief that the latter resembled nothing so much as a game of chance. More than once the *History* describes a military outcome as a lucky die roll. William once recovered a disputed horse by rolling eleven with two dice to beat a nine.

Battles involved moral hazard, besides material risks. Like trial by combat in legal cases, they represented the pursuit of justice by other means. Participants had to feel sure they were in the right. Robert of Gloucester expected divine assistance at First Lincoln, the king having attacked his son-in-law without provocation, besieged his daughter, and fortified Lincoln Cathedral. Winners and losers were viewed as righteous or impious respectively. Jordan of Fantôme had no doubt that the Scots' defeat at Alnwick reflected divine anger at their atrocities. Spiritual preparation for battle naturally included hearing Mass, but some combatants went further. The winners at Thielt (1128) cut their long hair and dressed as penitents. Sometimes the Church prevented battles altogether. The Truce of God or *Trux Dei* banned fighting from Advent until a week after Epiphany, from Lent through Easter Week, and from sunset Thursday to sunrise Tuesday. Such restrictions gave pause for thought. Before Bouvines, the Imperialists debated fighting on a Sunday, and only did so upon the urging of the godless *routier* Hugh of Boves.

The infrequency of medieval battles did not make them unimportant. Drincourt was not one of the world's decisive battles, but it spared the town a nasty ravaging, the grateful inhabitants treating the victors to costly wines and fruit. As in other periods, a battle might change the course of a war, or terminate a conflict already decided. Henry II's defeat at Le Mans persuaded him to abandon a losing struggle. The seneschal of an earlier Count of Anjou summarised the advantages of battle as follows: 'Battles are short, but the victor's prize is enormous. Sieges waste time, and the town is rarely taken. Battles overcome nations and fortified towns, and an enemy beaten in battle vanishes like smoke.' (*Gesta consulum Andagavensium*, quoted in Verbruggen p.280)

He might have been speaking of Saladin's dismantling of the Kingdom of Jerusalem after the Muslim victory at Hattin in 1187. Second Lincoln was one of a cluster of nearly contemporary battles that altered the course of European history: Las Navas de Toledo in 1212, which cleared the way for the Christian reconquest of Spain; Muret in 1213, which confirmed French domination of Languedoc; and the battle of Bouvines in 1214, which sealed the Angevin loss of Normandy.

Three of these four were victories for the attacker, a proportion reflected across the *History*'s land actions. The exceptions were Drincourt (1166), Gisors (1188), and Bouvines. Knightly armies were more than capable of effective offensive action, but they needed a good reason and a complaisant enemy. Three circumstances favoured acceptance of an offer of battle. Civil war, the usual form in England, inclined commanders to fight rather than watch their property being destroyed. Robert of Gloucester brought matters to a head at First Lincoln because 'he preferred risking extremities to prolonging the sufferings of the country' (William of Malmesbury).

Sieges frequently led to battles. A besieging army was fixed, its over-extended siege-lines vulnerable to surprise. The battles of Lincoln and Muret were both fought to raise a siege, as was the naval action at Dam. Henry II's sortie from Rouen in August 1174 almost provoked a battle, had not Louis VII and his men (probably including William) cowered in their tents. Investing armies caught by a relieving column left smartly to avoid being cut to pieces like the Angevins during the Rout of Winchester. John abandoned his tents and siege engines at La Roche-au-Moine and ran for La Rochelle. Three of the *History*'s actions arose from sieges. Four took place in an urban setting that sits uneasily with the stereotype of knightly warfare as a country pursuit. Jousting down Lincoln's streets was by no means the abnormality Sir Charles Oman suggests. William performed similar exploits on at least three other occasions: Drincourt, Le Mans, and Montmirail. King John's knights did the same at Mirebeau. The nobility of Cologne crushed a citizens' revolt in the 1260s by spurring on their destriers to break through chains blocking the streets. Charging down streets on horseback was the natural result of mounted troops' monopoly of the tactical offensive. The best way to assert control of a town was to ride through it, just as the Red Army drove tanks through Berlin in 1945, or the British did through Basra in 2003.

Another circumstance favouring battle was the ambush, surprise pre-empting escape. John Marshal got his revenge for Wherwell Abbey somewhere in the Test Valley, between Winchester and Ludgershall. Challenged by a royalist force under his future brother-in-law Patrick, John intimated that he would not await their coming. Instead of retiring, he got up at midnight and ambushed the road. Catching his disarmed prey at dawn, still in their padded linen armour, he took numerous prisoners and much booty. This anonymous skirmish, known only from the *History*, illustrates the devious nature of the chivalric warfare of which William became an exemplar. Such tales, reinforced by bitter experience, underlay his caution at Le Mans and Fréteval. Only Bouvines, of all the *History*'s land actions, resembles the conventional knightly battle, honestly fought in the open.

The four-fold predominance of sieges in William's career reflects the density of fortified sites across Western Europe. Archaeological surveys reveal a castle for every 40 square miles (104 square km) of Hertfordshire countryside, implying 1,250 across England, an estimate similar to Robert of Torigny's contemporary figure. Every lay and ecclesiastical baron expected to have a castle, as did most county towns. Twelfth-century improvements in construction favoured the rich, as stone replaced earth, and square towers shed their corners to baffle miners. William's castles at Chepstow and Goodrich still sport their bluff Norman keeps, but at Pembroke he built a great round tower in the latest style. Smaller round towers were distributed along the outer curtain, allowing archers to cover the base of the walls from defiladed slits invulnerable to the attacker's missiles. Such improvements might have increased the defence's existing advantage, but new siege techniques ensured they did not.

Castles were capital-intensive devices that substituted money for manpower. Unlike linear defensive systems they required small garrisons. Roger of Howden's semi-official numbers seldom reach three figures: Henry II left thirty knights and sixty sergeants in Le Mans castle. Sixteen knights and twenty-five sergeants held Pembroke Castle. Investing armies needed far more, such as the 500 Welsh and 500 Marshal retainers who besieged Windsor in 1194. Like personal armour, protective walls reduced the owners' casualties and boosted morale. Only one of Wark's defenders was killed during a three-week siege in 1138. When the Scots stormed Brough in 1173, a single knight defied them all, hanging his shield over the battlements and throwing down sharpened stakes, until he was smoked out. High walls maximised the effect of kinetic weapons, such as the wooden blocks thrown down at Milli, or the millstone with which William was menaced at Newbury. In a well appointed castle, projectiles would be pre-positioned, like the piles of stones Count Richard found on the parapets of Taillebourg's triple-moated castle in 1179.

Fortified towns and castles might hold out for months, if not stormed by a coup-de-main like Milli or Taillebourg. A sample of nearly fifty notable sieges from Norwich in 1075 to La Rochelle in

1224 suggests a thirty-eight-day average. Antioch and Château Gaillard held out longest at 226 and 187 days each. Average duration falls to a month if these freaks are omitted. Three-quarters of investments succeeded, more by negotiation or starvation than by assault. Besieged a second time, Wark's English garrison surrendered after eating all their horses, the King of Scotland giving them more so they could ride out with dignity. An honourable defence did not have to be successful. The gallant commander of La Ferté in 1189 won great esteem for his unavailing resistance.

The French historian Philippe Contamine diagnosed a medieval siege mentality, a form of military agoraphobia which impelled combatants to shut themselves up in their most defensible strongholds. Barring the gates was the pragmatic response to porous battle-fronts. Medieval armies were too small and ill-informed to secure their home base by presenting a continuous front, or intercepting a fast-moving enemy as modern armies might do. Point defence was, therefore, the most effective way to protect key assets, whether personal, material, or topographical. Castles bought time to react to an enemy incursion, while invaders who bypassed unreduced garrisons faced losing their communications. A mounted garrison could cause trouble up to 10 miles (15km) away. Castles also provided bases for offensive raiding. The *Anglo-Saxon Chronicle* describes this in Normandy in 1090, when William Rufus's 'riders' at St Valéry and Aumale 'did harm in the land by raiding and by burning'. Sieges had disadvantages, however. They were time-consuming and expensive, and rarely succeeded against a dynamic commander like Henry II at Rouen in 1174 or Count Baldwin at Arras in 1197. The Young King's Revolt saw many sieges, but the battles at Fornham and Alnwick were decisive. Philip Augustus' Norman siege strategy only succeeded because John ran away.

The aggressive use of castles by William Rufus is a reminder that formal battles or sieges were a minor part of a knight's career. They provided the beans in the stew, titbits for knights like William and his biographer to pull out. The daily reality of war was raiding. When fighting started between Henry II and Philip Augustus in July 1188, the *History* comments that the land was ravaged and cruelly harmed. Wasting an enemy's land was more than an unfortunate side-effect of a medieval army's need to forage for the tons of fodder it required for its horses. The mounted raid or *chevauchée* was policy, sanctioned by the highest echelons of chivalric society with the avowed intention of harming their enemies. Medieval wars were mainly fought over economic issues – feudal property rights – not abstract national interests, and their conduct reflected this. Ignored or misunderstood by battle-oriented historians, raiding targeted civilians in order to destroy an enemy's economic resources and undermine his authority, a concept familiar to Second World War bomber barons.

William may have learned this fundamental principle of medieval warfare from the master strategist who inspired his tournament tactics: Philip of Alsace, the worthy Count of Flanders, 'who surpassed everyone then living through his wisdom'. Jordan of Fantôme quotes Philip's advice to William the Lion's Scots emissaries during the Young King's Revolt. The Marshal may well have been at the French court to hear it:

> *Destroy your enemies and waste their country,*
> *That by fire and conflagration all may be kindled;*
> *That he* [the Scottish king] *may leave them* [the English] *nothing,*
> *either in forest or in meadow,*
> *Of which they may in the morning have a dinner.*

The Marshal adopted a similar line in Henry II's councils when advising the raid that avenged the Gisors Elm. So much were such affairs an accepted part of knightly warfare that Henry could style William's advice as *molt corteis*, most courtly. The inseparability of warfare and raiding in Henry's mind is shown by the safe conduct he granted William in 1183, permitting the Marshal to fight the king and burn royal property.

The Montmirail *chevauchée* of 1188 exposes the true nature of such destructive expeditions. Henry II himself gave the orders to burn and destroy the whole region, sparing none, 'for sparing the wicked achieves nothing'. The town's destruction would be a feat of great chivalry. William rode directly to Montmirail without stopping for sleep, burning and taking everything within reach, leaving nothing behind. The Milli *chevauchée* of 1197 was similarly undertaken on royal orders, marching by night to achieve total surprise, inflicting damage out of all proportion to the forces engaged. Mercadier took so many prisoners that there was no room in Milli to stand. Raids did not always go to plan. When the French withdrew after demolishing Fontaine castle in June 1194, Robert Earl of Leicester, William's diplomatic companion in April 1204, set off after them. Leaving Rouen by night in the approved manner, Robert strayed too far, was captured, and was forced to surrender his castle at Paçi-sur-Eure as ransom.

It may be argued that the rapid passage of small medieval armies did little permanent damage. Ralph of Coggeshall's claims of Norman depopulation in 1197 may be a chronicler's exaggeration, but he is supported by other evidence outside his period: Domesday Book's sparse population figures for counties bordering Wales, or the brambles that infested northern France during the Hundred Years War. The *History* describes raiding's effect in 1140s England as follows:

> ... *cruel war, by which the land was ruined,*
> *The people dead or downcast, and all joy melted away,*
> *All gain turned to loss, and riches to poverty;*
> *When the poor folk cannot harvest, and have nothing to pay*
> *their rents,*

They must leave the land and seek their bread elsewhere.
Whence the lord is impoverished …

Jordan of Fantôme witnessed similar distress in Northumberland:

The land which was full of such prosperity
Is now destitute of all riches.
There is no drink but spring water,
Where they used to have beer in the week.

Economic warfare was indecisive with a high collateral cost, like William's slaughtered retainers at New Ross. The Church tried to protect non-combatants under the Peace of God or *Pax Dei*, but Jordan of Fantôme thought such restrictions not worth 'a single clove of garlic'.

Atrocities were usually blamed on Scots rabble or King John's alien mercenaries, but the knightly class profited from their misdeeds. Guilt by association sapped the chivalric ideal. When William, in his knight errant days, encountered a runaway monk eloping with the sister of a distant acquaintance, he had no qualms about confiscating the money on which they intended to live by usury, then forbidden by the Church. The *History* treats the affair as a joke; now it looks more like highway robbery. Matthew of Boulogne, who sought to plunder Drincourt in 1166, had gained his county by kidnapping its heiress from a Hampshire nunnery. Pillage was politically and morally corrosive.

Medieval commanders did not limit themselves to military means, but wove sanctions, subversion, and shady deals into a very modern pattern. Sanctions could be material or spiritual. Richard I blackmailed Baldwin of Flanders, by denying Flemish weavers access to English wool, hanging the sailors he caught running the blockade. Philip Augustus was adept in black propaganda, claiming to be the target of Assassins hired by Richard from the Old Man of the Mountain. Treachery was the best way to end a siege, from Antioch in 1098 to Wiston Castle, on William's Pembrokeshire doorstep, captured bloodlessly by the Welsh in 1194.

On the diplomatic front, the Church played a mediation role similar to the United Nations today, with similarly mixed success. Philip Augustus habitually rejected papal mediation in his domestic quarrels with the Angevins, except when it suited him. Mediation was most effective when neither side had realistic hopes of success, as before the Treaty of Westminster that ended the Anarchy in 1153. If the Church was on side, the enemy might be excommunicated before a battle to undermine their morale. Both sides at Thielt were excommunicate, but God's position was clear; it was the losers' commander who fell sick. As the Church's temporal ambitions grew, it extended Crusading privileges to its supporters in conflicts between Christians, saving them the inconvenience of overseas travel. The Albigensian Crusade of 1208 against Languedoc is the most notorious example, but the idea was widely adopted and abused.

Earthly inducements remained significant. Henry of Huntingdon recalled William Rufus intriguing against Philip Augustus's great-grandfather, whose army vanished, 'obscured by dark clouds of money'. England's financial resources enabled Henry I to buy Robert Curthose's Norman supporters in the same way that Henry II isolated the Young King, by oiling the palms of French magnates. Richard I was similarly generous, paying the Count of Flanders 5,000 marks, even while the *History* mocked the Papal Curia's reverence for Saints Ruffin and Albinus, red gold and white silver respectively. Peace deals and truces involved payments running into thousands of marks. The *deniers* generated by the twelfth-century economic recovery had more direct strategic uses than hiring mercenaries.

ARMS AND MEN

Medieval authorities took a binary view of armed forces. Socially they distinguished *Le grand peuple et le commoune gent*, the great and the common folk. Tactically they differentiated *equites* from *pedites*, mounted men from foot. The command hierarchy reflected this division. William's grandfather had once marshalled the horsemen, leaving the Constable in charge of the foot. Terms like 'cavalry' and 'infantry' are modern coinages, inappropriate in a medieval context. Knights were skilled warriors, not professionals in any modern sense.

There were two further distinctions: between armoured foot-men, usually known as sergeants but including town militia, and the *inermes* or naked irregulars, such as the Welsh who swam the Seine in August 1174 to raid Louis VII's camp outside Rouen. Equally significant was the distinction between troops with weapons designed for close quarters shock action, and sharpshooters equipped with longer-ranging missile weapons. This was another binary split, the types not being interchangeable, unlike modern infantry who may fight at a distance with mortars and machine guns, or close up with bayonets and grenades. Individual combatants rarely combined missile and shock action, although the *History* mentions sergeants armed with bows and spears at a tournament, and Richard I once stalked Nottingham Castle's defenders with a crossbow. It was difficult to provide missile support for mounted troops, as sharpshooters could not approach hostile shock troops, without being overrun. This would remain a problem even after the so-called infantry revolution of the fourteenth century. William was one of the few medieval commanders to use missile troops offensively in battle.

Medieval armies in Europe comprised three main troop categories in the field: mounted shock troops, dismounted shock troops, and dismounted missile troops. Each individual category included several sub-categories, as shown below:

MEDIEVAL TROOP TYPES

Mounted?	Weapon System	
	Shock	Missile
Yes	Knights	n/a
	Sergeants	
No	Sergeants	Archers
	Welsh Irregulars	Crossbowmen
	Miners	Engineers

The *History* mentions representatives of all three main troop types – as the poetic meter required: 'knights, and sergeants', 'good sergeants and good archers', or 'knights, and sergeants, and crossbowmen'. William would have seen mounted archers in Outremer, but these never featured at home. Engineers were international specialists who built and operated siege engines, like Master Urric *ingeniator* who served Richard I at Nottingham in 1194, alongside a Saracen and a Greek. Miners were humbler exponents of pick and shovel who undermined castle walls, the most certain way of making a breach. Philip Augustus was never without them.

The mounted arm shaped medieval warfare to such an extent that knights came to monopolise the term *miles*, the Latin for any soldier, implying an unbridgeable gulf between themselves and lesser warriors. Mounted troops enjoyed a tradition of victory dating from Roman defeats by German and Persian horsemen. Their technical superiority over the cavalry of antiquity had been consolidated by the adoption of stirrups, a wrap-around saddle, anchored by harness round the horse's breast, and horse-shoes. Unlike foot-sloggers, mounted warriors reached the battlefield fresh, an advantage they increased by monopolising the available horseflesh. William's contemporaries rode to battle on a palfrey and carried their armour on a pack horse, saving their destriers for more serious work. The 1106 Treaty of Dover, when Henry I hired 1,000 Flemish knights with three horses each, may reflect this arrangement. Hard working knights needed more than one destrier, however. William had three after his first tournament success at Ste Jamme in 1166.

The best horses came from Europe's southern fringes, exposed to Arab bloodstock. Lombard horses were particularly prized. William remembered capturing one during the St Brice tournament in 1166. Richard I rode another at Gisors in 1198. An Angevin knight repeatedly passed the French siege-lines at Verneuil in 1194 on a Lombard, and was never caught. A temperamental Italian destrier would kill Gilbert Marshal. The *History* quotes prices of £30–40, presumably Angevin money, equivalent to £7–10 sterling. It valued the two that William left with Henry II in 1184 at £100 each (£25 sterling). Good horses brought social prestige, as well as military advantage. Philip Augustus was mocked for riding a ten-year-old chestnut during the retreat from Vernon. Not the least of William's embarrassments as a Poitevin prisoner was having to ride a donkey.

A destrier was not the cart-horse of popular misconception. The dimensions of maritime horse transports suggest an animal of 15–16 hands like a modern hunter or Welsh cob, combining a good turn of speed with the strength to carry a knight in armour. War horses needed to be stout hearted and biddable. William's mount at the Épernon tournament of 1179 was struck repeatedly without budging, until his master applied the spurs. In battle, war horses were sacrificed ruthlessly. William I lost three at Hastings. Even the peaceable Henry III had two killed under him at the battle of Lewes in 1264. The Marshal recalled losing two horses killed in action, one at Drincourt and one outside Lusignan. Two more were wounded at

Le Mans and Montmirail respectively. John of Earley counted seven wounds to the latter's shoulders, neck, and breast.

The other professional trademark of the knight was his armour. For William this meant the *lorica* or hauberk, a long mail shirt made of up to 200,000 interlinked iron rings, worn over a padded undergarment or *pourpoint* that absorbed the energy of blows deflected by the hauberk. Weighing 25–30lb (12–14kg), far less than a modern soldier's combat gear, mail was flexible and well distributed, especially when worn with a belt, allowing easy movement. Inured to arms from youth, knights can have experienced little difficulty wearing armour. The *History* twice admits to William becoming out of breath, once after climbing a motte during a tournament in 1179, and again after scaling the walls of Milli Castle, aged fifty.

Proof against sword blows, mail was less effective against pointed weapons. The Syrian memoirist Ousama al Munquidh recalled thrusting his lance through a Christian knight's haunches in 1119, tearing through two layers of mail to protrude a cubit beyond, similar to William's wound in 1168. The decisive advantage conferred by wearing mail in combat is evident from the short-lived resistance offered by disarmed knights, from Earl Patrick's *mesnie* in the Test Valley to Henry II's escort at Le Mans. The *History*'s account of Mirebeau suggests the punishment mail had to absorb: 'blows given, returned and repaid with interest, many hauberk links cut through, helmets beaten down, mail hoods sliced through to the head'. Nevertheless, hauberks might be removed for speed in reconnaissance or pursuit, as William did before and after Le Mans, and again at Arques.

Twelfth-century improvements to personal protection included closer fitting hauberks with longer sleeves and mittens, and leg guards or *cuisses*. Preparations for the Ste Jamme tournament included polishing the latter. Exports embargoed at Southampton by the regent's government in 1217 included armoured shoes.

Helmets underwent dramatic improvements. William's effigy shows a simple mail coif or hood, exposing his face, but he wore something more substantial in action. Helmets were a natural target, hostile knights seeking to pull them off or twist them back to front to blind the owner, as happened to William during the St Brice tournament. The conical Norman helmet worn over a coif at Hastings acquired a domed or flat top and facial protection, evolving towards the cylindrical great helm shown on Richard I's second great seal. William had one at Le Mans, where a burning mattress flooded his helmet with smoke, nearly choking him. His son Gilbert fatally lost control of his destrier, partly because he was blinded with dust and sweat, oppressed by the weight of his helmet. The inconvenience of the enclosed helmet explains Richard I's preference for an open iron cap, and William remaining bare-headed to the last moment at Le Mans and Lincoln.

The rising cost of protection encouraged the appearance of a new class of mounted warrior: mounted sergeants, from the Latin *sirvientes* or serving men. Sergeants were socially inferior to knights, but functionally identical. At Muret sergeants formed up with the French knights as supplementary heavy cavalry. Jordan de Fantôme credited a sergeant with bringing down William the Lion's horse at Alnwick. When the Abbot of Bury St Edmunds could not persuade knightly tenants to serve Richard I in Normandy, he hired sergeants. Known as *servientes loricati*, i.e. wearing hauberks, they were by no means light cavalry. Their equipment resembled that of the eleventh-century *miles*, as shown on the Bayeux Tapestry. Paid half the wages of a stipendiary knight, sergeants made up half to two-thirds of the mounted arm. A prestigious force like a French royal army might have less. A fifth of the French mounted troops at Bouvines were sergeants, a higher proportion serving on the Dauphin's secondary front on the Loire.

A major difference between knights and sergeants was the horse armour that the former adopted during the late twelfth century. At Bouvines, Flemish knights received a charge by French sergeants at a stand, stabbing the latter's unprotected horses with their lances. Horse armour's evolution is unclear, concealed by silk trappings, and consisting of perishable chain mail. Romans and Persians had both used horse armour, suggesting an Eastern origin. An eyewitness of the First Crusade describes Muslims with horses covered with dazzling iron plates. Turkish horse archers may have encouraged Western knights to protect their horses, but they took their time. The first European reference to horse armour is in 1187, when the Count of Hainault in modern Belgium fielded 190 knights, 109 of them on barded horses. William's horse at Montmirail clearly had no armour beneath its trappings, although a fast moving raid was not the occasion for such an encumbrance. Richard's account of Gisors in 1198 says that 140 of the 200 French prisoners had covered horses, a similar proportion to the Lombard League's order of battle in the 1250s. Horse armour was perhaps the mounted arm's most significant advance in William's life-time, reinforcing its predominance by protecting the source of its mobility.

Footmen were socially and militarily inferior, sometimes able to resist knights, but having little offensive capability. The secret of drill was lost with the Romans, leaving bodies of foot easily disorganised and vulnerable to faster, better armed horsemen. Three hundred foot sergeants failed to block a street against William and the Young King at Anet in 1176. Nevertheless, William's career provides numerous references to well-armed foot. Apart from killing his horse at Drincourt, sergeants chased knights into the *recet* during the tournament at Eu, halted a French charge at Gisors (1188), stormed up ladders at Milli, and captured the French flagship at Sandwich. Sometimes styled *pedites loricati*, they wore the shorter mail shirt known as a haubergeon or *loricella*.

The best foot were Flemish. Never conquered like the English at Hastings, the Flemings maintained a Germanic infantry tradition against the knightly warfare imported from France. Many hired themselves out to Henry II and his enemies as Brabançon mercenaries. They made cheap garrisons, but fought too few battles to prove their value in the open. Surprised on the march at Fornham they were broken by a mounted charge, and massacred by angry peasants. More perished at Alnwick next year. Otto of Brunswick's Brabançons held out to the bitter end at Bouvines. Typical weapons included pikes longer than a knight's lance, and *gisarmes* with curved blades resembling halberds. William was well acquainted with Flemish foot. The *History* praises the Count of Flanders's proud and haughty commons at Arras, eager to fight. As Earl of Pembroke, William had Flemish tenants. Welsh Annals for 1193 describe their defeating a Welsh force at Llanwhaden, killing sixty in a wolf-like pursuit.

The other source of Angevin foot soldiers was Wales: spearmen from the north, archers from the south. Unlike sergeants they were lightly armed, capable of swimming the Seine to raid the French camp outside Rouen. Discipline was poor. Richard I interrupted his hunting to stop his Welsh and Brabançons fighting at Portsmouth. The spearmen had an undistinguished combat record. The Earl of Chester's Welsh spearmen were scattered at First Lincoln. Henry II lost all of his retreating from Le Mans. The princes of Gwynedd usually avoided direct confrontation with English armies, retreating into their barren mountains.

Their bow-armed compatriots from South Wales would one day revolutionise English warfare. Archery during William's lifetime, however, resembles the dog that failed to bark in the night. A cheap, simple, rugged weapon up to 6 feet (1.8m) long and made from elm, the longbow had a range of 200 yards (180m) and a theoretical rate of 20 shots a minute. Its power is attested by Gerald of Wales's often quoted accounts of arrows left sticking through Abergavenny Castle's oak door, or penetrating a luckless knight's *cuisses* and saddle to pin him to his horse. Few bowmen feature in William's career, although his father introduced archers of unspecified origin into

Newbury Castle. A Welsh archer precipitated the skirmish at Gisors in 1188 by shooting an insolent French knight in the head, though not fatally. King John hired some for his last campaigns in Normandy. His father, however, had not thought them worth regulating in the 1181 Assize of Arms.

The neglect of archery, following its prominence at Hastings, demands explanation. Social prejudice may have inhibited celebration of low-status troops. The Bayeux Tapestry's depiction of short bows drawn to the chest is often interpreted as evidence of poor material and defective technique. Thirteenth-century sketches of Welsh archers, however, look much the same, while Iron Age bows found in peat bogs are no shorter than Tudor ones from the *Mary Rose*. Longbows are sometimes represented as a regional speciality limited to Wales, but they were not. Archers were an essential component of Crusading armies recruited across Europe, and featured in the communal disturbances before Thielt. Yorkshire archers formed the English second rank at the battle of the Standard. Wealden archers from Kent, sometimes misconstrued as Welsh, picked off intruders in 1216 and 1264.

A combination of factors explains their neglect. A high rate of fire is useless without an adequate ammunition supply. Wark's commandant told his garrison in 1173 to shoot sparingly, and save arrows for important targets. Later medieval kings supplied thousands of arrows for their campaigns. If used to screen advancing knights, bowmen had little time to shoot, reducing their advantage over the slower shooting but more powerful crossbow. Fatalities caused by arrows hitting combatants' unprotected faces imply that arrows usually failed to penetrate chain mail. Henry I survived a direct hit over the heart during an ambush in Powys, 'from the goodness of his armour, for he was mailed, and the arrow turned and rebounded back' (*Chronicle of the Princes*). Longbows required large numbers to be effective. Twelfth-century Welsh princes could not mobilise enough to stop a knightly charge, as Gwenwynwyn of Powys found at Painscastle in 1198, when an army drawn from all over Wales fled a mounted charge at the first onset. The English, on the other hand, had yet to invent the Commissions of Array that Edward I would use to field thousands of archers. Longbows in William's time were most successful against unarmoured targets, like the Galwegians riddled like hedgehogs at the Standard, or in a guerrilla context as in Kent.

The twelfth century's missile weapon of choice was the crossbow or arbalest. Banned by popes, and popularised by Richard I, crossbows could break a limb or pierce a hauberk at 100 yards. The Byzantine princess Anna Comnena considered them diabolical weapons, a Crusader's bolt having pierced both the shield and scale armour of a Greek admiral. The *History* may reflect their rise in popularity with its shift from archers at Newbury to crossbowmen at Limoges, Nottingham, and Verneuil. The change may reflect the appearance of horse armour, which reduced longbows' effectiveness against mounted targets, or it may reflect an increased financial ability to hire specialist crossbowmen. Gervase of Canterbury records a royal escort of numerous armed men and crossbowmen during John's visit to Kent on 1209. John's reliance on foreign crossbowmen earned them a place in Magna Carta, among the other aliens to be expelled. A complex weapon, crossbows or arbalests were for professionals who rode to battle. Some of John's arbalestriers had three horses, as many as a knight. Like poorer foot sergeants, crossbowmen wore padded jackets known as gambesons or *pourpoints*. During the Fourth Crusade's assault on Constantinople in 1203, the crossbowmen were with the archers in the van, as they would be at Lincoln. Like longbows, crossbows were best in a static siege context, where they were less likely to be suddenly overrun.

The final element in a medieval array was the machines that played an increasing part in sieges, inhibiting a recurrence of the

Anarchy when Stephen's enemies had built castles faster than he could capture them. There were three types: devices for approaching walls, stone throwers powered by counter-weights, and torsion-driven catapults which play no part in our narrative. The first category attracted evocative names: belfries that overlooked enemy walls; sows, cats, and tortoises which provided a covered approach for miners or a battering ram. The *cleier* to which William was attached at Newbury was one of the latter, a moveable gallery made of wickerwork 'claies' or hurdles.

Counter-weight machines had a long arm or 'flail' pivoting over a vertical frame, the fulcrum nearer the weight than the sling to magnify the force imparted to the projectile. They fell into the following types, as recently recreated by Renaud Beffeyte:

SIEGE ENGINES

Designation	Range (m)	Projectile Wt (kg)	Rate	Crew
Perrière	40–60	3–12	1/minute	8–16
Bricole	80	10–30	1/minute	16
Mangonel	150	100 (max)	2/hour	12 plus
Trébuchet	220	125	1–2/hour	60 plus

Mangonels and trébuchets were large pieces of equipment, fitted with boxes of earth to provide the mass for the counter-weight. Perrières had no counter-weight, but depended on several people all pulling at once. They were less accurate than trébuchets, which could be adjusted to hit the same spot repeatedly by altering the amount of earth in the counter-weight box. The bricole combined teamwork with a small counter-weight to improve range and throw weight, while preserving a high rate of fire. None of these machines resemble the torsion-driven machines of the Romans which often appear in surveys of medieval warfare. They were a brand new type of weapon.

The *History* refers to perrières and mangonels, describing the weapon into which William was loaded at Newbury as the former. This appears small for a five-year-old weighing several stone (20–25kg), suggesting that Stephen had a bricole or mangonel. Trébuchets were copied from Muslim examples, reaching Western Europe in the 1190s. The first English use of the word *trebuca* occurs in the Dunstable annalist's account of Dover's second siege in 1217. Smaller machines could smash crenellations and wooden hoardings along parapets to stop defenders picking off miners or storming parties. Larger machines might breach town walls, as Bulgarian stone-throwers did when besieging Latin Crusaders at Demotika and Adrianople in 1206 and 1207. Siege engines could also start fires within the perimeter, as may have happened at Marlborough in 1194 when machines were sent from Reading in the abbey's carts with sulphur and pitch for incendiaries.

Complex weapons based on abstruse mathematical principles, trébuchets were imported into England rather than built locally. Lesser weapons were constructed as required, often in large numbers. Philip Augustus abandoned twenty-three perrières outside Rouen in 1193. The Bulgarians employed thirty at Adrianople. Either weapon was deadly against soft targets like people. Ousama remembered Christian mangonels at Shaizar in 1138 indiscriminately shattering heads, walls, and buildings.

PRACTICE OF WAR

Knightly armies were raised in various ways. At the heart of every military undertaking were members of a lord's household, acting as staff officers, junior leaders, and bodyguards. William was a household knight for over twenty years. In Henry II's last campaign he played all three roles: advising on the Mantes *chevauchée*, leading the Montmirail raid, and covering Henry's retreat at Le Mans. Households were small bodies of dedicated professionals, roughly 100 strong like the ninety-four who followed William of Tancarville's banner. They were instantly available, but too few for major enterprises. For these a great lord summoned a feudal host consisting of all those owing him military service with their own retinues. On the outbreak of the Angevin-Capetian war in 1188, Henry II summoned William with all the knights he could get. Richard spent the night after he broke with his father at Bonmoulins dictating over 200 letters to his adherents.

A feudal host provided useful numbers of competent warriors, and was cost-effective within a limited geographical range, but it lacked flexibility and staying power. The *History* claimed that Henry II fielded 20,000 men at Gisors in 1188. An unlikely figure, it suggests significant numbers, like those attributed to Richard in 1194. Feudal hosts had a mind of their own, however. French magnates disliked fighting Henry II, a fellow Crusader. English magnates objected to crossing the Channel. Service was in principle limited to forty or sixty days from joining the host. Angevin kings preferred smaller, more durable forces. John dismissed the host he summoned to Portsmouth in 1201, and spent their travelling money hiring three troops of 100 knights each for overseas service, one commanded by William.

The largest and least flexible part of the feudal array was the popular levy of all free men. The *History* called it the *criz de la terre*, proclamation of the land. This was not the ill-armed mob of peasants derided by anti-feudal historians, but a useful tool for local defence, as at the Standard. The 1181 Assize of Arms specified the same equipment for free laymen worth over 16 marks as for a knight. Anyone worth 10 marks or more needed a haubergeon, iron cap, and lance; poorer freemen a gambeson. Dunstable Priory purchased one hauberk, nine haubergeons, and nine gambesons for John's counter-invasion forces in 1213. His threats to declare defaulters serfs, *nithing* as William Rufus put it, persuaded so many to turn up that food ran short, and the least experienced were sent home. Roger of Wendover claimed that John had 60,000 men at Barham Down outside Dover, a logistically unsustainable figure symbolising unmanageable numbers. Such mass levies, of doubtful value, remained a feature of thirteenth-century invasion scares.

Alongside feudal arrangements based on personal obligation was a thriving trade in paid troops driven by the twelfth-century economic recovery. Never subject to the brutal demonetisation experienced in Europe, England led the way. William Rufus was known as *militum mercator et solidator* – a dealer and hirer of knights. Henry I so depended on his paid knights that at Christmas 1124 he castrated every moneyer in England for not making pennies of sufficiently good quality to satisfy his troops. Henry II boosted the market with the 1159 scutage, used to hire paid knights. We might call such troops mercenaries, a name they would have resented, *mercennarius* being then a term of abuse. Consistent classification is not straightforward. Household knights like William were rewarded in cash as well as in kind. His credit was always good, though he possessed not a furrow of land. Members of a feudal host might overstay their forty days if paid to do so. Remote or protracted campaigns were in effect conducted by paid troops.

The whole feudal structure was thus drawn into the cash nexus, long before Edward III invented bastard feudalism in the fourteenth century. Any fighting man of any social level from knight to archer might be in receipt of wages. King John hired Brabançon knights and sergeants to put down a Scottish rebellion in 1211. Mercadier employed sergeants and crossbowmen. Rates of pay varied. Henry II paid his knights 8d (3.3p) a day and his foot sergeants 1d (0.4p), an agricultural labourer's wage. Inflation pushed these rates up to 12d a day for knights and 4d or 2d for mounted or foot sergeants respectively.

The 2-mark scutage (320 old pence) which had once hired a substitute knight for forty days was no longer adequate in the 1200s.

There remained an essential distinction between those serving from feudal obligation while being paid their keep, and true mercenaries like Mercadier's men who fought to eat. True mercenaries were deracinated cut-throats named after their supposed origin: Basques, Navarrese, Aragonese, and always Brabançons. The lowest were the *cotereaux*, named after the knives they thrust through gaps in ill-fitting armour. *Routier*, a useful umbrella term, comes from *ruta*, the mercenary band. Sometimes the *History* lists *routiers* beside functional troop types, knights, sergeants, and crossbows, suggesting a spurious tactical distinction. A task force, like John's Irish expedition of 1210, consisted of three components: the royal household, the feudal host, and mercenary bands. William must have rubbed along with Mercadier, but the *History* minimises the *routier*'s contribution to Richard's victory at Gisors, and condemns John's use of mercenaries outright. They were essential, but politically and financially ruinous.

The armies raised by whatever combination of these methods were very small. Population was limited, political units modest, warriors expensive, and logistics undeveloped. Simon de Montfort won Muret with under a thousand men. The French army at Bouvines, the supreme confrontation of the age, consisted of 1,600 horse and 4,000–6,000 foot. Lack of numbers prevented armies establishing a continuous front line, and contributed to operational fluidity. Fighting was diffuse, spread out in time and space. Combined with the unceasing struggle for a myriad of strongholds this creates an impression of strategic chaos. The image is unfair. Like their modern counterparts, the best medieval commanders met the challenges of their day with ingenuity and skill.

It would have been strange if they did not. Warfare was the main activity of medieval Europe's secular elite, the most prestigious end of a spectrum of violence running from hunting through jousting and tournaments to war, domestic and foreign. Skills were transmitted verbally, a vanished oral discourse of which the *History* formed part. William would have absorbed this traditional expertise while daydreaming at Tancarville, or attending the courts of Philip of Alsace and Henry II. While in Palestine he formed a close attachment to the Templars, whose Rule represented the best of twelfth-century chivalric practice. After 1194 William was the constant companion of Richard Coeur de Lion, the foremost exponent of knightly warfare. Such a *curriculum vitae* demanded more than instinctual physicality. William's argument at Arras that 'Foresight, common sense and right, often accompany prowess' stuck in John of Earley's mind to reappear twenty-five years later in the *History*.

Comparison with twentieth-century military doctrine demonstrates the maturity of twelfth-century military expertise. The British Army's *Field Service Regulations* of 1924 reflected the experience of the greatest land war the nation has ever fought. They identified eight underlying principles of war. Medieval commanders would never have expressed themselves so succinctly, but their actions showed their instinctive understanding of the key ideas:

Maintenance of the Objective: Philip Augustus devoted his adult life to overthrowing the Angevin Empire. When Richard turned back from Jerusalem, he sacrificed a minor objective, the problematic recovery of the Holy City, to preserve a viable Christian enclave on the Palestinian coast. Medieval circumstances made it hard for commanders to pursue the destruction of enemy forces, the ideal aim of military operations today, but leaders like Saladin and Richard persistently sought to do so. As regent, William would show similar focus.

Offensive Action: It became a cliché in the later Middle Ages, when knights fought dismounted, that to attack was to court defeat. That was not so in William's day. Twelfth-century knights fought mounted, making the offensive the most effective route to tactical success. Henry II ended the Young King's Revolt not by sitting behind Rouen's defences, but by sallying forth to offer battle. Simon de Montfort twice reversed a dire strategic situation in Languedoc by resolute offensive action, first at Castelnaudary (1211) and then at Muret. William's insistence on the bold move at Arras won the day without a fight.

A knightly charge was not the pell-mell rush suggested by Anna Comnena's claim that 'a Frank on horseback would drive a hole in the walls of Babylon'. Started on the word of command, it began gently, as if carrying a bride in the saddle, then built up speed on a trumpet call to burst through the opposing ranks, as Team Angevin did at Joigny in 1178/79. When several bodies of knights were in line, they charged in successive echelons, usually starting from the right, to deliver a series of shocks and provide a rallying point for preceding waves. Philip of Alsace characteristically added his own twist, charging *à la traverse*, to roll up the Young King's disordered ranks from the flank.

Surprise: The first thought of every twelfth-century commander was to outwit his adversary. Almost every action mentioned in the *History* features surprise, which was always the best way to pre-empt a siege before it started. The *History's* account of Newbury uses three 'surprise' related words in twelve lines, the garrison's first warning being the appearance of Stephen's advance guard. William's capture of Cilgerran in Advent 1204 was equally sudden, catching its Welsh guards *inermis* – naked or unarmed – at a time when the *Trux Dei* outlawed military activity. Movement by night was common, from John Marshal's Test

Valley ambush, via the Montmirail and Milli raids, to King John's secret flight in December 1203. Twice the victims were caught eating breakfast.

Concentration: The *History*'s comment that the Imperialists lost at Bouvines because they attacked prematurely with a quarter of their numbers is statistically incorrect, but tactically astute. Otto's army arrived piecemeal, some of the leaders having ridden on ahead, among them the Earl of Salisbury from whom the *History*'s account may derive.

Medieval tactical organisation sought to prevent such dissipation of effort. Knights formed up for action in troops or *conrois* of twelve to twenty-four men each, like William's fifteen-strong banner at Lagny-sur-Marne. Several *conrois* formed an *eschiele* or *bataille*, commonly translated as a 'battle', fifty to sixty men in front and two or three ranks deep. These tactical units formed line or column depending on their numbers and situation. When they advanced, they did so in the tightest formation consistent with movement. Close order maximises the fighting power of short-range weapons, concentrating the maximum number of blows on the shortest frontage. The eyewitness *Itinerary of the Pilgrims* says the Crusaders at Arsuf were so packed that 'an apple, if thrown, would not have fallen to the ground without touching a man or horse'.

This compact formation appears repeatedly in the *History*'s accounts of tournaments, starting at Ste Jamme, where the chamberlain's *conroi* rode out *seréement & sanz desrei*, tightly and without disorder. The chamberlain pushed William back into line at Drincourt lest his enthusiasm disrupted the formation. When the chamberlain's men withdrew under pressure, they did so in serried ranks not dispersed like Cossacks. Tournaments were instrumental in developing this instinctive ability to maintain formation, the exact antithesis of modern caricatures of medieval battle as a disjointed series of duels.

Economy of Force: Medieval strategists were adept at preserving their own strength, while dissipating the enemy's. Raids weakened the enemy economically, and might compel his scattered forces to fight at a disadvantage. Richard captured the Marshal's great rival, William des Barres, near Mantes attended by just a few knights. Castles represented economy of force. Substituting money and labour for blood, they forced the enemy to waste time besieging them individually, or risk dispersing to attack several at once. Blockading a besieging army wore them out faster than fighting them, as Philip Augustus learned at Vaudreuil in 1194.

Security: The first responsibility of any commander is to guard against surprise. As early as the First Crusade, we hear of advance and rear guards protecting an army on the march. Archers and scouts preceded Stephen's host at Newbury. Reconnaissance was so painstaking that in 1173 Louis VII captured a town while Henry II's scouts were still feeling their way. The English commander at Alnwick 'prudently' sent a spy to reckon the Scottish forces. Richard I in Outremer dressed his scouts as Bedouin. His victory at Gisors followed careful reconnaissance, first by a veteran knight, who knew the country, then by the king. William's patrols at Le Mans and Arques place him in the same tradition of personal observation.

Mobility: Vegetius, one of the few classical authorities owned by medieval commanders, rated speed more highly than numbers. Small well-horsed medieval armies, not tied by the leg to an artillery train, could move at an astonishing rate. The Montmirail raid rode 70 miles (114km) from Chinon, stormed the town, and then marched another 26 miles (42km) to Châteaudun, apparently in two days and the intervening night. King John was almost as quick at Mirebeau, making 40 miles (60km) a day. Even infantry could cover the ground. Henry II's Brabançons marched 132 miles (210km) from Rouen to Dol to crush the Young King's Breton supporters, 19 miles a day (30km). High march rates help explain the frequency of surprise attacks, armies arriving before news of their coming, as at Drincourt. Socio-economic factors speeded operations: the survival of Roman roads, not yet plundered for building material, and the aristocracy's acquaintance with the countryside, ingrained by years of incessant hunting and perambulation between estates.

Co-operation: If the duelling model of knightly combat were correct, there would have been no mutual support on medieval battlefields. The *History* provides plentiful evidence to the contrary. Groups of knights continually join forces against single opponents, like the five who assailed William at St Brice, tearing at his helmet and pulling him back over his horse's crupper. Even as their *conrois* disintegrate under the shock of battle, individual knights cling together to protect their comrades. When forty knights set upon the Young King at Lagny, the Marshal rides to the rescue, laying about him with his sword, while a freelance prisoner on parole hauls at the royal reins, the helmetless prince covering them both with his shield.

Maintaining a reserve allows one part of an army to support the rest. It was common twelfth-century practice, which William learnt from Philip of Alsace and applied at Fréteval. Simon de Montfort withheld one of his three *eschieles* at Muret to turn the Aragonese flank. The 'feigned flights' that feature in so many medieval battles are no more than the use of a reserve to restore the fight, in accordance with nineteenth-century cavalry practice, where up to half a mounted force might be kept as a support.

Inter-arm co-operation was problematic and probably under-reported, given the mounted arm's social dominance. Nevertheless it happened. Dismounted knights and archers together formed the front ranks at the Standard; sergeants and crossbows at Jaffa in 1192. Horse and foot in Outremer were so accustomed to working together that the latter opened their ranks at Arsuf for the knights to charge out through the gaps. Before Muret, Count Raymond of Toulouse proposed drawing the Crusaders onto a line of crossbowmen behind a palisade, but was laughed at by Peter of Aragon. William would not be such a fool at Lincoln.

The conflict that followed John's ignominious return from Poitou late in 1214 conformed to customary patterns. Both sides used blackmail and devastation to intimidate their opponents, and sustain their own troops. Much effort was expended in sieges. Battles remained a last resort. Dirty tricks featured prominently. A profoundly conservative society utilised its traditional weapons and military organisation. Hostilities were conducted by heavily armed cavalry and professional crossbowmen drawn from magnate retinues and mercenary bands. Commanders followed principles absorbed over twenty-five years of Angevin-Capetian conflict. It is not surprising that the royalists, with their *routier* captains and the Marshal's unequalled experience, came out on top.

I V

KING JOHN AND
THE DAUPHIN

Civil war was a frequent consequence of royal failure in pre-modern England. The Barons' War that followed John's return from Poitou in October 1214 would have been predictable in other, less fraught circumstances. For John it was the fitting climax of an appalling reign; for William it was a dramatic pause, before he emerged centre stage as saviour of his country. The *History* glosses over the Marshal family's role in the conflict. Other sources reveal the older William's complicity in John's counsels, an embarrassment for his son whose loyalty was less certain.

The poet observed that John's troubles began with his allies' bad day at Bouvines, and continued until his death. Those whom the king had injured turned against him, followed by others with less excuse. Both sides committed excesses that were unbelievable, had they not been seen. William's conciliatory attitude as regent suggests he shared the poet's ambivalence. The barons held the initiative, compelling John to grant the concessions framed in Magna Carta. As John mobilised his superior financial and political resources, however, he gained the upper hand, besieging Rochester in October 1215 and a launching a *chevauchée* through northern England at Christmas. Only French intervention in May 1216, led by Philip Augustus's son Louis, stemmed the royalist tide. Reduced to roaming the country like some bandit, John died at Newark in October 1216, ending the first instalment of hostilities.

THE BARONS' REVOLT

The baronial movement originated in the conspiracy of 1212, whose exiled leaders returned after John's submission to the Pope. The royal climb-down brought together an explosive combination of lay and clerical malcontents. Throughout the crisis, John's enemies posed as defenders of the liberties of both Church and kingdom, a potent mixture. Their personal grievances were less exalted. Professor Holt, Magna Carta's great historian, described the Barons' War as a rebellion of the king's debtors. Magnate indebtedness to the Crown quadrupled between 1199 and 1209. Robert fitz Walter, a ringleader, was deeply in debt to the king, as was Geoffrey of Mandeville, who owed 20,000 marks for the hand of John's cast-off queen. As son of John's long-serving justiciar, Geoffrey fitz Peter, Mandeville was a natural royalist, but his debts drove him to revolt. Indebtedness was more than just a financial hazard, as the Braose affair showed. It was a life-threatening condition.

The rebellion's hard core lay in the north, so much so that Northerner became a general term for the dissidents. Ralph of Coggeshall called them Northumbrians, but the dividing line lay further south, at the Wash rather than the Humber. Many rebels came from East Anglia, explaining Lincoln's strategic importance astride Ermine Street, the main road between the revolt's main foci. The Northerners had refused to follow John to Poitou after the naval victory at Dam in 1213, claiming to be exhausted after defending the coast all summer. Next year they would neither serve, nor pay the 3-mark scutage demanded of defaulters. Nearer home, they resented the intrusion of alien royal servants into county administration, hard-faced men such as the Tourangeau Philip Mark, the real-life Sheriff of Nottingham, or Philip of Maulay, Arthur's alleged assassin. Unrestrained by local ties, such men had no compunction about extracting every penny John demanded for his foreign adventures. Between 1199 and 1212 Yorkshire's tax revenues trebled, in line with inflation but not custom.

Menaced by debt and excluded from office, magnates and gentry were also exposed to John's whimsical application of legal process. Partly this arose from his transferring legal business from fixed courts at Westminster to the peripatetic royal court; partly it resulted from his confusing the administration of justice with money raising, magnates having to offer large sums for the king's favour. More than one chronicler cited John's arbitrary dispossessions without prior judgement as a grievance; 'thus was tyrannical will the law for him' (*Waverley*). More than one rebel leader nursed claims to a castle withheld by a suspicious monarch: Robert fitz Walter to Hertford, Saer of Quincy to Mountsorrel in Leicestershire, Geoffrey of Mandeville to the Tower of London.

The war was also a rebellion of cuckolds. Some reports of John's affairs emerged later, and may be dismissed as fabrications. Walter of Guisborough, for example, told a bizarre tale of a raddled harlot smuggled into the royal bed in place of Eustace of Vesci's wife. Better documented, though equally odd, is the fine of 200 chickens that Hugh de Neville's wife offered the king for a night back home. Hugh would abandon John in June 1216, handing Marlborough Castle to the French. Allegations of sexual misconduct were a common feature of thirteenth-century political discourse. Poitevin rebels had accused Richard I of debauching their women, before marrying them off to his mercenaries. John's misconduct, however, was flagrant. The Brabançon minstrel who wrote a *History of the Dukes of Normandy and Kings of England* (known as Anonymous of Béthune) was no unworldly monk. He thought John *de bieles femes ... trop convoiteus* – too desirous of fair women: 'by which he brought great shame upon the highest men of the land, for which he was much hated'. The *Melsa Chronicle* from Yorkshire says that John 'deflowered the wives and daughters of the nobility, [and] spared the wives of none whom he chose to stain with the ardour of his desires', a claim echoed at Waverley in Surrey. Even rumours of sexual misconduct with a high-status woman could prove devastating, as William had found in 1182. Three major aims emerged from this maelstrom of grievances: to limit John's exorbitant financial demands; to regain control of the localities; and to restrain the arbitrary application of royal justice. The conflict's personalisation, however, made John's disappearance the only sure way of ending it.

William's role in the crisis reflects a personal ambivalence. Like other magnates he had suffered confiscation of castles and lands, demands for hostages, and the wasting of his lands. But he owed everything to the Crown. A younger son made good, William was as much a parvenu as John's less savoury supporters, making him a natural *curialis* or member of the court party. John emphasised where William's material interests lay by granting him Cardigan and Carmarthen in January 1214. As the *History* commented, it was John's custom to keep his *prud'hommes* at arm's length, until he needed them. When the barons presented John with their charter of liberties at Epiphany 1215 (6 January), William acted as a surety for the king's answering their demands the Sunday after Easter (26 April). Another guarantor was Stephen Langton, the archbishop wished upon John by the Pope. Roger of Wendover stresses Langton's leadership in the negotiations leading to Magna Carta, but William was Stephen's constant companion. Together they represented society's twin pillars, the churchmen and the knights. John sought delay, arguing the novelty and time-consuming nature of the baronial programme. The Barnwell chronicler, our surest guide, said that John had other ideas in his mind, however. Recruiting officers, like Hugh of Boves, began hiring French and Flemish mercenaries, of which the barons were soon aware. Royal letters to the Pope denounced baronial disloyalty. Sheriffs imposed oaths of fealty, backing John against the charter. John boycotted further meetings, using William and Langton as intermediaries.

William's diplomatic skills emerge no more brightly from these deliberations than from his abortive missions to Philip Augustus. In neither case did he hold winning cards. He would do better after John's death, playing his own hand. Meanwhile, John prevaricated, hoping to provoke his opponents into violence. On Ash Wednesday (4 April), the king and his household put on the English Crusaders' traditional white crosses. He thus gained three years' immunity from attack, pleased the Pope, and infuriated his enemies. They asserted that 'he had not done it out of feelings of piety or the love of Christ, but in order to cheat them of his promise.' (*Barnwell*). After the Epiphany conference, the barons had formed a *conjuratio*, a sworn league, to demand redress. Almost by accident, they became the first rebels with a cause greater than mere self-aggrandisement. Being practical men, they fortified their castles, and despatched their own envoys to the Pope.

Distrusting John, the dissidents foregathered, 'with horses and arms', at Stamford in Lincolnshire, a tournament venue on England's main north–south road. On Easter Monday (20 April) they moved to Brackley, a day's ride from John's location at Oxford, 'committing no warlike acts, beyond the mere appearance of war' (*Barnwell*).

Brackley was the seat of Saer of Quincy, Robert fitz Walter's companion in dishonour at Vaudreuil. John had paid their ransoms and made Saer Earl of Winchester, but he failed to secure their loyalty. Like William, Saer was a self-made man with links to the Young King's household. He had vouched for the sufficiency of William's hostages in 1210. Matthew Paris thought there was no more handsome knight in the world. Heavily indebted to the Jews, Saer played a leading role throughout the rebellion. The slide to war gathered momentum as the barons threatened to withdraw fealty, the formal prelude to hostilities. William and Langton rode between Oxford and Brackley, returning with a written statement of the barons' demands. Failing agreement, the dissidents threatened to seize John's fortresses. According to the plentiful but unreliable Roger of Wendover, the king refused in a rage. On 5 May, the barons withdrew homage, and marched off, banners flying, to attack Northampton, 18 miles (29km) to the north-east.

The baronial démarche caught John at a disadvantage. Roger of Wendover identified forty-four 'chief promoters of this pestilence', who mobilised 'two thousand knights, besides horse sergeants, attendants, and foot soldiers ... variously equipped'. As Magna Carta's twenty-five enforcers promised to provide nearly 1,200 knights, 2,000 knightly followers does not seem excessive for forty-four magnates. A third of the English knight service, it explains John's unwillingness to take the offensive. It also bears comparison with the 1,380 knights later named in writs of restitution as dispossessed for rebellion. It is, however, more than Philip Augustus concentrated at Bouvines, while specific references to baronial armies range from 500 to just over 1,000.

The arch-traitor Robert fitz Walter was appointed commander-in-chief as 'Marshal of the Host of God and Holy Church'. Represented on his seal brandishing a sword and sporting one of the latest flat-topped helmets, Robert also held Castle Baynard, London's second strongest fortress after the Tower. The Barnwell chronicler confirmed widespread rebel support, 'especially younger sons and nephews ... seeking to make their military reputation'. Older men, with more to lose, supported the king. Others, 'friends of fortune or lovers of novelties', went with the tide. Among the families thus divided were the Marshals. Roger of Wendover's list of rebels includes the younger William, who no doubt resented seven years spent as John's hostage. Alternatively, the family may have backed both horses. William and his brother John were accused of doing so in 1194, and Scottish families did likewise during the eighteenth-century Jacobite risings. The alliance of Alexander II, the new King of Scots, and Llewelyn of Gwynedd with the malcontents had the advantage for John of consolidating the Marcher lords behind him. If the rebels enjoyed quantitative superiority, the king had quality: the Earls of Salisbury, Chester, Pembroke, Derby, Warenne, Aumale, and Cornwall. John pawned his jewels, including Matilda's imperial regalia, to the Templars to hire mercenaries. He had fewer men, but the simpler aim of gaining time until the barons tired of besieging royal strongholds, and went home. The *History* glosses over the fighting: 'there were too many dishonourable circumstances to relate', and the author feared for his safety if he dwelt upon them.

Northampton was a washout. Lacking siege engines, the barons made no impression on the castle, which lay at the south end of town, near today's railway station. Northampton was an important communications centre. Its position ensured further fighting there during the Second Barons' War of 1264 and the Wars of the Roses. Lying clear of the wetlands that stretched inland from the Wash, possession of Northampton would have secured the Northerners' retreat to Stamford, past the Fens. John's garrison proved unco-operative, however. A crossbowman shot Robert fitz Walter's standard bearer in the head, and the barons decamped to Bedford, held by a friendly castellan. Here they met envoys from London, offering to surrender the city. John had issued a charter confirming London's ancient liberties, but concessions extracted under duress enjoyed little credibility.

Five hundred knights set off at once for Ware near Hertford. Next day, Sunday 17 May, they pressed on 20 miles (30km) to the capital ready for battle. While the population were hearing Mass, the rebel advance guard scaled the walls using scaffolding erected for maintenance work, and let in their friends. The intruders plundered royalist merchants and Jews, and rifled the usurers' document chests, a common target during attacks on Jewish communities. Jews were especially vulnerable during civil wars when royal protection became a liability, while the destruction of credit agreements also hurt the king, who inherited the debts of dead Jews. In this holy campaign, remarked Ralph of Coggeshall, the invaders filled their empty purses many times over. Taking control of the city, the rebels appointed a new mayor, placed guards around the perimeter, and pillaged stone from Jewish houses to repair the walls. Only the Tower held out against them.

London's capture was a fatal blow to the king. Cities were almost impossible to besiege. Antioch resisted the First Crusade for 226 days, and only fell through treachery. Jordan de Fantôme, writing in the 1170s, claimed that no-one had ever besieged London. Since his day fresh ditches had been dug outside the Roman walls, most recently in 1213. The 'head and crown' of the kingdom, London provided a sure refuge for the baronial party until the last days of the war. Its loss to the barons was decisive for the first round. When they issued letters threatening to destroy the manors of those who supported the king, including William, most of John's supporters changed sides. Only the staunchest *curiales* remained loyal.

The collapse of John's position in England was mirrored in Wales. While John had focussed on Europe in 1213–14, Llewelyn gained ground in North Wales, taking John's new castles, 'by force, one by one, the townsmen partly killed, partly ransomed and partly ordered to depart' (*Welsh Annals*). As royal difficulties intensified, Llewelyn allied with the Northerners and Giles of Braose, Bishop of Hereford. 'One of the first confederates against the king', Giles drove John's bailiffs out of the Braose family castles at Abergavenny, Brecon, and Builth. Towards Ascension, as the rebels took London, Rhys ap Gruffydd's descendants marched through William's recent acquisitions in Cardiganshire, to take Kidwelly in South Wales. Entering the Gower peninsula in force, they 'carried out lootings and burnings, and burnt and cast down the castles, not without loss of life' (ibid.). Carmarthen's English colonists burnt their town rather than see it fall into enemy hands. Llewelyn himself burst out of North Wales to capture Shrewsbury, Shropshire's county town. It was an unprecedented English humiliation, the timing too good to be coincidental.

Reduced to seven household knights, while rebel armies ranged about despoiling royal manors and hunting lodges, John hid in Windsor Castle, not daring to step outside. Philip Augustus increased the pressure by denying him French recruits, and offering to send the barons volunteers, money, and siege engines to batter the Tower. In Whit Week (7–14 June), the Northerners occupied Lincoln town, and blockaded the castle. William had already ridden into London seeking an armistice. John's delaying strategy had failed. He had no choice but to accept the barons' terms, or at least pretend to do so.

THE GREAT CHARTER

Magna Carta has become the corner stone of English constitutional law. In 1215 it was a temporary expedient, like most of the treaties that punctuated medieval conflicts. The original agreement was overthrown within months, denounced by the Pope, its undertakings and guarantees declared null and void for ever. It acquired its name and significance later. What Bishop Stubbs called the Great Charter of Liberties, contemporary sources knew as the *concordia de Runingemede*, or *carta de Runemede*, from the place where it was agreed.

The Charter differed in substance from contemporary international treaties, dealing with feudal custom, legal process, and economic regulation rather than lands, castles, or marriages. Its sixty numbered chapters and three supplementary clauses made it the longest piece of English legislation since Cnut's reign. No individual could claim sole responsibility for its content. John had been outmanoeuvred not defeated. His forces remained in being. The document was a compromise, reflecting common ground between loyalist and rebel barons, the bishops, and John's officials. Stephen Langton had the intellect to draft the charter, and may have produced an Unknown Charter of 1213–14, found 650 years later in the French national archives. Even a vengeful King John, however, could find no evidence for his authorship, however hard he tried. Sidney Painter credited Langton and William jointly, but the Marshal's role remains opaque. Age, prestige, and experience made him an essential interlocutor in the three-week negotiations, but the *History* is silent.

Peace talks were always held at secure locations to ensure that neither side took advantage of the other. Henry II and Stephen discussed terms across the Thames at Wallingford; Richard went to Le Goulet in 1198 by boat. Runnymede was a traditional meeting place on the southern bank of the Thames, between the rival headquarters at Windsor and Staines. Lying on the Roman road from Silchester to London, low marshy ground protected it to south and east, while the river covered the barons' advanced base at Staines. Ponds and streams along the river's old course provided further security, making the area a virtual island.

John arrived from Windsor on 10 June, and camped at one end of the field, the barons at the other, 'with a multitude of distinguished knights, all well armed' (Coggeshall). Matters were sufficiently advanced by 15 June for John to admit his recent enemies to the kiss of peace, whereupon they renewed their homage and fealty. Barnwell makes it clear that peace was restored before John '[granted] them all what they wanted, confirming it with his charter', thus preserving the legal fiction that the agreement was by mutual consent, not extracted under duress. John did not sign Magna Carta. Kings did not do things like that. Royalist witnesses included eleven bishops led by Langton, followed by the Master of the Temple, and sixteen *curiales* led by William. The loyalists were balanced by twenty-five *barones electi*, magnates chosen to oversee the charter's implementation. Originally unnamed, the subsequent list includes such committed rebels as Robert fitz Walter, Eustace of Vesci, and the younger Earl Marshal.

Magna Carta lacks the ringing statements of principle fashionable in more recent constitutional documents. Both sides' leaders were concerned with practical issues. Neither anarchists nor reactionaries, they sought to preserve the positive features of Henry II's legal innovations while protecting themselves against the abuse of royal power. The opening chapters reasserted existing ecclesiastical and feudal rights, limiting the royal exactions that drove so many into debt. Scutage was to be levied by common counsel of the realm, the thin end of a constitutional wedge that would eventually broaden into 'no taxation without representation'. Chapters 39 and 40 placed real limits on the arbitrary exercise of power. No free man might be imprisoned, dispossessed, outlawed, banished, or otherwise ruined without lawful judgement. The nature of that judgement was unspecified, legal process being in flux between the old-fashioned ordeal favoured by William in his confrontations with royalty, and the evidential procedures favoured by canon law. Chapter 40 comes nearest to a statement of principle with its terse promise that 'To no-one shall we sell, refuse, or delay right and justice'.

Other chapters reflect the charter's conflictual origin. Property confiscated before or during hostilities was to be restored. The winners' allies were rewarded. London got standard weights and measures and guarantees of freedom of movement, including removal of fish weirs from the Thames. Welsh and Scottish hostages were to be freed. Magnates passed on royal concessions to their knightly accomplices in rebellion. John's alien servants, 'knights, crossbowmen, sergeants, mercenaries, who had come with horses and arms to the harm of the kingdom', were to be expelled. This was not just xenophobia. Gerard of Athée from Touraine, one of those mentioned by name, had played a leading role in destroying the Braose family. The *History* describes him plotting William's ruin in 1207. The Barnwell annalist summarised contemporary priorities:

> *And the king immediately gave back his right to everyone, the hostages whom he held, the castles and estates which he had long held in his hand … and even those which his brother Richard had carried off …*

Recent enemies restored peace with traditional conviviality, eating and drinking together. John wore his grandmother's regalia, redeemed from the Temple. A day was set to finalise implementation, peace declared, and those besieging Lincoln and the Tower told to stop. It was too good to last.

CIVIL WAR

Magna Carta was a victory for John's moderate supporters, who probably included the Marshal. Extremists on either side saw it as a breathing space. John stands accused of dragging his feet, but he was prompt enough to dismiss expensive mercenaries, and restore castles and estates. He was less willing to replace trustworthy foreign officials with disaffected Englishmen. Gerard of Athée and his colleagues remained in post. John's immediate request for papal dispensation from his oath to observe the charter, however, casts serious doubt on his sincerity. The rebels were no better. Some left Runnymede early, making their absence a pretext for continued dissidence. As cover, they arranged a tournament at Stamford, the prize a live bear, an appropriate symbol of England's descent into chaos. Mistrust was mutual: 'neither did he [John] entrust himself to them, nor did they come to him' (*Barnwell*). Some rebels returned to London, others to their castles. Some built *munitiunculae*, minor strongholds like those that plagued Stephen's reign. In areas dominated by dissidents, royal servants were beaten up and imprisoned.

Magna Carta subordinated John to a committee of twenty-five, a revolutionary constraint that a milder king might have found intolerable. Baronial intransigence made matters worse. When John lay sick of gout, they had him carried into court to give judgement, recalling Count Richard's shameful treatment of Henry II. 'Of such pride and such outrages,' wrote Anonymous of Béthune, 'there was great plenty'. The bishops sought to mediate. William participated in one last effort at Oxford on 16 July. John stayed away, claiming that the presence of so many armed men made it unsafe. Meetings in August were equally fruitless. The Twenty-Five instituted a parallel administration, appointing themselves sheriffs to eastern and northern counties. William withdrew to his estates to co-ordinate action against the Welsh.

Meanwhile, John gathered shipping, blockaded the south coast, and summoned fresh mercenaries. Hugh of Boves preached a Crusade in Flanders with papal letters of doubtful authenticity, inviting 'all those trained to arms [to] come to England for the remission of their sins, and hand out death there' (Coggeshall). Real papal letters were equally deadly. Consistently out of step with events in England, the Pope became increasingly peremptory. Langton and the moderate bishops ignored papal demands for widespread excommunications while continuing mediation. Late in August they were overtaken by a papal bull addressed to the Bishops of Norwich and Winchester. The former was the Italian legate who had ended the Interdict in 1213, and was now a royal favourite. The latter was Peter des Roches, a hard-line royalist, who exploited the Pope's commission to unleash counter-revolution. On 5 September he suspended Langton and excommunicated anyone attacking the king, propelling the archbishop into exile and England into civil war. The *History* says little about the conflict that would eventually bring William to the supreme moment of his career, either from embarrassment, or because John of Earley was on the Marches, away from events. Its course must be told from other sources. Anonymous of Béthune fills many gaps. Writing with a soldier's eye of events that he had often seen for himself, he complements and confirms much of the *History*'s often sparse account.

Raiding began immediately, 'the king holding out in his strongholds … the barons roving freely about the country, although so far they had spared the people on account of the harvest' (*Barnwell*). Royal estates and forests were particular targets, the rebels selling the king's timber and killing his deer. John lurked at Dover, commanding the narrow seas across which he looked for support. Meanwhile, the arrogance of the Twenty-Five drove moderate magnates into his arms, much as intransigent Parliamentarians created a Royalist party in 1642. Summoned with dire threats to discuss John's deposition, a substantial number of magnates objected, 'especially as he had pronounced himself ready to observe the agreed peace. And so they were divided among themselves, and the ills of the land were multiplied' (ibid.). 'Of all this evil,' the *History* assures us, 'nothing was undertaken or done by the Marshal's advice.' Known at the time as *Regales* or *Reaulx*, the royalist hard core included eight earls, among them William. Their opponents included six earls, besides Robert fitz Walter and Eustace of Vesci, 'and many others whom it would be tedious to enumerate' (ibid.).

Such generalities illustrate the problematic nature of medieval orders of battle. Roman numerals were difficult to manipulate, muster rolls scarce, and unworldly monks less numerate than merchants or architects. Roger of Wendover wrote with spurious precision of 'three battalions of sergeants and crossbowmen', thirsting for human blood. Less inventive chroniclers wrote of Gascons, Poitevins, and Brabançons pouring in, lured by promises: 'foreign barbarians and a great multitude of different tongues steered for England, encouraging the king in his error' (*Waverley*). The *History* specifies Flemings, 'foreign knights and sergeants, who wanted to plunder every day. They hardly thought of helping him [John] win his war, but only of spoiling his country.' Estimates reached 15,000, a figure comparable with the 14,000 *routiers* that Henry II paid off after the Young King's Revolt.

Figures from record evidence are generally lower. Gilbert of Mons, the Count of Hainault's chancellor in the 1180s, quotes Flemish comital forces of 700 to 1,000 mounted men. Fewer made it into the front line. Villehardouin estimated the Fourth Crusade at 20,000 overall, but specifies battlefield contingents in the low hundreds. Lack of money limited army sizes, and drove them to plunder. Professor Carpenter reckons that John fielded 800 mounted men in late 1215. Garrisons absorbed considerable numbers, although individual detachments were small, like the three knights and ten sergeants captured at Odiham in June 1216. Literary references suggest that average wartime garrisons were nearer 100. Even at half that figure, John needed 7,500 men to hold the 150 castles he is believed to have owned in 1215, a figure comparable with Professor Barlow's estimate of 6,500 for Henry II's total establishment. These static forces must have sustained themselves from local resources. Deployed across a much smaller area than Henry's empire, John's larger establishment supports contemporary perceptions of a militarised despotism.

John's opponents appear simpler to assess, the Twenty-Five guaranteeing contingents totalling 1,187. The most notorious did not make the largest contribution: Robert fitz Walter and Eustace of Vesci supplied fifty and thirty knights respectively. Geoffrey of Mandeville and the younger Marshal were joint top with 200 each. The latter's contribution matches the *mesnie* his father led to North Wales in 1212. It also explains the *History's* reticence concerning 1215–16. None of these figures includes foot. Mounted troops, knights and sergeants, provide an index of an army's fighting value, but infantry always surpassed them in numbers. Richard held Saintonges against his father in 1174 with sixty knights and 400 crossbowmen, and shipped 2,100 Welsh from Portsmouth in 1196, compared with a few hundred knights. The role of infantry was significant but unquantified.

The nascent conflict escalated with rebel sieges of castles at Oxford and Northampton, while the barons in desperation offered the throne to the Dauphin. The *History* dismissed the decision as *granz folie*, but it did ensure a supply of French artificers to build siege engines. Meanwhile, John suffered his usual bad luck. On 26 September, Hugh of Boves and a large party of Flemish mercenaries were shipwrecked off Dunwich, their bodies washed up along the east coast. Then a rebel party occupied Rochester Castle, perhaps as a staging post for French reinforcements, or to block a royalist advance on London. The Sheriff of Kent, Reginald of Cornehull, was holding it for the Archbishop of Canterbury pending legal consideration of its rightful ownership. At Michaelmas, he admitted

William of Aubigny, one of the Twenty-Five and sponsor of the Stamford tournament. Finding Rochester destitute of warlike stores, the rebels considered returning to London, until William appealed to their honour as knights. They ransacked the town for provisions, but John left them no time to gather booty from further afield.

The king, 'who for some days had been as it were skulking at Dover now began to raise his head' (*Barnwell*). The loyal Earl of Salisbury took some mercenaries to relieve Oxford and Northampton, while John tackled Rochester. Lying east of the ancient bridge where Watling Street crosses the Medway on the way from Dover to London, Rochester was a strategic sore point, like Northampton. The scene of a Roman victory of AD 43, it was besieged by William Rufus in 1088, and Simon de Montfort stormed the bridge in 1264. A rough diamond shape, the castle's corners were oriented to the main points of the compass, its outer bailey surrounded by deep ditches and crenellated stone walls on an earth bank. Its curtain, as yet, lacked towers to enfilade the perimeter. The keep in the southern corner was 70 feet (21m) square, rising 113 feet (34m) to the parapet, with walls 12 feet (3.6m) thick strengthened by corner towers.

John's first step was to isolate the defenders from their friends in London by burning the wooden bridge. He presumably attacked downstream along the west bank opposite the castle, 'the river flowing between' says Coggeshall. Robert fitz Walter, however, 'with 60 knights and sergeants and trusty crossbowmen held the bridge and put out the fire, compelling the king, foiled in his intentions, to flee'. Regrouping, John returned on Sunday 11 October, 'and bursting in, besieged the castle, attacking the defenders with all kinds of machines'. Five of these were on Boley Hill south of the castle, whence they showered the defenders with stones, covered by relays of crossbowmen and archers. Rochester's defenders fought back, 'with over a hundred knights and sergeants and many stout crossbowmen', inflicting heavy losses. Between spells in the line, the attackers stabled their horses in the cathedral, 'and there indulged in eating and drinking, whoring and lewdness, with none of the usual respect for saints or holy places' (ibid.).

A fortnight into the siege, the London barons rode down to Dartford with nearly 700 knights, intending to lift the siege: 'but when they heard the king had set out in battle order to meet them, having left no fewer continuing the siege, it was agreed to await a better time, because they had few infantry, and the king a great multitude' (*Barnwell*). Returning to London, they proposed a further expedition on St Andrew's Day, choosing to believe that the besieged could hold out until then. John, however, urged on the siege, using miners to bring down the outer wall. Ralph of Coggeshall describes the technique used by Richard I at Chalus-Chabrol:

> *So the king attacked them himself with crossbows, while others dug around, so that hardly any dared to appear on the tower battlements, or defend it in any way. Nevertheless, they threw large stones off the top of the battlements, which falling down with great force, terrified bystanders, but could not injure the miners in the least or prevent the works, since these were protected on all sides …*

When the bailey fell, Rochester's defenders withdrew into the great tower: 'All else broken down, only the keep stood, to which, on account of the age and solidity of the work, the hurling of stones did little damage' (*Barnwell*). Miners dug beneath the keep's southeast corner, since rebuilt with a telltale cylindrical tower. Orders despatched to Dover on 25 November commanded the justiciar 'to send us … with all haste 40 bacon pigs of the fattest and those less good for eating to use for bringing fire under the tower'. At La Roche-au-Moine John had experimented with sulphur, pitch, and mercury. Now he reverted to more traditional incendiaries.

Even when John's men entered the shattered keep, the defenders held out north of the cross-wall, whose imbedded well shaft spared them thirst if not hunger:

> *Nor does our age record another siege more vigorously pressed nor so bravely defended. For no rest was allowed them for days on end, also within the keep they suffered the pangs of most bitter hunger, lacking anything else they lived on horse meat and water, which was hard for those brought up on delicacies.*
>
> (Barnwell)

John's rapid investment, denying the garrison time to plunder the locality, paid off. On 30 November, St Andrew's Day, the garrison surrendered for want of food. Those who could not claim benefit of clergy were thrown into chains, while John considered their fate. Eventually the commons were released, the gentry held for ransom. John wanted to hang the lot, as Stephen did at Shrewsbury in 1138 and Henry III would do at Bedford in 1224, but Savari of Mauléon, the Poitevin commander, urged restraint. The war had just begun, and the enemy might retaliate in kind. Finally, just one crossbowman was hanged, whom the king had brought up from a boy. Otherwise, only one of the garrison was killed, though many 'useless mouths' expelled during the siege had their hands or feet cut off.

The capture of Rochester has attracted much favourable comment. The Barnwell annalist thought it struck terror amongst John's enemies, who took refuge in religious houses, as 'few ... would trust themselves to fortifications'. The *History* was less positive, focussing on the financial cost: 'in five weeks [*sic*], he had spent all the riches he used to have in his treasury ... whoever lays out much and gains little and allies himself with evil people is soon reduced to the dregs'. Ralph of Coggeshall estimated the operation's cost at 60,000 marks, a third of John's war-chest in 1214. So expensive a victory was both an opportunity and a spur to action. His treasury empty, John had to end the war while his opponents were cowed, or seek the means of prolonging it. His solution was a *chevauchée* through northern England to bring the rebels to terms, while maintaining his army at their expense. William Longsword, Earl of Salisbury, stayed behind to keep the Londoners in check with a handful of *routier* captains. The Marshal remained in the west, where Giles of Braose's submission in October may represent a local success. Neither side sought battle: the barons awaited the outcome of their negotiations with Philip Augustus; John, as always, preferred to put off a decision.

Leaving Rochester on 6 December, John split his forces at St Albans on the 20th, heading north with 450 knights. In sixty-five days he marched to Berwick and back to Bedford, nearly 600 miles (900km) as the crow flies. Slower than William's raids on Mantes and Montmirail, but more extensive, John's winter campaign bears comparison with the Black Prince's Languedoc *chevauchée* of 1355. John spent Christmas at Nottingham, 'not as customary, but as if on campaign' (*Barnwell*). Pro-forma charters were issued for repentant rebels to abjure their oaths to Magna Carta, for John's aims were political as well as punitive. The day after Boxing Day, he persuaded William of Aubigny's garrison at Belvoir to surrender, to save their lord being starved to death. Passing through York, Newcastle, and Durham, John reached Berwick on the 14th, an average of 12 miles (19km) a day. None stood against him. The King of Scotland who had besieged Norham in October retreated across the border, leaving the citizens of Berwick, then a Scottish town, to face John's wrath. Ralph of Coggeshall claimed that John penetrated as far as 'the Scottish Sea' – the Firth of Forth – depopulating baronial lands, spreading destruction and levelling castles. Everyone fled his face, 'except a few who gave themselves up to the mercilessness of his mercy'.

Closely formed *conrois* of knights pursue fleeing opponents with lances couched for maximum impact. Mail shirts are longer than at Hastings, but helmets remain open. One knight (left) has lowered his lance to finish off a dismounted enemy. (M.736 f7v – Life of St Edmund, twelfth century. New York, The Pierpont Morgan Library. ©2013. Photo Pierpont Morgan Library/Art Resource/Scala, Florence)

The Young King's effigy at Rouen cathedral – overshadowed by his younger brother Richard even in death. The inscription reads:

Whose brother was called the Lion Heart
Henry the Younger sought a place in Normandy by right of arms
In the year 1183 cruel death took him hence

Effigy of Richard I in Rouen cathedral: only Richard's heart is at Rouen; his body was buried at Fontevraud beside his parents. Like the Young King's effigy this is a nineteenth-century impression of the dead man's appearance, which is unknown. (Author's photo)

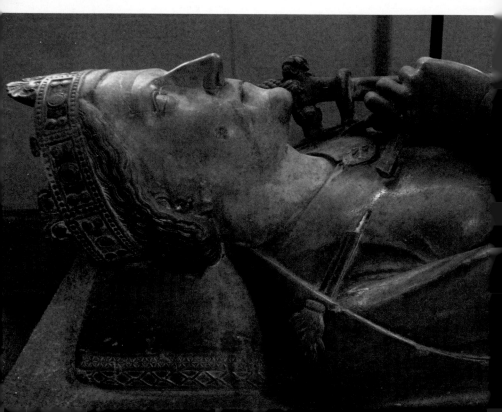

The keep and ruined inner ward of King Richard's saucy castle at Château Gaillard, perched high above the River Seine. Built at enormous expense as a jumping-off point for an Angevin counter-offensive, Château Gaillard fell to the French after a six-month siege in March 1204. (Author's photo)

One of King John's favourite objects, a *denier* or silver penny: John hoarded so many, he precipitated a liquidity crisis. The royal portrait and the name *Henricus* remain unchanged from the reign of John's father. Original size about 1cm.

(Author's photo; original coin courtesy of Mark Wingham)

The overgrown ruins of Tancarville Castle: the square tower where William lived as a squire is tucked away behind the seventeenth-century *Château Neuf*, and the whole site remains difficult of access.

(Photo courtesy of Marcel Barbotte and *Les Amis du Château de Tancarville*)

A nineteenth-century impression of a Crusader's first sight of Jerusalem, suggesting the emotional nature of a moment shared by every pilgrim. Intended to represent the First Crusade of 1099, the armour depicted is nearer that worn by William's contemporaries. (Postcard in author's collection)

Chepstow Castle on the River Wye in the early twentieth century: William added the gatehouse with its revolutionary drum towers in the 1190s when he extended the lower bailey towards the landing area below the cliffs; the square keep pre-dates the Marshals by a century. (Postcard in author's collection)

The Marshal's Tower at Chepstow Castle, seen from the barbican. Believed to have been built for William and Isabel as a personal apartment, the accommodation comprised a ground floor kitchen and a first floor private chamber lit by elegant west-facing windows. (Author's photo)

William's castle at Kilkenny converted into an eighteenth-century Irish Ascendancy mansion: only the massive drum towers recall the stronghold that his countess defended against the assaults of King John's henchmen in the dark winter of 1207–8. (Postcard in author's collection)

The murder of Thomas Becket in 1170, after a thirteenth-century image. Note the variety of protective headgear – round and flat-topped helmets and a chain mail hood caught up at the front to cover the mouth. The leftmost figure has mail leg guards and an early heraldic device on his shield.

(Author's collection)

Twelfth-century blacksmiths forging the tools of war, including a rare representation of horse armour: the helmet on the anvil is a reminder of the occasion William required a blacksmith to remove his much-battered helmet.

(MS 0.9.34 f24r, by kind permission of the Master and Fellows of Trinity College Cambridge)

No longbowmen are recorded fighting at either battle of Lincoln, but one appears amidst the decoration of the cathedral's western porch, a reminder of their ubiquity in English society. Allowing for distortion inherent in the medium, the archer is clearly pulling the string to his ear.

(Author's photo)

Rochester Castle from the side attacked by King John, engraved in the eighteenth century before the gatehouse (right) was demolished: the two square towers in the curtain wall were added after the siege, when miners undermined the walls and brought down the keep's leftmost corner. (Postcard in author's collection)

Dover Castle from the east showing the depth of the fortified area: the French attacked from right to left. They broke through the first line of defences on the site of today's Norfolk Towers, but were driven out again in fierce hand-to-hand fighting. (Postcard in author's collection)

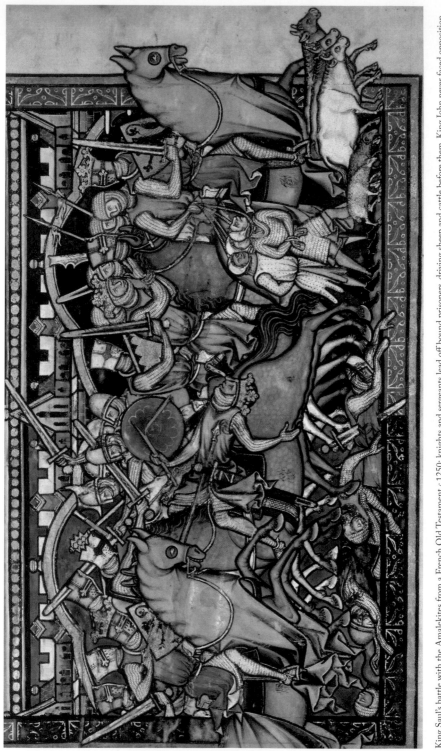

King Saul's battle with the Amalekites from a French Old Testament *c*.1250: knights and sergeants lead off bound prisoners, driving sheep and cattle before them. King John never faced opposition like this during his *chevauchées*, his opponents fleeing his anger. (M.638 f24v – New York, The Pierpont Morgan Library. ©2013. Photo Pierpont Morgan Library/Art Resource/Scala, Florence)

Newark Castle, the scene of King John's death and the Marshal's last military enterprise, is seen from the bridge whose medieval predecessor gave the town its name. Most of the present structure was built later, but the square keep and gatehouse on the left is twelfth-century. (Author's photo)

Goodrich Castle was in the front line of the Welsh uprising of 1215–17. Llewelyn's men attacked it on the eve of Henry III's coronation, forcing William to interrupt the feasting and send a rescue party. The keep is the only part of the castle left from William's custodianship. (Author's photo)

Joshua's Conquest of Ai showing all the horrors of a medieval siege: knights repulse a sortie; sergeants in gambesons scramble up ladders; miners set to work covered by crossbowmen; a captured leader is loaded into a trébuchet, recalling William's childhood experience at Newbury. (M.638 f10v – New York, The Pierpont Morgan Library. ©2013. Photo Pierpont Morgan Library/Art Resource/Scala, Florence)

Three generations of Marshals besieged the Bishop of Winchester's Wolvesey Castle: William's father in 1141; the Regent and his son in 1217. Both the structures seen here, the East Hall (left) and Wymond's Tower (right), were built during the reign of King Stephen. (Author's photo)

THE SOUTH-WEST PROSPECT OF THE CITY OF LINCOLN.

Lincoln from the south-west in the eighteenth century, hardly altered since the Middle Ages: castle and cathedral on the skyline dominate the lower city which runs down the slope towards Brayford Pool (left); Wigford's church towers are centre right, behind the trees. (Image courtesy of The Collection: Art and Archaeology in Lincolnshire (Usher Gallery, Lincoln))

One of the fine medieval townhouses attributed to Lincoln's thirteenth-century Jewish community perched on the aptly named Steep Hill. Armoured knights once battled past their front doors; today they house a bookshop and the Society for Lincolnshire History and Archaeology. (Author's photo)

Lincoln Castle and Cathedral in the twelfth century, showing the former's West Gate entered by Peter des Roches and Fawkes of Bréauté during the battle's opening moves. The round shell keep is the Lucy Tower, the square Norman keep the Observatory Tower. (Drawing by David Vale; courtesy of the Society for Lincolnshire History and Archaeology and the Usher Gallery)

Lincoln's northern gate at Newport Arch, the last Roman gate in England still in use for traffic: the medieval structure was deeper and higher, while the street level was eight feet lower than today, making it a tough nut for the assaulting Royalists to crack – if they ever did. (Author's photo)

The West Gate of Lincoln Castle retains its original box-like structure, beyond the modern bridge. The massive simplicity of the twelfth-century walls and the height of the Norman embankments defied every attempt by the Dauphin's supporters to break in. (Author's photo)

The exterior of the Lucy Tower after an eighteenth-century sketch made before housing blocked the view: the original shell keep had an extra storey, dominating Lincoln's skyline. The postern gate's inaccessibility makes it an unlikely route for troops entering the castle. (Original watercolour courtesy of Eileen Brooks)

Lincoln Castle's East Gate through which Fawkes attacked the Franco-rebel knights on Castle Hill: the original structure was simpler, similar to the West Gate. The turrets, which have lost their upper floor, were added later as part of general upgrade of the defences. The cannon were captured in the Crimea. (Author's photo)

Castle Hill, the scene of the main action viewed from the castle walls: Fawkes sortied bottom left, to be joined by William from Bailgate, left of centre next to the black-and-white half-timbered Tourist Information Office. The enemy commander was killed near the cathedral porch, beyond the later medieval Exchequer Gate. (Author's photo)

The Siege of Lincoln as imagined by Matthew Paris: a crossbowman directs a parting shot at fleeing rebels, while the Angevin leopards fly over an expiring Count de la Perche. The text above describes the fugitives' difficulties negotiating the *flagellum* gate at Lincoln's southern exit. (MS 16 55v, by kind permission of the Master and Fellows of Corpus Christi College Cambridge)

The probable site of the rebels' attempt to rally at the junction of Steep Hill and Christ's Hospital Terrace (right foreground), looking up to the top of the rise (left). The medieval townhouse is attributed to Aaron, Angevin England's greatest money-lender. Note the gradient. (Author's photo)

A modern impression of the East Bargate after an eighteenth-century sketch. Now demolished, the two Bargates and the waterlogged Sincil Dyke were a serious obstacle for anybody wanting to leave Lincoln in a hurry. The turrets may be those repaired in 1228. (Original watercolour courtesy of Eileen Brooks)

The quay at Sandwich was still in commercial use at the turn of the twentieth century. This would have been the nearest point for William to have observed the progress of the battle. The Barbican gate beside the bridge in the background is later medieval. (Courtesy of Sandwich Museum)

The River Stour's winding course today, looking back towards Sandwich: in the Middle Ages these reed beds were open sea. The medieval town was located around St Peter's Church behind the trees (left centre). Stonar, where Prince Louis landed, is across the river to the right. (Author's photo)

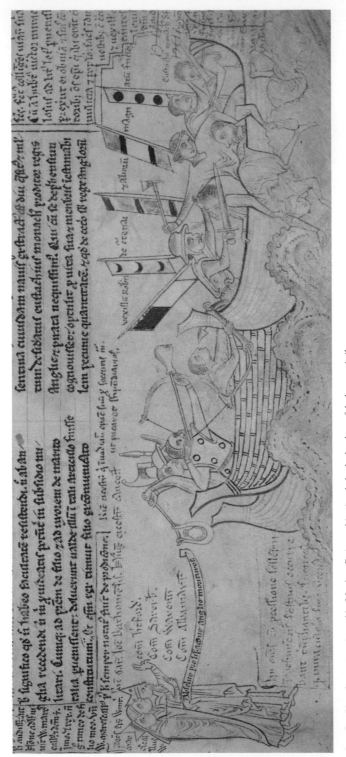

A medieval boarding action pictured by Matthew Paris, resulting in wholesale slaughter of the losers: missile weapons include a staff-sling and longbow projecting a jar of some unspecified substance. The list of earls present, beside the trio of bishops (left), omits William, epigraphic evidence of Matthew's unremitting bias.

(MS 16 56v, by kind permission of the Master and Fellows of Corpus Christi College Cambridge)

An early twentieth-century reconstruction of the capture of a French vessel by Henry III's great ship the *Queen* in the Bay of Biscay in 1225. Painted by Charles Dixon, this was one of a series linking Victorian and Edwardian naval vessels to their heroic predecessors. (Author's collection)

The chapel at St Bartholomew's Hospital: material evidence for the battle's location off Sandwich. The chapel was restored by Sir Gilbert Scott, designer of the Albert Memorial in the 1880s, and its associated almshouses still shelter the Brothers and Sisters, remote beneficiaries of the battle. (Author's photo)

The circular nave of the Temple Church was inspired by the Church of the Holy Sepulchre in Jerusalem that William visited in the 1180s. Henry III added the Gothic chancel (right) in the 1240s. Such a prestigious resting place, overshadowing the family mausoleum at Bradenstoke, is material proof of William's contemporary reputation. (Author's photo)

Inside the Temple Church: William's effigy lies nearest the font accompanied by his sons William and Gilbert on his left and at his feet respectively. The exact site of the Marshal's grave is lost, but the setting retains an elegant dignity appropriate to the knight who saved England. (Photo by Christopher Christodoulou, courtesy of the Temple Church)

GILBERT MARSHAL
fourth Earl of Pembroke died 1241

EFFIGY OF A KNIGHT

William's sorely damaged effigy suffered worse injuries during the Blitz than the Marshal ever did in his lifetime. One of the earliest such portraits of a layman, the stylised image suggests how a thirteenth-century warlord might wish to be remembered. (Author's photo)

The Flower of Chivalry: part of a modern tapestry celebrating the Marshal's part in the foundation of New Ross in Leinster. The panel shows his three manifestations as the Young King's guardian, knight errant, and magnate, and is edged with chivalric scenes from William's early life. (Reproduced by kind permission of The Ros Tapestry Project Ltd. ©The Ros Tapestry Project Ltd, New Ross, Co. Wexford)

Ralph lived 14 miles (20km) down Stane Street from Robert fitz Walter's castle at Great Dunmow, and saw royalist depredations in East Anglia for himself. Defying meteorology and military convention, Salisbury's southern task force stormed Geoffrey of Mandeville's castle at Pleshey in Essex on Christmas Eve, devastating his tenants' estates. Next day they moved on to the Cistercian Abbey at Tilty north of Great Dunmow. Bursting in during Mass, they 'destroyed all its furnishings, and breaking into the numerous cellars looted and carried off many merchants' deposits'. Ralph's own abbey was raided on New Year's Day and twenty-two horses taken. Turning north through Bury St Edmund's, the royalists then attacked the Isle of Ely, where many knights and ladies had sought refuge. Bitter cold froze the surrounding marshes, allowing the *routiers* to bypass rebel roadblocks, and storm the cathedral swords in hand, plundering refugees and monks alike. Some escaped across the ice, while 'the worthy Earl of Salisbury' extended his protection to the ladies. William Longsword is one of the *History*'s favourites, 'the good earl', one who 'made largesse his mother, and whose banner untarnished prowess bore before him'. Matthew Paris styled him 'the flower of earls'. The presence of such a paragon of chivalry at such scenes highlights the intense moral paradox of knightly warfare.

Damage to life and property during these operations remains speculative. There was no thirteenth-century Domesday Book to assess devastated manors, as the original had done after William the Conqueror's depredations. Ecclesiastical sources were loud in their lamentations, particularly Roger of Wendover, but rarely specific. Monks were John's natural enemies; their treasure an irresistible temptation to a cash-strapped regime. It is hard to know how far clerical accusations of cruelty were just monkish propaganda. John maintained some discipline, punishing a soldier for stealing goods from a churchyard. Violence may have been more threatened than applied. The Abbot of St Albans, 'lying open to the to-ing and fro-ing of the many', preserved his abbey's assets by paying protection money to both sides: £951 in total (*Gesta Abbatum Monasterii Sancti Albani*). Besides taking cash, armies stole untold quantities of livestock and inflicted random destruction. St Albans lost over 100 horses in a year. King John took three from Redburn, with an iron-shod cart. Fawkes of Bréauté's men burnt three houses at Langley, with thirty-five pigs. John Marshal and Anonymous of Béthune both accompanied John's winter campaign, but neither military source mentions it, whether from embarrassment or acceptance.

King John resurfaced at Bedford on 22 February, after an absence so protracted he was rumoured to be dead. Advancing into Essex, he met no resistance except at Colchester, which fell after a short siege. Apart from Mountsorrel and Helmsley Castle in Yorkshire, only London held out against him. Leading rebels, including Eustace of Vesci, considered making terms. Late in March John reached Waltham, 12 miles (19 km) outside London. The capital remained defiant, as in 1471, when menaced by another raiding army after the second battle of St Albans. Learning that John had primed his mercenaries to attack the city, the citizens opened their gates to give battle: 'the king recognising their hostility, and numbers, and readiness to fight wisely withdrew from danger' (Coggeshall). He was probably right. Jordan of Fantôme comments how every Londoner of military age was armed to the teeth. As Savari of Mauléon rode past the suburbs, he was ambushed and badly wounded. John had rallied waverers throughout the Midlands, and brought the rebels to the brink of defeat, but it was too late. Another player was about to enter the game.

INVASION

One reason for John's success was the absence of an opposing field army. Castles must fall if unrelieved, but barons never fought kings.

Norman magnates had avoided confronting Philip Augustus at Fontaine in 1194, because their own king was elsewhere. The Young King's supporters only fought Henry II's lieutenants, and fled his face at Dol. Robert of Gloucester was exceptional in attacking Stephen twice, but Robert was himself of royal blood, defending his half-sister's right to the throne. The rebels in 1215 needed a royal figurehead, as the rebels of 1173 needed the Young King.

Arthur's murder and Otto's humiliation at Bouvines narrowed the field. The most hopeful claimant was Blanche of Castile, John's niece, whom he had carelessly allowed to marry Philip Augustus' son Louis in 1200. The title of Dauphin used by the heir to the French throne really does derive from the Provençal *dalfin* for dolphin, symbol of the lords of Vienne in the Dauphiné. Born in 1187, the future Louis VIII grew up with Arthur, and nursed a lifelong hatred for King John. A sickly youth, Louis matched the Capetian stereotype of piety and sexual continence better than his father. Unlike his great-uncle Philip of Alsace, he never risked his neck jousting, watching helmetless from the sidelines. Count of Artois from 1212, Louis became his father's substitute field commander after Bouvines, earning the surname of the Lion. His claim to the English throne was equally improbable. The manifesto that his envoys presented to the Papal Curia in May 1216 was a model of diplomatic chicanery, even by French accounts, its arguments vague, false, and contradictory.

Rumours of baronial appeals for French help went back to 1212. The following year, before the Interdict's sudden end, Philip Augustus planned to put Louis and Blanche on the English throne, creating a united Anglo-French realm after his own death. The renewed negotiations of October 1215 progressed slowly, however. A direct assault on a papal vassal was a risky business. When agreement seemed near, John threw a spanner in the works, sending bogus letters under his enemies' seals, claiming that all outstanding issues had been amicably resolved, and apologising for any expenses the French monarchy might have incurred. Saer of Quincy, the barons' leading negotiator, swore that the letters were false, allaying Philip's suspicions with fresh oaths and hostages.

The first French contingents reached England in December and January 1216. Some 250 knights altogether with similar numbers of crossbowmen and more sergeants, they were insufficient to challenge John in the field. Short of money, they stayed in London grumbling about the food and their hosts: 'The French rabble,' said the *History*, 'drank many a barrel and cask of fine wine ... full of boasting, they said England was theirs, and the English would have to quit the land, for they had no right to it.' When John took Colchester, he sowed fresh discord between the allies by releasing his French prisoners while keeping the English. Back in London, the French were first threatened with hanging, then kept in irons pending the Dauphin's arrival.

This was long delayed. While Louis struggled to raise troops by a mixture of bribery and threats, a papal legate appeared. Guala Bicchieri was a cardinal tasked with frustrating French designs on England, now part of St Peter's patrimony. He would become the indefatigable ally first of King John, and later of the Marshal. At Melun in April 1216, Guala strove unsuccessfully to prevent the Dauphin's departure for England. Learning from spies of Louis's plans, John despatched William and the Bishop of Winchester to remind Philip Augustus of the truce made after Bouvines, 'but they returned without being heard' (Coggeshall). It was William's last cross-Channel excursion. Planned for January, promised for Easter, the Dauphin's expedition finally sailed the Friday evening after Ascension, from the traditional embarkation points: Calais, Boulogne, Gravelines, and Wissant. The expedition featured 1,200 knights, as many as Philip Augustus deployed at Bouvines, in up to 800 ships. Eustace the Monk, *pirata fortissimus*, who had conveyed French military aid to the barons the previous summer, directed naval operations. The crossing was rough, the ships blown along by the 'euro-eagle', a stiff north-easterly, which next morning (Saturday 21 May) brought Louis off the North Foreland with just seven ships.

John had been patrolling the Kent coast, assembling ships from Yarmouth, Lynn, Dunwich, and the south coast towns named the Cinque Ports. His plan was to repeat the pre-emptive strategy of 1213, when English galleys savaged French shipping from the Seine round to Dieppe. The principle that England's front line was the enemy coast later became a strategic commonplace. Drake and Nelson both tackled invasion fleets in port, but as usual John was unlucky. The gale that brought Louis struck the English shipping on the night of 18/19 May, and 'wrecked most of the fleet through collisions, sunk them, or blew them far to the south' (Coggeshall). Running downwind, Louis landed unopposed at Great Stonar. Just north of Sandwich, Stonar is now several miles inland, separated from the sea by the Sandwich Flats. A friendly crowd was on hand to greet the invaders, a comment on John's popularity. Anxious to be first ashore, Louis fell in the sea and stumbled dripping up the beach to kiss the crucifix held out to him by a local priest.

Ralph of Coggeshall claims that John might have attacked Louis and his men while exhausted from the crossing, before other French ships came up. John, however, had spent the night at Canterbury. By the time he reached Sandwich, it was too late. Besides, John was paralysed by doubt:

> 'since he had foreigners and mercenaries with him, for the most part of French allegiance, he did not consider opposing the landing nor attacking [them] once on the beach'
>
> (Barnwell)

The Dunstable annalist attributes the decision to William: 'King John hurrying up with a great army … withdrew (on the advice of William Marshal) for he did not have much trust in his own troops.'

John's distrust and William's caution combined to postpone a decision. William had argued at Arras that foresight and common sense were the complement of courage: fighting at a disadvantage was no part of his military credo. Anonymous of Béthune describes John riding distractedly up and down the shore, before leaving his *routiers* in the lurch. Unpaid for some time, they presented a shabby appearance, and needed more than a few trumpet blasts to cheer them up. His plans in ruins, John fled westwards in tears, slighting Hastings and Pevensey Castles as he went. Boldly sending back his ships, Louis advanced on London. Bypassing Dover, he took Canterbury and Rochester, to link up with forces summoned from London. Numerous English magnates did homage, including the younger Marshal. On 2 June, Louis was received in London amidst general rejoicing, the burghers swearing fealty in St Paul's. The Tower held out as usual, with the monks of Westminster Abbey; 'and it was imagined the whole island was about to fall' (*Barnwell*).

Wasting no time, Louis followed the king, taking castles at Reigate, Guildford, and Farnham: 'and wherever John's alien supporters were caught, he hanged them' (*Melsa*). John and William retreated 120 miles (180km) west to Winchester, England's second capital. Arriving on 28 May, they 'raised the dragon flag of war as if to crush Louis in battle if he should come' (Coggeshall). But, before Louis arrived, John threw down his standard and fled, leaving Savari of Mauléon to defend the city. His men fired the suburbs, withdrawing into Winchester's two castles: the 'castle in the town', i.e. the royal castle near Westgate at the top of the High Street, and the bishop's palace, or Wolvesey Castle, beside the River Itchen. The citizens extinguished the flames, and greeted Louis enthusiastically. He approached cautiously and under arms, drawing up his *batailles* and making them advance in *conrois*, suggesting a formation in column of squadrons equally appropriate for movement or fighting. Louis stationed men in the town to stop the defenders burning what was left, while his perrières and mangonels battered the castles. Ten days later, Savari evacuated his men in exchange for surrendering the palace and castle. Louis moved on to Odiham, where the tiny garrison held out for a week, capturing a dozen prisoners during a sortie, and eventually 'saving their horses and arms, to the great admiration of the French' (Wendover). Meanwhile Hugh Neville surrendered Marlborough Castle, Louis's westernmost conquest and the culminating point of his offensive.

The invasion wrought a strategic revolution. Confronted with overwhelming numbers, John was physically and psychologically incapable of fighting back. The only coherent royalist response came from the legate. The day before Louis landed, Guala arrived at Romney (Kent) dressed in papal robes, riding a white palfrey. Avoiding capture at Canterbury, he followed John to Winchester, excommunicating Louis and his supporters on arrival. This had little immediate effect, church services continuing in occupied London. Meanwhile, Louis and the barons 'prevailed to such an extent that the king did not know where he should turn' (*Melsa*).

John's winter triumph had proved shortlived. Those who had fled his face soon raised their heads. The Northerners surrendered Northumberland, Cumberland, and Westmorland to Alexander of Scotland. Robert fitz Walter regained control of Essex and Suffolk. The south-coast Cinque Ports changed sides, to protect their trade from Eustace the Monk. By August 1216, John was directing merchant shipping west of the Isle of Wight, as Portchester and Southampton fell to Louis's blitzkrieg. John's mercenaries were first to go: 'when the king had no more wealth, few remained who were there for money: they took off with their winnings' (*History*). Among them was Anonymous of Béthune, who joined a company led by the Avoué of Béthune, a brother of William's old friend Baldwin. Some of John's closest associates betrayed him. The Earls of Salisbury and

Warenne could both resent John's attentions to a wife or sister, and had territorial interests threatened by Louis's advance. According to the *History*, only William, 'who had a pure and untarnished heart', stood by him to the death.

This was not strictly true. The Earls of Chester and Derby remained faithful, for their own reasons, while the Marshals played a double game. In July, the younger William occupied the city of Worcester in the rebel interest:

> *But on St Kenelm's day* [17 July], *the Earl of Chester, Fawkes, and others faithful to the king riding up, despite the citizens' bravely defending themselves, much to the astonishment of the besiegers, at last broke into the town, through the castle not being carefully guarded on all sides, and took the citizens, hitherto defending themselves on the ramparts, by surprise, and by exquisite torments extracted from them whatever they had, and more.*
>
> (*Worcester Annals*)

The younger Marshal's soldiers were dragged from the cathedral, where they sought sanctuary, but he escaped, 'heeding his father's warning by flight, as it is said' (ibid.).

Worcester lay deep in John's redoubt of western counties, outside which he controlled only the neighbourhood of his surviving castles. Most of these lay in the Midlands, with outposts at Lincoln, Windsor, and Dover. Their resistance amply justified Angevin expenditure on castles and *routiers*. The most significant was Dover. Blocking Louis's direct communications with France, Dover was 'strongly fortified by art and nature' (*Barnwell*). Matthew Paris described it as 'the front door of England'. It was held by Hubert de Burgh with 140 Poitevin and Flemish knights, and a profusion of sergeants and supplies. Justiciar of England since 1215, Hubert had defended Chinon long after Rouen fell, being wounded and captured in a hopeless sortie in June 1205. If anyone could hold Dover he could.

Louis occupied Dover Priory below the castle, while his men built a hutted camp outside, complete with shops to demonstrate their intention to stay. Unimpressed, the garrison launched ferocious counter-attacks, to which Louis replied by threatening to hang the defenders. He then launched a co-ordinated attack from the high ground to the north-west, while troops demonstrated from the town, and ships cruised offshore to cut off all hope of relief. Crossbowmen shot at the defenders, and perrières and mangonels battered the walls. Engineers constructed a tower of hurdles and a 'cat' to protect miners entering the ditch to dig beneath the barbican, a palisaded fortification before the gatehouse. The avoué's company took the barbican, killing the sector commander, but when their miners brought down one of the gatehouse towers, the defenders repulsed the storming party, and blocked the breach with oak beams and tree trunks. After twelve weeks both sides were ready for a truce.

The sieges of Lincoln and Windsor were equally futile, though financially more advantageous for the attackers. The chatelaine of Lincoln, Lady Nicola de la Haye, bought off the Northerners, who rode to Dover with the King of Scots to do homage. They were followed in September by the Count of Nevers, whom Louis had sent with many English barons to take Windsor. This was defended by Enguerrand of Athée, fresh from the defence of Odiham. His garrison of sixty knights launched violent counter-attacks, twice cutting through the French perrière's arm. The French commander battered the walls for two months, but 'when they were on the point of the castle giving up, having accepted a bribe from the castellan, he treacherously withdrew with the army.' (*Dunstable*). On 14 October, Louis agreed a truce with Dover's undefeated garrison, consummating his triple failure.

JOHN'S LAST RIDE

For nearly two months, John lurked in Corfe Castle, on the remote and swampy Isle of Purbeck, while the shock of the French intervention wore off. Then, realising that Dover would occupy Louis for some time, John went to secure his rear in the Marches. His presence was overdue. Exploiting the unusually mild winter of 1215–16, Llewelyn had led an army drawn from all Wales to Carmarthen, which he took and destroyed after a five-day siege, 'having expelled the French [i.e. English] not in warlike conflict, but solely from fear' (*Welsh Annals*). Newport fell before Christmas, with half a dozen other castles. Only Pembroke held out. On Boxing Day Llewelyn took Cardigan and Cilgerran, both in William's keeping: 'whence the Welsh went home rejoicing. The French, however, sorry and everywhere driven out, were scattered here and there, like birds'. The New Year saw further Welsh gains, with the capture of Swansea Castle 'at the first onset', the defenders of Ros offering hostages and 1,000 marks, 'because they could not resist' (ibid.).

Llewelyn's winter campaign does little for William's military reputation. His defence might be that Wales was a side-show, its light infantry unlikely to leave the shelter of their native hills. What mattered was to hold the frontier. He was at Hereford in July 1216 to join John's counter-offensive, the Dunstable annalist claiming that they 'took and destroyed the castles of Reginald of Braose [Giles's nephew] and his other enemies in the Welsh Marches'. The Welsh *Book of the Princes* was less positive: John 'came to Hereford accompanied by many armed men', and ineffectually summoned Reginald and his allies to make peace, 'after which he burned, ravaged, and destroyed Oswestry'.

Back at Corfe on 25 August, John set off next day to relieve Windsor, already past the average term of a siege. He was at Reading on 6 September, 18 miles (27km) up the Thames from Windsor. Anonymous of Béthune claims that the opposing armies were so close that John's Welsh archers shot into the rebel camp by night, 'inspiring great fear'. When the rebels offered battle, John veered off north of London to ravage their East Anglian estates, as William had thought he might back in 1194. Burning their engines, the barons followed, John retreating before them:

> *And wherever he came across the lands of his enemies in this march,*
> *he gave them over to plunder; and they were given over to burning*
> *and food for the flames, so that our age cannot remember such fires to*
> *have been made in our part of the world in so very short a space of*
> *time.*
>
> (Barnwell)

Monasteries were particularly targeted, as dissident refuges. The day after Michaelmas (30 September), Savari of Mauléon's men:

> *... came unexpectedly to Crowland [in the Fens], and not finding*
> *there those whom they wanted, burst into the monastery. Knights*
> *and horses charging through the church, cloister, and monastic*
> *buildings, they seized men from the very altar itself, amidst the holy*
> *sacrament of the Mass, and dragged them from the church. In their*
> *withdrawal, they carried off with them an incalculable booty, as*
> *much herds of cattle as flocks of sheep.*
>
> (ibid.)

The first signs of dysentery interrupted John's career at King's Lynn on 9 October. Ralph of Coggeshall blamed over-eating in general; Roger of Wendover new cider in particular. Monastic rumour, followed by Shakespeare, claimed that a black monk poisoned John for threatening to raise the price of a halfpenny loaf to one shilling.

Turning back into Lincolnshire, the king lost part of his baggage crossing the River Wellstream, final proof of incompetence. He was bled at Sleaford, aggravating his condition, and carried to Newark. Here John died during the night of 18/19 October, during a storm so terrible the townspeople feared for their houses. The dead king's attendants plundered his personal effects, as usual, but the Bishop of Winchester was nearby, as were a 'great body of armed men ... nearly all of them mercenaries and foreigners' (*Barnwell*). William was directing operations on the Marches, a more fitting role for a septuagenarian than galloping across East Anglia. John Marshal was present, however, with two of William's Marcher associates: John of Monmouth and Walter of Clifford, near Hay-on-Wye. They seem to be the source of the *History*'s account of John's last words.

Part of a broader confession, these were carefully edited to emphasise William's pre-eminence. First, John asked those present to seek the Marshal's forgiveness for the wrongs inflicted upon him. Then, because he had more faith in his loyalty than anyone else's, John asked them to persuade William to take care of his son, 'for never will he keep his lands through anyone, if not through him'. John's will, which survives, shows that William was in fact one of thirteen executors appointed to assist John's sons in the defence and recovery of their inheritance. Anonymous of Béthune, however, repeats John's specific request for the Marshal to take his eldest son Henry under his protection. Partial as the *History* may be, it reflects the political reality that would allow William to assert his leadership over John's other supporters, and lead them to unexpected victory.

V

WILLIAM'S WAR

ohn's death altered the tone of the war. His savage policies
had achieved little at great cost. There would be no more
punitive *chevauchées* now. Fire-raising razzias made way for
a stubborn struggle for advantage, characterised by the
Marshal's quiet but purposeful leadership.

RECTOR REGIS

John was buried in Worcester Cathedral, the first Angevin to rest on
English soil. As Newark lay within enemy territory, John's remains
had to be escorted to safety by the 'great body of armed men attending
him, nearly all of them mercenaries and foreigners ...' (*Barnwell*).
William and the legate met the cortège outside Worcester. William
had been observing the Welsh battle-front from Gloucester. Now he
took command.

We may doubt the *History's* claim that William regretted John's
passing. The king's death certainly gave his followers a problem,

similar to those that William had confronted during previous changes of regime. This time, however, he was well placed. His own men held Gloucester, the Severn's lowest crossing place. Savari of Mauléon, another of John's testamentary executors, held Bristol, ensuring maritime communications with Chepstow. Beyond the Severn lay the Forest of Dean with its coal and iron, essential ingredients for crossbow bolts, lance-heads, and armour. Relative to his only serious competitor on the royalist side, the Earl of Chester, William enjoyed what a later age called interior lines, with ready access to the queen and her children, held at secure locations in the south-west.

Events moved swiftly. John received proper burial on 26 October, William sending John Marshal to fetch the rich cloths appropriate for a royal funeral. Immediate steps were taken to fill the lacuna in royal authority by crowning John's heir, just four weeks past his ninth birthday. The royal sergeant responsible for Prince Henry's personal security was sent to collect him from Devizes Castle. William met the royal party 'on the plain outside Malmesbury', escorted by 'a great company of armed men … as was proper'. There followed the first of several affecting scenes. Unlike Roger of Wendover's synthetic speeches, the *History's* exchanges are credible and moving, preserved by John of Earley. Too young to ride solo, Henry was carried in his custodian's arms, like one of those precious brides that medieval manuals enjoined knights to imagine they were holding when beginning a charge. The boy was well drilled, greeting William politely and recommending himself to the Marshal's keeping: 'As God has my soul', replied the old man, 'I will stand by you in good faith and not fail you, as long as I have strength'. At which, everyone burst into tears. This touching encounter had a serious aspect. Devizes lay within easy reach of Louis's outpost at Marlborough. It made sense to remove John's heir to safety under as strong an escort as possible.

There seems to have been no idea of abandoning Henry in return for a peace deal, as Stephen's partisans had done with his heirs in 1153. Perhaps John's supporters felt they had nothing to gain from such treachery. For William, it would have betrayed a lifetime's service. There was anxious discussion of whether Henry should be crowned at once, before the arrival of the Earl of Chester. Expediency won, 'for nobody knows what may happen'. Only one person could possibly knight the little prince first – William Marshal, who forty-three years earlier had girt the Young King with his own sword, and would thus have knighted two kings.

Two days after his father's funeral, on 28 October, Henry III was anointed and crowned in Gloucester Cathedral. It was William's fifth coronation, if one includes Philip Augustus in 1179. The legate sang Mass, then commanded the Bishop of Winchester to place a gold circlet donated by the queen mother on the new king's head. The ceremony was a wartime improvisation: Westminster Abbey was in enemy hands, the crown jewels in pawn, and the Archbishop of Canterbury in exile. Only seven bishops attended, with William and one other earl; 'the rest of the earls and barons supported Louis' (*Waverley*). It was a far cry from Richard I's splendid coronation, when William processed in style with fifteen other magnates. As if making up the numbers, the Melsa chronicler counted William twice, once as Earl of Pembroke and again as Earl of Striguil. Nevertheless, the ramshackle affair gave Henry III a sacral quality the Dauphin never enjoyed.

Afterwards, Henry's knights bore him into the banqueting hall on their shoulders, led by Philip of Aubigny, Constable of Bristol. Others held out their hands, said the *History*, but were of little help. As they sat down to dinner, a rider came from Goodrich Castle, 17 miles (25km) to the west between Ross and Monmouth, blurting out his message, 'more like a fool than a wise man'. Welsh patriots had attacked the castle that morning, and the constable urgently required help. William reacted promptly, despatching knights, sergeants, and arbalestriers to ride through the night to the rescue. Some thought it a bad omen for the reign. It was a salutary reminder of problems ahead.

Henry III was England's first minor king since the Conquest. With no precedent to guide them, beyond customary notions of feudal wardship, his supporters took just over twenty-four hours to put in place the troika that would defeat the Dauphin: 'By common consent, care of the king and the kingdom was entrusted to the legate, the bishop of Winchester, and William Marshal, Earl of Pembroke' (*Barnwell*). John of Earley's eyewitness account fills in the detail, showing medieval decision-making at its best: the search for consensus; the elaborate courtesy that masked the jockeying for position; the Church's practised mediation. William's handling of the discussions shows his maturity as a *prud'homme*, and how far he was from the intellectually challenged knight errant evoked by Painter and Duby.

The coronation feast concluded, a preliminary council urged William to take immediate charge of the king, but the Marshal refused to be rushed. He was old and feeble, he said. They should await the Earl of Chester. As a good lord should, William withdrew to take counsel with his retainers: John of Earley, John Marshal, and Ralph Musard, Castellan of Gloucester Castle. Tempted by the fruits of office, the latter two pressed William to accept. More concerned for the Marshal's personal well being, John of Earley sought to dissuade him. Facing contradictory advice, William sought refuge in sleep: God would provide counsel and peace of mind.

Ranulf Earl of Chester arrived next morning. Half William's age, his loyalty was equally impeccable, and his English possessions even more extensive, including the semi-autonomous County Palatine of Chester, and the honours of Lancaster and Bolingbroke in Lincolnshire. Erstwhile Duke of Brittany by marriage, his claims to Richmond in Yorkshire brought him into irreconcilable conflict with the Dauphin's half-brother, the current duke. Politically, Ranulf was a moderate, having already extended Magna Carta's guarantees of good lordship to his own vassals. His ready acceptance of the need to crown Henry before his own coming augured a realistic approach to the matters in hand.

When deliberations resumed under the Bishop of Winchester's chairmanship, Sir Alan Basset, one of John's senior household knights, suggested there were but two possible royal guardians: the Marshal or the Earl of Chester. This was not strictly true. In other circumstances the legate or Queen Isabel, even Hubert de Burgh, the kingdom's chief political and judicial officer, might have had a claim. Guala was no soldier-administrator, however, and if England was a papal fief, it was not an Italian colony. Queen Isabel later became one of the century's most remarkable women as Countess of Angoulême. Matthew Paris styled her 'more Jezebel than Ysabel'. Her part in her son's minority was almost nil, however. John had denied her the financial means or opportunity to develop an affinity of her own, cheating her of her dower and guarding her closely. Hubert, as John's last justiciar, might have taken a lead as Richard's justiciars did in the 1190s, but he was occupied at Dover, deep in enemy territory, and lacked the two earls' territorial base.

William stood firm, declining so great a charge. He was past eighty, or so he said, and broken down with age. He offered Chester his wholehearted support, as long as God gave him grace. Chester responded as if reading a script. The choice could only fall upon the Marshal, 'so worthy a knight and a proven counsellor, as much feared as loved, and so wise ... one of the finest knights in the world'. Compliments over, the legate took the candidates aside with the other chief men, but could not overcome William's resistance. The breakthrough came when Guala invoked his delegated papal authority to offer William full remission and forgiveness of his sins.

This was too good a bargain to miss. Nearing the end of a long, violent, and acquisitive life, William must have known how far short he fell of the Christian ideal. Some veteran knights sought absolution in the cloister. King John was said to have been buried in the cowl of a Benedictine monk, perhaps hoping to slip past St Peter in disguise. If the price of salvation was to take charge of the kingdom, William would pay it. Even at this exalted moment, his political instincts remained sound. To preserve his personal freedom of movement, and broaden the basis of his support, he asked Peter des Roches, the hard-line royalist spokesman, to retain his oversight of the king's safety and education.

William was now regent, a title then unknown. Contemporaries used the Latin expression *regis rector et regni*: keeper or guardian of king and realm. The Middle French *History* speaks of William receiving the king and *la baillie*. The modern English 'bailiff' has squalid overtones of eviction and repossession; in French it implies a judicial officer acting for the Crown, not unlike the justiciarship. A few documents even called William justiciar, a practice abandoned when Hubert surfaced from Dover. Anonymous of Béthune styled William *maistres* or *souverains baillius de regne*, 'lord or sovereign custodian of the kingdom'. Emphasising his pre-eminence, the title recalls the *History*'s earlier sobriquet, *Sire et mestre de son seignor*, used in connection with a previous Young King. The precise extent of the Marshal's powers was uncertain. He would struggle to subdue rebels or control John's unruly servants. He was, however, the mainspring of what government there was. Whatever taxes there were passed through his hands. The first letter 'by the Earl' went out within days of the coronation. If William sometimes struggled, it is more remarkable that he prevented a repetition of the anarchy that characterised his childhood.

The common people outside rejoiced at this lucky roll of the dice; God had looked upon them kindly, for no one in England could resolve the situation more successfully than William. The poet's eulogy was not overdone. Nobody on the royalist side combined so much military and political experience, with service stretching back to Richard's and Henry's successes against Philip Augustus and beyond. As long ago as 1183, William's enemy, Geoffrey of Lusignan, had sworn he was the only man able to help the Young King, offering to fight anyone who disagreed. At the same time, William's semi-detached attitude during much of John's reign distanced him from the worst excesses of Angevin despotism. He was the perfect figure to reconcile the warring factions.

Even so, when William withdrew to take counsel of his men, the task ahead brought tears to their eyes. They were embarked on a bottomless sea, from which it were a miracle if they ever reached harbour. Above all: 'the child has no money'. John of Earley took a more positive view. If the worst came, and William had to retreat to Ireland, he would still win great honour; on the other hand, if he succeeded how much greater the renown. 'By God's sword,' swore the earl, 'that counsel is good and true.' If everyone else failed the boy, he would carry him on his own shoulders from island to island, even if he had to beg for their bread. On which stirring note, they retired to bed, trusting that God would aid those faithfully seeking to do right.

STRATEGIC BALANCE SHEET

The younger son of a minor robber baron, William had reached such heights that he might be excused an attack of vertigo. Later regents were almost always members of the royal family: Queen Isabella in the 1320s or the Duke of Bedford a century later. But was the situation as desperate as William feared? Did the *History* exaggerate to magnify his achievement? The next few months suggest that the Marshal's trepidation was not unjustified.

Contemporary assessments of the strategic situation in November 1216 vary. Roger of Wendover reported that while John's supporters adhered to his son more firmly, Louis and the barons 'confidently expected that they now had the kingdom of England in their own power'. Those dependable analysts, the Barnwell chronicler and Anonymous of Béthune, disagree. The latter saw John as 'disinherited of the most part of England'. If the king was unbeaten, it was only because he had avoided a military decision that must have been unfavourable. The Exchequer was closed, and the treasury empty. Royalist forces were too attenuated to risk a battle or siege. But at some point one or both of these would be necessary to expel the French and cow the rebels. The fringes of the British Isles were in uproar, Llewelyn's raiding parties a day's march from William's headquarters. Nevertheless, 'rumours of the king's death cheered the whole country' (*Barnwell*). They also undermined the rebel narrative: Louis was no longer the noble defender of English freedom, but a foreign usurper. Henry III was by contrast: 'an innocent youth, [who] had offended nobody, [and] many who were hostile to his father, began to adhere to him' (*Dunstable*). A review of the strategic balance suggests that while conventional forces momentarily favoured the Dauphin, popular feeling and the soft power of the Pope tended the other way.

Sidney Painter counted ninety-seven barons in revolt at John's death against thirty-six royalists, implying that Louis disposed of nearly three-quarters of England's feudal levy, an ostensible 3,500 knights. Such numbers never took the field, but they give a sense of the royalist disadvantage. The disparity was increased by whatever remained of the French invasion forces. These had initially totalled 1,440 knights plus sergeants and crossbowmen, plus defectors from John's service. Unspecified French reinforcements arrived in August, under Count Peter of Brittany, pursuing his Richmond inheritance as brother-in-law to the murdered Arthur. Even without a major battle, the wear and tear of campaigning soon diminished these numbers. Geoffrey of Mandeville died in a tournament; Eustace of Vesci was shot dead outside Barnard's Castle. Many French and Flemish departed in the summer, fighting their way past English pirates in the Channel. The Barnwell chronicler thought the French too few to occupy such a large kingdom: 'Realising this, Louis hovered round the coast, so that if by chance something untoward happened, his men and he would have an easy way home.'

Supported half-heartedly by his father, Louis depended on his own County of Artois for money and troops. He had financial difficulties from the start. The *Dunstable Annals* comment that many of the knights that he sent ahead to London were ruined and begging for want of wages. Roger of Wendover describes French troops with insufficient clothing, 'to cover their nakedness'. Compelled to reward his French supporters with English lands, Louis risked alienating the English, who were often fighting to recover fiefs or castles lost over the preceding eighty years of revolt and confiscation. William Marshal the Younger launched his ill-fated Worcester adventure after the Dauphin granted Marlborough Castle to his own half-brother Robert of Dreux. The *History* describes the Count of Nevers, commandant of Winchester, as proud and cruel, guilty of numerous unspecified excesses. The *Dunstable Annals* agree, claiming that Nevers 'inflicted such tyranny upon the people, that his name and that of his lord made a stink in their sight'. Many accounts of Anglo-French discord were shameless inventions, however. One of Roger of Wendover's finest was a deathbed confession of Gallic treachery attributed in September 1216 to the Viscount of Melun, who survived to accompany the Dauphin to Winchelsea the following April.

The country was still in dispute, despite John's losses during the initial French onset: 'For there were many royal castles strongly garrisoned, maintaining control of nearly the whole kingdom'

(*Barnwell*). Self-sustaining, through ransoms and local extortion, these formed a barrier across the country from Bamburgh to Corfe, inhibiting attacks on the Angevins' last-ditch position on the Severn. Many dominated river crossings or strategic defiles, as Newark did the intersection of the Fosse Way and the Trent. Anonymous of Béthune listed eleven, a figure which can easily be trebled:

ROYAL CASTLES 1216–17

Region	Location	Lost to Dauphin?	Date
North	Bamburgh		
	Barnard Castle		
	Knaresborough		
	Newcastle upon Tyne		
Midland	Bedford		
	Buckingham		
	Lincoln	Besieged	
	Newark		
	Northampton		
	Nottingham		
	Oxford		
	Sleaford		
East Anglia	Cambridge	Surrendered	Jan 1217
	Colchester	Exchanged for truce	Jan 1217
	Ely	Besieged	
	Hedingham	Exchanged for truce	Jan 1217
	Norwich	Exchanged for truce	Jan 1217
	Orford	Exchanged for truce	Jan 1217
	Pleshey	Captured	Jan 1217
South	Berkhampstead	Exchanged for truce	Dec 1216
	Dover		
	Hertford	Surrendered	Dec 1216
	Tower of London	Surrendered	Nov 1216

	Windsor		
South-west	Bristol		
	Chepstow		
	Corfe		
	Devizes		
	Exeter		
	Gloucester		
	Goodrich	Besieged	Nov 1216
	Worcester		

Many of these places were commanded by professional military men, entirely dependent on royal favour, 'foreigners, who frequently ranged about the country laying it waste and taking plunder' (*Waverley*). Foremost was Fawkes of Bréauté, Sheriff of Oxford, Northampton, Buckingham, Hertford, Bedford, and Cambridge, the war's central front. Fawkes also controlled the Isle of Wight, through his wife, commanding the approaches to Portsmouth Harbour. A poor royal sergeant of Norman origin, Fawkes 'so bettered himself that he was one of the richest men in England. Small he was of body, but most valiant' (Anonymous). Matthew Paris and the Waverley annalist were less enthusiastic, describing him respectively as 'a rod of the Lord's fury', or *quidem furiosus* – a lunatic.

Medieval public opinion is hard to assess, as most people were never asked. This did not stop the Barnwell canon claiming that 'Few in these times were seen to approve of Louis or his coming into England, or that he should get the kingdom, as those who brought him in had promised'. The English, moreover, were changeable and fickle. A paradox familiar from modern invasions ensured that the invaders were blamed for collateral damage, even when they came by invitation, and most of the harm was caused by the incumbent regime. Knights and sergeants, in the sense of minor landowners, hid themselves to avoid fighting on either side. Common folk, unable to escape, turned on their perceived tormentors. The *History*'s informants remembered seeing a hundred French corpses eaten by dogs between Winchester and Romsey.

The chief focus of popular resistance lay on the Kent/Sussex border. West of the prosperous Watling Street corridor and the Channel ports, the ancient forest of Andredsweald filled the great valley between the South Downs and Surrey Hills. Its uncleared woodland, sparse population, and difficult access made it a classic refuge for guerrilla forces. Kentish dissidents would harass Henry III's forces there before the battle of Lewes in 1264. They were so successful in 1216 that their leader's name has been preserved, in some thirty different spellings. He is most securely identified as William of Kasingeham or Cassingham (now Kensham), a manor in the Kentish hundred of Rolvenden. The *History* calls him Willekin de Wauz or Willy of the Weald, French tongues struggling with Kasingeham. Refusing to acknowledge Louis, Willekin recruited a thousand archers, who harassed the French from the woods, 'and slew many thousands of them' (Wendover). Anonymous of Béthune confirms that Willekin's exploits were more than patriotic propaganda. Unfortunately for theories of spontaneous popular resistance, this real-life Robin Hood was a royal official, an erstwhile Flemish mercenary, of uncertain expertise with the bow.

The balance of external forces favoured the royalists. Philip Augustus refused to make the invasion a French national cause for fear of papal disapproval. Scottish knights were scarce, their footmen only suited to plundering the north of England, which belonged to the Dauphin's allies. Alexander II had ridden to Dover to do homage, but it was a perilous journey. Eustace of Vesci was killed on the way, and John nearly intercepted the party going back. The Welsh had no knights at all, and their foot were commonly massacred whenever they strayed into England. This weak hand, two kings and a jack, was trumped by the Pope's unwavering support for the other side. Innocent III had been 'feared by everyone above all who preceded him for many a year'. His death in July 1216 encouraged John's enemies, 'speculating that the new pope would make a new policy, and would not follow in his predecessor's footsteps' (*Barnwell*). They were disappointed.

Innocent's successor, Honorius III, learned of John's death early in December 1216. He boldly decided to make a stand on behalf of the orphaned boy king, 'the cause to be supported not only with words, but if it were necessary, with arms as well' (*Barnwell*). Like his predecessor, Honorius was organising a Crusade to recover the Holy Land, and needed to terminate Christian disputes as soon as possible. Given time, papal support would alter the war's moral and numerical balance. The process was slow to take effect, however, as events on the ground would show.

The minority government lacked the resources for active campaigning. William used John's last reserves of jewellery and rich fabrics to pay the bills due at Michaelmas, including wages and supplies for the Dover garrison. His well-documented distaste for both sides' excesses suggests that the regency had no appetite for extensive raiding. It pursued the war by other means, opening a peace offensive on three fronts. Two were business as usual; the third was game-changing. John's policy of issuing safe conducts and offers of pardon to potential rebel defectors continued under the Marshal's name. Guala maintained the spiritual pressure, rallying the bishops to the new king. Within a fortnight of the coronation, would-be royalists were invited to swear fealty to their new king at Bristol on 11 November. Eleven bishops attended, four more since the coronation, nearly all those in post and not in exile. Wales and other areas under the Dauphin's control were placed under an Interdict, and Louis and his followers excommunicated again.

The Bristol Council's most dramatic measure was to reissue Magna Carta in the new king's name. Sealed by William and Guala, for want of an authentic royal seal, it was witnessed by eleven bishops, four earls, and eighteen other magnates and *curiales*. Among them were Hubert de Burgh, fresh from Dover, and the Earl of Aumale, one of the Twenty-Five and the first magnate to abandon the rebel cause. William employed his new title for the first time: *rector nostri et regni nostri* – 'guardian of ourselves and our kingdom'. Having helped draft the original charter, William now rescued it from the oblivion into which Pope Innocent had consigned it, with the active assistance of the Pope's personal representative.

The new document's contents reflected its official origin. Enforcement clauses and attacks on specific royal servants were dropped, while 'weighty and doubtful' issues as scutage and forest laws were reserved for future consideration. The crucial feudal and judicial reforms survived the exigencies of war, however, a commitment to civil liberties which compares favourably with modern governments' readiness to curtail them during emergencies. The new document clearly reflects a desire for reconciliation, born of William's own resentment of royal tyranny and his loathing of the excesses of civil war. There is every reason to believe that his views were shared by other loyal magnates, who had supported John out of habit and self interest rather than absolutist conviction. The incoming government's bold statement of its programme suggests a remarkable confidence in final victory. In the short run it stole the rebels' thunder. In the longer term it foreshadowed a new style of more responsible government based on co-operation rather than coercion.

Royalist Midwinter

The enemy were unmoved. Hearing of Henry III's coronation, they had solemnly sworn 'that no descendant of King John, formerly king of England, should ever hold the land, for the same were not worthy to bear the name of king' (*Barnwell*). As for the legate, Louis denied his authority, and threatened church leaders who bound themselves to Henry, ordering them to swear fealty to himself instead. The diocesan authorities, however, took the royalist side. Rebuffed diplomatically, Louis and his allies withdrew from Dover, 'determined to reduce the smaller castles throughout the country, so that after the lesser fortresses were in their power, they might attack the larger ones' (Wendover). As Louis left, Dover's undaunted garrison emerged to replenish their supplies by plundering the neighbourhood. The Dauphin's withdrawal from Dover may be seen in Clausewitzian terms as the campaign's culminating point. The invaders had exhausted their initial impetus, leaving them over-stretched and vulnerable.

Reaching London during the first week of November, Louis took the Tower on the 6th. The *Barnwell Chronicle* implies treachery, but this is the common medieval attribution of military outcomes to personal frailty rather than the objective balance of forces. The Tower's fourteen-month siege was well past the norm. Pursuing his strategy of consolidating the south-east, '[Louis] shifted his quarters from London into the interior of the country, dragging throwing engines after him and the instruments of war' (*Barnwell*). While the royalists gathered at Bristol, he opened siege operations against Hertford Castle. North of London near the head of the Lea Valley, a little west of Ermine Street, Hertford's capture would safeguard Louis's northern communications. It would also protect the rebel heartland, blocking the Roman road from St Albans into East Anglia, which William Longsword had taken the previous winter.

Hertford Castle lies on the River Maran's east bank. Once an Anglo-Saxon *burh*, its features are obscured by the urban development that occupies most of the semicircular outer ditch. The mound measures 100 feet (30m) across the base, and 22 feet (6.5m) high. Its commander was one of Fawkes' household knights, Walter of Godardville, who had recently shaken down the Abbot of St Albans for 50 marks, a gold cup, and a palfrey worth 5 marks. Louis surrounded the castle with machines to batter the walls, presumably on the east side to avoid attacking across the river. Roger of Wendover assures us that the garrison made great slaughter amongst the French, before surrendering on 6 December, saving their lives, arms, and property. The *History* claims that the garrison requested a twenty-day truce, expecting no relief, but as we shall see the poet's informants found this part of the war deeply confusing.

Louis moved on to Berkhampstead, 22 miles (35km) further west. Another of William the Conqueror's royal castles and site of the English surrender in 1066, Berkhampstead lies 10 miles west of St Albans, and six from Roger of Wendover's birth place (15km and 10km respectively). It occupies a well-chosen position commanding the narrow valley through the Chilterns taken by Akeman Street, the Roman road from Aylesbury to London, and the modern railway. Strategically, Berkhampstead covered Watling Street, which runs north-west from St Albans towards Saer of Quincy's estates in Leicestershire. It might also provide a jumping-off point for a rebel advance into Oxfordshire, bypassing Windsor Castle in the Thames Valley.

Berkhampstead Castle's outer perimeter is one of the largest surviving in England, its oblong embankment 150 yards (135m) north-to-south topped with a flint rubble curtain wall. The mound in the north-east corner is even bigger than Hertford's, 180 feet (54m) across the base and 45 feet (13.5m) high. It featured a circular shell keep, with walls 7 feet (2m) thick, an economical way of upgrading the original palisade. Thomas Becket had built the walls and keep in the 1150s. Since then little work had been done, before John had the defences repaired with timber from nearby woodlands. A wet ditch surrounded the whole site.

The garrison was commanded by a German *routier* called Waleran, and offered a vigorous defence. While the barons were still pitching camp, the defenders sallied forth, seizing baggage and a standard. Waleran's men sortied again at dinner-time, flying the captured banner in hopes of catching the besiegers by surprise. The main and south gates faced away from the French approach, so these stirring events may have occurred to the north outside the Derne Gate beside the motte. Next day, Louis set up his machines to launch a destructive shower of stones. Eight mounds along the outer bank to north and east are sometimes identified as the firing platforms, but archaeological excavations disagree.

Meanwhile, William and the king hovered around various royal strongholds in the south-west. Lack of money hampered vigorous action outside the belt of south Midland castles. Tradition and common sense, however, dictated that unrelieved garrisons should surrender in good time to preserve their lives, arms, and horses. William made the most of Berkhampstead's hopeless situation by exchanging the castle for a Christmas truce lasting until 13 January 1217, the week after Epiphany. Its hero's inaction puzzled the *History*'s author, whose garbled account deepens the chronological confusion: the *Waverley Annals* dates the surrender to St Lucy's Day or 13 December, perhaps when a truce was first proposed; Roger of Wendover's date is a week later, perhaps reflecting the physical transfer of custody.

The royal party spent Christmas at Bristol, after which both sides summoned a council of their supporters: Louis at Cambridge, the guardians of the kingdom at Oxford. Roger of Wendover makes much of the rebels' predicament, disillusioned with Louis, but unwilling to give him up, 'lest they should be like dogs returning to their vomit'. In reality, they could no more change sides than their opponents. Both factions were competing for the same limited set of territorial assets. Neither would budge until compelled by a shift in the military position. Only two prominent rebels had changed sides since the Marshal's peace offensive, the weathercock Earl of Aumale, and Rochester's gallant defender William of Aubigny, grown weary of Corfe's compulsory hospitality.

The rebel garrison of Mountsorrel in Leicestershire celebrated the end of the truce by raiding the Trent Valley on 20 January. Alerted by scouts, the Nottingham royalists killed three of them and captured thirty-four. Louis resumed operations by besieging Hedingham in Suffolk. Once more William exchanged a threatened castle for a truce, this time until 23 April, four weeks after Easter. Colchester, Norwich, and Henry II's polygonal castle at Orford all surrendered at the same time. Lincoln and Ely were also under pressure, the city and Isle under rebel occupation, their castles closely invested. William seemed incapable of stemming the Dauphin's advance. Nine out of thirty-two royalist castles held at Henry III's accession changed hands by the end of January: 'Thus all the eastern part [of the country] fell into Louis's hands' (*Barnwell*).

Medieval motivation is hard to fathom from the sources available. Intentions have to be deduced from actions, or the guesswork of contemporaries and earlier historians, who may have been worse informed than we are. The *History* blamed the Hertford garrison's unauthorised negotiations for the loss of other eastern castles, a view which might pass muster if William's written orders had not survived in the Rolls of Letters Patent. When Sidney Painter disparaged royalist strategy as over-cautious, he was unaware of the regent's crushing financial difficulties as revealed in Exchequer records published after he wrote. William's threat to burn Worcester in December unless the city paid £100 that it owed King John, is not a story the *History* might celebrate. His inaction during the winter of 1216–17 bears a depressing resemblance to John's inertia in Normandy in 1203 or at Stonar in 1216, episodes for which William bore some responsibility. In both cases, however,

John had lacked the material means to offer effective resistance. Decisive action is only justifiable if attended by reasonable hopes of success. William had been more aggressive in earlier conflicts, on a more even playing field.

As Chapter Three's discussion of knightly warfare suggests, medieval commanders did not lack strategic resource. William was more than a baronial Micawber waiting for something to turn up. Painter himself advances two good reasons for the regent's inactivity. Firstly, East Anglia's garrisons might be more useful elsewhere. William had never entertained exaggerated notions of the value of isolated strongholds. He had advised Richard I to let Philip Augustus keep the Vexin's disputed castles in 1198, as long as he held the surrounding countryside and its revenues. Richard's *routiers* beset the French garrisons so closely that winter that they dared not water their horses outside their own castle gates. The tables in 1217 were turned. It was Angevin garrisons who were unable to venture out. Men and supplies were better transferred to more important sectors, as they were from Norwich and Orford to Dover, the war's strategic pivot. Secondly, yielding indefensible castles bought time for negotiations with uncommitted magnates in the far south-west, consolidating the Angevin position in that quarter.

The *Barnwell Chronicle* adds a third consideration: 'It was rather hoped that Louis would return home during the truces, and it might easily happen that the royalist side would gain [some] chance advantage through this', a precociously Clausewitzian analysis of the importance of gaining time when on the defensive. William's main aim was to maintain the regency as a going concern, avoiding risky adventures in areas dominated by the Dauphin's friends. His first sortie to Nottingham in early January, to organise help for Lincoln's hard-pressed garrison, stayed safely within the Angevin castle belt. William took steps to encourage other threatened garrisons, writing to Bedford and Northampton to thank the constables for their efforts, assuring them that reasonable ransoms would be paid for anyone taken prisoner.

LENTEN AUSTERITY

Medieval truces rarely lasted. The *History* blamed the customary arrogance of the French for William's refusing further negotiations. The *Barnwell Chronicle* says it was the English who broke the peace. Everyone agrees that hostilities restarted around Quadragesima, the first Sunday in Lent, which that year fell on 12 February. Gervase of Canterbury records a French defeat near Lewes, probably at the hands of William of Cassingham. High-status prisoners included two nephews of the Count of Nevers. About the same time, the royalists regained control of Rye, one of Louis's few Channel ports, *par engien* or by cunning.

Louis had been thinking of returning home to confront a papal diplomatic mission, and gather reinforcements. His English supporters smelt a rat, and made him swear on the sacraments that he would return before the truce's scheduled end. As he prepared to sail, bad news came from Sussex, 'whence Louis angrily moved the army thither, although he had few men' (*Barnwell*). Anonymous of Béthune confirms Louis's march to Lewes, and then Winchelsea, the next place to Rye. Cassingham's men, 'retreating into the woods, broke down the bridges behind him [Louis], and laid ambushes, so that he could not bring up supplies behind him' (*Dunstable*). The stage was set for an obscure episode that might have brought the war to a sudden and embarrassing conclusion – for the French.

The *History* naturally attributed the Sussex campaign to the Marshal's 'prudent and high-minded counsel'. Assembling every royalist capable of bearing arms, he sent Philip of Aubigny, who held the king aloft after the coronation, to occupy Rye with combat-hardened knights and sergeants. As royalist warships cruised offshore, William approached with a great host, gripping Louis so tightly he did not know which way to turn. The French historian Charles Petit-Dutaillis dismissed such claims of co-ordinated action as '*fantaisistes*', but some documentary evidence suggests pre-planning. The regent sent letters in December to Irish shipmen on the Norman coast to gather at Winchelsea by 13 January, the end of the first truce. Philip of Aubigny took command in Sussex a week later, a suggestive coincidence. William remained in the Thames Valley gathering reinforcements, but it is hard to deny him credit for a strategic combination carried out under his overall direction.

William's ability to confront Louis in the field was a product of Guala's tireless preaching and its dramatic effect on public opinion: 'those who had formerly called themselves the army of God, and boasted of defending the freedoms of the church and kingdom, were [now] counted as the sons of Belial' (*Barnwell*). As days grew longer, 'Many, nobles as well as commons, placed the sign of God's Cross on their breasts that they might eject Louis and the French from England, preferring to have a king of their own country than a foreigner' (*Waverley*). Played down by sceptical Protestant English historians, Crusading ideas and rhetoric were fundamental to the royalist war effort. Henry III had renewed his father's Crusading vows, soon after his coronation, reinforcing the respect due to royalty with Crusader immunity. Henry's opponents were now the enemies of God and the Church. Where Robert fitz Walter once posed as 'Marshal of the Host of God and Holy Church', Philip of Aubigny was now 'leader of the army of Christ'. Rebel defectors or *reversi* took the Cross as a condition of absolution. Those who had done so already postponed their departure overseas to join the royalists. When the war ended, combatants from both sides left for the Holy Land to fulfil their vows. While Guala played the

Crusade card, his clerical opponents attacked his moral authority, accusing him – and the Pope – of accepting bribes and trampling justice underfoot.

Winchelsea and Rye were two of the Cinque Ports, an association of towns on the south coast. Founded before the Norman Conquest, they originally numbered five towns, hence their collective name. Prospering from fishing and piracy, they dominated cross-Channel traffic. In return for royal recognition, they 'defended the sea-coast from the attacks of the enemy' (Gervase of Canterbury). Winchelsea and Rye joined the confederation during the twelfth century, providing five and ten ships respectively. They were tiny places. Domesday Book records sixty-four burgesses at Rye, implying a population of just over 300. Thanks to a shifting coastline, the two towns now lie a mile or two inland from Rye Bay, halfway between Hastings and Dungeness. Rye stands above the surrounding countryside on a hill surrounded by rivers: the Tillingham to the west, the Brede to the south, and the Rother on the east. Their confluence with Wainwright Creek formed an excellent harbour known as the Camber. Land access was limited to the narrow isthmus from Rye Hill to the north. Anonymous of Béthune describes Rye as a strong place, although today's defences are thirteenth century. Modern Winchelsea was rebuilt west of Rye after thirteenth-century floods destroyed the original town. In 1217, Winchelsea lay east of the Camber, a mangonel's throw across Wainwright Creek from Rye to the north.

The loss of Normandy lent the Cinque Ports a new significance, converting them from a transportation facility to England's first line of defence. John recognised this by confirming their charters in 1205, styling their burgesses 'barons', like London's leading citizens. As usual, however, he alienated essential allies. The *History* tells us that in the summer of 1217, the men of Sandwich still resented the injuries John had done them nine years earlier. Gervase of Canterbury describes him hanging some on the gallows, slaying others by the sword, imprisoning more in fetters, exacting heavy ransoms and hostages. The Cinque Ports' initial resistance to Louis was minimal.

Courted by royalist diplomacy, the Cinque Ports were among the earliest defectors from the Dauphin's camp, essential allies for William's Sussex campaign: 'Louis ... having not confirmed the truces he granted earlier, went to Winchelsea near the Cinque Ports, which had abandoned him. Our men intercepted him, and having broken down the bridges, kept him in dire straits' (*Worcester*). Anonymous of Béthune, who witnessed the siege from inside Winchelsea, observed Louis's difficulties at first hand. The townspeople had fled on board ship, smashing their mill stones as they went. There was plenty of corn, but no way of grinding it for flour to bake bread, the medieval soldier's staple. The French tried rolling grain between their hands and fishing, but English boats shot them up. The best food was a store of nuts. The *History* confirms the Brabançon's account. William was on one side, at a distance; on the other side was Philip of Aubigny's chivalry, who killed many of Louis's men, while the fleet injured them from the sea. In the countryside, Willekin of the Weald harassed them mercilessly, cutting off many heads to show he was not playing.

The Dauphin was caught, as his father had been amidst the Flemish polders in 1198. Courageous French sergeants ran the gauntlet to fetch help from London, which came slowly. The Castellan of St Omer set off with insufficient numbers to risk entering the Weald. His knights rode east down Watling Street to Canterbury, then turned west past Romney, where they found Rye blocking the land route into Winchelsea. Frustrated, they retreated to Romney, and summoned naval assistance from Louis's vassals in the Boulonnais region across the Channel. Several hundred ships set sail, but only one ran the English blockade, 'through the courage of the sailors' (Anonymous). The others stopped at Dover, where

Louis had left a detachment when he abandoned the siege. The Romney force rode back to Dover, but storms prevented them from going aboard. For a fortnight, Louis and his men endured an unusually rigorous Lenten fast.

The ship that did reach Winchelsea was commanded by Eustace the Monk, who promptly justified his reputation for maritime ingenuity. Winchelsea had been a royal dockyard, constructing ten galleys for King John in 1213. Eustace constructed a floating siege tower from local material, planning to tow it across the Camber with his own galley, to engage the English beyond. On top of a captured boat, he built a fighting castle, 'so big that everyone stared at it in astonishment for it overhung the ship's sides in every direction' (Anonymous). He then placed a perrière on a second ship lashed alongside to provide covering fire. Meanwhile, Louis mounted two more perrières to shoot across the creek. Before Eustace was ready, however, an English raiding party destroyed the galley under the very eyes of the starving Frenchmen, only four of whom had been fit to stand guard.

The *History* speaks of a thousand French killed over the course of the siege, 'as soon as they strayed from the ranks', suggesting they were cut off while out foraging, and never properly counted. It was a large number, equal to the infantry force John took to Ireland in 1210:

> *and so were ruined and routed the lowborn troop,*
> *who made such excessive boasts of having England at their disposal.*

Louis himself might have been captured, had Fortune not turned in his favour. The day after Eustace's galley was destroyed, the French relief squadron broke through from Dover. The reinforcements, says the *History*, brought Louis's numbers up to 3,000, not an impossible number if it includes sailors and infantry. Louis launched an amphibious assault across the creek to drive out Rye's outnumbered defenders, capturing welcome stores of wine and food, and the English ships, whom the new arrivals had cut off from the sea.

Louis sailed off home on 27 February. Next day, when it was too late, William addressed a letter to Rye's erstwhile defenders urging them to hold out, promising 'greater succour than they could believe possible'. All the royalists' secular leaders were assembled, four earls, half a dozen Marcher barons, and a troop of mercenary captains, followed by a multitude of knights, sergeants, crossbowmen, and loyal Welshmen, 'together with the lord legate, the clergy, and a host of Crusaders'. William's army, however, was still at Dorking, several days' march away. Rye was in French hands and Louis safely overseas. Nevertheless, the Sussex campaign had two lessons. Firstly, the French were not invincible. Secondly, medieval strategic combinations lacked neither scale nor ambition. Land and sea operations extending from the Thames Valley to the south coast and across the English Channel had aimed at nothing less than the wholesale decapitation of the Franco-rebel army.

SPRINGBOARD TO VICTORY

The Dauphin's departure restored the initiative to the royalists, and undermined his political position. The following month saw 150 safe-conducts issued to rebel defectors. The most significant *reversi* were the Earl of Salisbury and William Marshal the Younger. Avoiding inconvenient details, the *History* suggests that they simply fell in with the regent near Shoreham-by-Sea in Sussex, and went off to besiege the old Braose castle at Knepp. Their change of allegiance had been under discussion for some months. John's death had assuaged their personal grievances against the Crown, and both men nourished claims to castles that Louis had granted to more reliable supporters. Salisbury was especially valuable. An experienced commander, he would play a significant part in the closing stages of the war, leading a royalist *eschiele* at Lincoln.

William would have known of Louis's oath to return in late April. This gave him seven weeks to regain lost ground. The French field army being absent, rebel-held castles became vulnerable. Garrisons were small and exposed. Mountsorrel's numbered just ten knights, plus sergeants. Deep in hostile country, with little prospect of relief, they were easily intimidated. Louis had left his nephew Enguerrand de Coucy to safeguard London during his absence, and the latter took a narrow view of his responsibilities. Until Louis returned, William had a free hand.

He began with Farnham and Winchester. Carrying the war into Hampshire, away from the solidly fortified Thames Valley, William opened a new front and menaced London's communications with the south coast. Sir Ralph Hopton's Cavaliers would try a similar manoeuvre in the 1640s. The two sieges were mutually supporting, a day's march apart along a good road. Farnham lies at the western end of the Hog's Back, forming an advanced post for England's second capital, and the Solent ports. The castle belonged to the Bishop of Winchester, the king's tutor, another good reason for taking it. Its great central motte was not at one end as usual, but in the middle of a tear-shaped embankment, the eleventh-century earthworks surmounted by a polygonal shell keep and a curtain wall of flint rubble. The *History* gives no details of events at Farnham, a particular loss as other chroniclers are equally uninformative. Documentary evidence shows that William was there 7–12 March, when the garrison received a safe-conduct back to London. The Dauphin's rapid recapture of the bailey after his return, but not of the keep, suggests the latter suffered little damage.

Winchester was a more serious proposition, with two castles and extensive walls. Lying at the junction of Roman roads from Portchester, Southampton, Salisbury, and Marlborough, it was a major centre of government, and Henry III's birthplace. The ancient walls formed an irregular quadrilateral stretching half a mile (880m) westwards up the slope from the River Itchen. In 1141, William's father had helped besiege Wolvesey Castle, whose square keep and gatehouse still stand in the south-east corner of the walls. William the Conqueror's royal castle lay at the other end of town, overlying the south-west corner of the city walls near the Westgate. The royal castle occupied an elliptical mound 300 yards (270m) long north–south and 100 yards (90m) across, separated from city and countryside by a wet ditch 30 feet (9m) deep and wide. Stone walls had been added in the late twelfth century, John spending 100 marks on repairs in 1215. A cluster of square towers occupied the motte at the southern end of the bailey, a square great tower standing at the northern end, near the section of city wall leading to the Westgate. Today, the site is occupied by the Law Courts and the old Peninsula Barracks. The only medieval structure left is Henry III's Great Hall, built after the siege in the 1220s.

Salisbury and the younger Marshal established themselves at Hyde Abbey, a good spot north of Winchester for directing operations against either castle. Wolvesey fell almost immediately. Then, for a week, the two friends beset the royal castle so closely by day and night that the garrison could neither rest nor show their faces. The *History* does not mention engines, but references to both shooting and throwing imply bows and machines. The defenders probably had engines too. Castle accounts from the 1190s include payments for a *mangunel* and a *petraria*. The attackers' best firing position, by analogy with John's practice at Rochester, would have been to the west, on the higher ground beside the Romsey Road. The presence on that side of the castle's main gate, always a weak point, would also invite attack from that direction. The gate's subsequent reinforcement with a barbican may not have been coincidental.

Operations were momentarily interrupted by an urgent summons from the Marshal, during which the garrison came out to punish the citizens for siding with the royalists. Winchester's suburban inhabitants joined in the looting, suggesting tension between those living inside and outside the walls. The *History* puts the interruption early in the siege, but the return of Salisbury and the younger Marshal on hearing that Farnham had fallen suggests a date nearer 12–13 May. The regent arrived on the 14th, 'with such a company of knights the river banks and countryside were full of them and the town all round'. There were already enough royalists to bottle up the defenders, so William despatched his more active associates to recover Southampton, Portchester, Chichester, Odiham, and even Rochester. The *History* never explicitly mentions Winchester's capture, suggesting a gap in the text, which suddenly jumps to describing how the poorer royalists enriched themselves at their enemies' expense. The castle held out as long as was prudent. When Louis returned, Anonymous of Béthune reveals that he found much of the wall collapsed by mining, and had to fill the breaches with stout oak palisades. The defenders presumably gave up towards Easter, for shortly after that the Marshal divided the army. The Earl of Chester headed north to pursue his claim to Mountsorrel Castle. Fawkes went to relieve his garrison at Ely. Blending family concerns with the national interest, the younger Marshal invested Marlborough Castle the Friday after Easter, which he took, 'though not without great trouble'.

Louis was back in England by then, ready to take the gloss off the royalist recovery. His trip home had mixed results. Philip Augustus was mending fences with the Pope, and pretended not to be on speaking terms with his heir. The *History* claims that Louis returned with a large and warlike army, but Anonymous of Béthune says he 'brought but few knights', seven score of them besides some mercenaries. More interesting was the *Trebuket*, something 'much spoken of for at this time they had been little seen in France'. Among seventeen named magnates was the ill-omened Thomas de la Perche, the French commander at Lincoln.

The date on which Louis returned has caused much confusion, but the *Worcester Annals* support Anonymous of Béthune's timetable, placing it on Saturday 22 April, the eve of St George's Day. A favourable wind carried the French fleet past Dover so close that Louis could see the huts left from last year's siege. He did not land for Willekin of the Weald chose that day to attack the caretakers and burn the huts, while country people lined the cliffs ready to shoot down into the ships. Louis landed further north at Sandwich, not without further loss from English galleys lurking offshore. Here he received intelligence that Winchester, Southampton, Marlborough, and Mountsorrel were all besieged, diverting him from his immediate objective of renewing the siege of Dover. Keeping the pick of his knights and sailors, he patched up a local truce with Hubert de Burgh and marched top speed for Winchester. Before leaving he fired Sandwich, a gratuitous atrocity reflecting the deterioration in Anglo-French relations. The Brabançon's timetable provides a rare insight into the marching powers of a medieval army under pressure:

LOUIS'S MARCH FROM KENT TO HAMPSHIRE APRIL 1217

Date	From	To	Miles (km)
Tuesday 25th	Canterbury	Malling	28 (45)
Wednesday 26th	Malling	Guildford	42 (67)
Thursday 27th	Guildford	Farnham	10 (16)
Friday 28th	Farnham		
Saturday 29th	Farnham	Winchester	25 (40)

Wednesday was qualified as a long march. The transport stopped overnight at Reigate protected by the rearguard, and caught up next day, while Louis stormed the bailey at Farnham. The daily average of 26 miles (42km) compares favourably with nineteenth-century march rates. The British General Staff in 1914 advised that only small commands of seasoned troops could cover such distances, under favourable conditions. John did 40 miles (65km) a day at Mirebeau in 1202, but Louis was held up by his train: 'carters, sergeants and crossbowmen, mercenaries and riffraff' (*History*). At vespers on the 26th, the sun appeared red as blood, and remained so for many days, celestial confirmation that dreadful deeds were afoot.

Still at Farnham, Louis was joined by Saer of Quincy, with *grant chevalerie d'Englois*. Of the rebel strongholds under siege, only Mountsorrel still held out. A bone of contention between the Earls of Leicester and Chester during the Anarchy, Mountsorrel lies 8 miles (13km) north of Leicester in the Soar Valley. Standing on high ground south of the village, the castle was situated near the intersection of the boundaries of Leicestershire, Nottinghamshire, and Lincolnshire. Not far from Fosse Way, the great highway that runs diagonally across England from Exeter to Lincoln, it menaced Chester's communications with his honour of Bolingbroke in south Lincolnshire. Forfeited to the Crown after a previous Earl of Leicester was captured at Fornham, fighting for the Young King, the castle had been returned to Saer following Magna Carta. Saer's support for Louis gave Chester a fine chance to reassert a claim dating back to his great-grandfather.

Roger of Wendover's statement that the siege was undertaken on William's orders affords it wider strategic significance than a baronial property dispute. The only rebel castle south of the Humber to escape John's clutches in 1216, Mountsorrel's capture would ease pressure on the Lincoln royalists, 45 miles (72km) to the north. Chester's army included Fawkes and a swathe of Midland castellans with their garrisons. Battered by machines, the defenders 'courageously returned stone for stone and shot for shot' (Wendover). Having demonstrated their mettle, they called on Saer for help, who appealed to his own feudal lord. Focussed on the southern theatre, Louis had little to send. 'Unable to get rid of him otherwise', he gave Saer permission to relieve Mountsorrel with his English chivalry, supported by seventy French knights led by de la Perche. More Brabançons might have gone, but the Avoué of Béthune was not asked. Two other leaders lacked the men.

The rebel army divided next day, 29 April. Saer returned to London; Louis headed for Winchester, hoping to win the war at a blow by capturing the boy king. Squires riding ahead to seek billets caught some royalist stragglers, but king and regent had gone, retreating to Marlborough along the road that John Marshal had traversed so painfully seventy-six years before. For all William knew, Louis's whole army was present including Saer's English, while he had only part of the royalist array. By luck or cunning, the younger William Marshal persuaded Marlborough's defenders to surrender just before the Dauphin's return became common knowledge. The garrison saved their lives and bodies, avoiding death or mutilation, but were deeply embarrassed. Frustrated in his wider aims, Louis spent several days restoring Winchester's defences:

> *Rebuilt the keep and the high walls richly with stone and mortar,*
> *And all the breaches in the walls and the damage*
> *Made well and truly good, as if they were all brand new.*

He then returned to London en route for Dover, leaving the Count of Nevers to hold Winchester with a strong garrison. When Louis sat down before Dover on 12 May, it was as if the royalist spring had never happened.

Saer of Quincy's column left London on Monday 1 May, 'pillaging all the places they passed'. Roger of Wendover put their numbers at 600 knights, which is credible, and 20,000 infantry, which is not. Roger, who saw them ravaging the vicinity of Belvoir Priory, described them as the refuse and scum of France, 'their poverty and wretchedness ... so great that they had not enough bodily clothing to cover their nakedness'. Marching via St Albans and Dunstable, Saer approached Mountsorrel on the Wednesday. If Chester's force represented half the royalist troops present at Lincoln three weeks later, it would have been outnumbered two-to-one in knights. For all the royalists knew, Louis was coming with his entire army. After the war, some commentators still thought he had been there. Warned by scouts, the royalists burnt their machines and huts, and withdrew to Nottingham to await events. The rebels re-provisioned the castle, repaired mangonel damage, pillaged the local churchyards, and marched off to Lincoln. Hugh, Castellan of Arras, and Gilbert of Ghent, Louis's candidate for the Earldom of Lincoln, had been besieging the castle since Lent. With Saer's reinforcements, they felt sure of liquidating its gallant defenders.

The crisis of the war had come. Both sides had divided their forces, but the royalists occupied a central position between the enemy corps at Lincoln and Dover, able to strike a concentrated blow at either before the other could come to its aid. William, lying at Oxford, enjoyed easy communications with the Earl of Chester at Nottingham. The situation called for extreme measures. The rebels were pinned down in sieges, their nearer detachment commanded not by the Dauphin but by magnates inferior in status and reputation to the Marshal. They were ripe for slaughter.

V I

LINCOLN FAIR

he second battle of Lincoln was fought on Saturday 20
May 1217, the eve of Trinity Sunday. The climax of the
Marshal's military career, it was the consummation of
six decades of chivalry and 16,000 lines of poetry. The
debates surrounding the action are surprising given the
extensive sources, not just the *History*, but also Roger of Wendover's
unwontedly factual narrative. The most serious deficiency is lack of
testimony from the defeated side. As if struggling to digest the rare
surfeit of information, historians have disagreed over operational
responsibility for the action, the wisdom of its conduct, the means
by which the royalists gained access to the city's interior, and the
significance of its outcome. The *History's* author set the pattern by
admitting his own difficulties reconciling the contradictory accounts
circulating in the 1220s. These problems can be reduced by adapting
contemporary accounts to the ground, as it stands and as uncovered
by archaeological investigations. The urban setting makes this easier
than for a conventional encounter fought in some meadow, lacking
permanent structures like castles and cathedrals.

LOCATION

The ancient city of Lincoln occupies a dominating position on the narrow limestone ridge known as Lincoln Edge, just north of the gap through which the River Witham turns eastwards to gain the Wash. A northerly spur of the Northamptonshire uplands, the Edge divides reclaimed Fen country to the east from the Vale of Trent to the west. Just short of the obstruction, the Rivers Till and Witham flow into Brayford Pool, the source of the city's medieval prosperity. This inland harbour also gave Lincoln its name, its first syllable deriving from the Celtic for 'pool'. The ill-drained swamps and ponds south of Lincoln would exert a powerful negative influence on the course of the battle.

The intersection of ridge and stream made Lincoln an early communications centre. Just short of the Humber, it was a natural anchor point for the invading Romans' right flank, their headquarters above Brayford Pool shielding the junction of Ermine Street, running northwards, with Fosse Way, the only Roman road in England not leading to London. The two roads join just south of Lincoln, and continue north along High Street and across the Witham, before climbing the Strait and Steep Hill, gaining 175 feet (53m) in 660 yards (600m) – a 9 per cent gradient. Beyond Lincoln, Ermine Street continued northwards to the Humber ferry, en route for York. Three miles (5km) north of Lincoln, another Roman road forks left. Crossing the Trent by the paved ford at Littleborough to reach York via Doncaster, Tillbridge Lane had witnessed several Dark Age confrontations. Harold II, England's last native king, marched down it for Hastings, sleeping at Lincoln on the way.

Lincoln's prosperity, however, derived from water communications. Eastwards, the Witham led to markets in Europe and Scandinavia. Westwards, the Fossdyke assured communications with the Trent and the Midlands. Once a Roman canal, this reopened in the 1120s, to make Lincoln the third- or fourth-richest town in England. Physical evidence for Lincoln's medieval wealth survives in its architecture: the Norman vaults beneath High Bridge; St Mary's Hall in High Street; the townhouses on Steep Hill attributed to the Jewish community. Its Domesday Book population of some 6,350 compares with that of Norwich.

Commercial success was a mixed blessing: Lincoln was attacked nine times between 1141 and 1265. Nearly a third of the pre-Conquest city was demolished to make room for the castle in 1068. Five years later, however, William I transferred the seat of England's largest bishopric from Dorchester-on-Thames to Lincoln, initiating two centuries of spectacular architectural development. Henry II granted the citizens their first royal charter in 1157, which Richard I confirmed in 1194 for 500 marks. William Marshal was among the witnesses. As at London, civic pride bred disaffection. John fined the city £1,000 in February 1216, its mayor being absent, apparently serving with the rebel army. Since then, Lincoln had attracted the largest concentration of rebels outside London: 'every day, many great men flocked there with their wives and children, as they made out it was safer to stay there, as much from the strength of the place, as the presence of powerful men' (*Barnwell*).

The thirteenth-century city comprised three main areas spread along Ermine Street, measuring 2 miles (3km) north to south but less than a mile (1.5km) wide. The upper city or Bail was the original Roman fortress. A sparsely populated government quarter in 1217, its square walls enclosed the castle and St Mary of Lincoln's Cathedral in their south-west and south-east corners respectively. South of the Bail, the lower walled city ran down the slope towards the Witham. Divided from the upper city by an internal wall and gate, this formed the commercial quarter with wharves along the modern Pool side. Outside the walled city and south of High Bridge lay the *History*'s Wikefort or Wigford, a suburb housing the weavers

THE KNIGHT WHO SAVED ENGLAND

who made Lincoln Green cloth. Wigford extends a mile (1.5km) along High Street to the Great or West Bargate whose mechanism would baffle rebel fugitives and historians alike. This, and a connecting wall to the nearby Little or East Bargate, was Wigford's only formal defensive work. The suburb's flanks, however, were protected by water features: the Witham to the west and Sincil Dyke, a drainage ditch carrying excess river water, to the east. An enemy from the south faced sufficient obstacles to deter any army.

Lincoln remained a walled city into the nineteenth century. Roman in origin, its walls had been rebuilt in the fourth century: 10–13 feet (3–4m) thick, 23–27 feet (7–8m) high, behind an 80-foot (25m) wide ditch. A few slabs of rubble core are still visible from East Bight. They should not be confused with the less substantial wall built later around the Cathedral Close. Lincoln's walls constituted a significant military obstacle in 1217, contrary to the opinion of Professor Tout who believed that they were low and easily surmounted. The only place this may have been true was to the east, where the Bail walls had been breached to extend the cathedral.

Access to the city was controlled by a number of gates, many of which would play a role in the battle or in the subsequent debates. Those extant in 1217 are shown below, in clockwise order:

LINCOLN CITY GATES

Location	Name	Fate
North wall – Upper City	Newport Arch	Roman Gate still in use today
East wall – Upper City	Eastgate	Demolished 1764
East wall – Lower City	Clasket/Claxledgate	
South wall – Lower City	Stonebow	Fifteenth-century rebuild still in use
West wall – Upper City	West Gate	Demolished c.1700

The castle had its own gates, discussed below, and more gates were built later, for example Exchequer Gate near the cathedral, and Newland Gate leading from the Lower City to West Common. Several historians assign the latter a role in the battle, but Sir Francis Hill, medieval Lincoln's great historian, found no evidence for its existence so early. For added confusion, many of Lincoln's streets are named 'gate' in the Scandinavian manner. The most important here is Bailgate, running between Newport Arch and Castle Hill.

Adjacent to the open space of Castle Hill lies the castle itself. Archaeologists disagree over its original extent and building sequence. By 1217, however, it was firmly established in its modern form in the south-west corner of the Bail. Looking out across the Vale of Trent, it was an uncompromising statement of power, visible for miles. Earth embankments probably date from the castle's foundation in 1068: 50–80 feet (25m) broad and 20–30 feet (9m) high, they slope gently within, falling steeply into ditches outside. The curtain was built along the embankments when the earth had settled, some time before 1115 when the fortress is first described as walled. The walls today stand 30–40 feet (9–12m) high and 20 feet (6m) thick. The masonry is rough and hasty, but well grouted with good mortar. Lincoln has none of the geometric appeal of Edward I's Welsh castles, resembling a crushed parallelogram bulging out to the south and east. Its overwhelming effect, as the walls curve round out of sight, is of unyielding brute strength.

The bailey is large for an urban castle, roughly 200x150 yards (180x135m). As if to emphasise its scale, Lincoln has two mounds instead of the usual one: the only English castle to do so beside Lewes. Sequence and nomenclature are controversial, but the larger Lucy Tower is probably earlier. A classic motte, sitting astride the south-west enceinte, it is crowned by a polygonal shell keep with an internal diameter of 64–74 feet (19–22m) and walls 8 feet thick (2.4m). Now reduced to one storey, in 1217 it was a floor higher. The Observatory Tower to the south-east is less impressive, a much amended rectangular tower, with an irregular heap of earth around its base. Lincoln's only other tower is Cobb Hall at the perimeter's north-east corner. Constructed after the battle, it is significant for what it suggests about the location of the fighting.

The castle's size reflects its intended use as a base for mounted columns, riding out to intercept hostile parties observed from the lookout post atop the Lucy Tower's mound. This offensive function is reflected by its two major gateways. Built originally to a common box-like pattern, they allow independent access to Castle Hill on the east, or to open country on the west. Both feature prominently in the battle, the west gate often confused with its civic namesake which penetrated the city wall just beyond the castle's north-west corner. Smaller postern gates existed, west of Cobb Hall and in the Lucy Tower's south-west face, but they were narrow and difficult of access for bodies of troops. The extensive bailey, however, allowed ample space for the halls, kitchens, and storehouses that subsequent surveys describe, administrative features which helped the garrison ride out the protracted sieges of 1215–17.

Lincoln's twin mottes reflect twelfth-century territorial and jurisdictional conflicts. The Anarchy saw a complex three-cornered struggle for the castle, the county, and its shrievalty. Breaking out afresh in 1217, the contest illustrates the difficulties that William experienced in keeping his own side together. The triangle's weakest point was Gilbert of Ghent, nephew of King Stephen's ephemeral Earl of Lincoln. A prominent rebel who owed the Jews £800, Gilbert had been trying to capture 'his' castle since the summer of 1216. The strongest contender was the royalist Earl of Chester. Ranulf's claim derived from his great-grandmother, the eponymous Lucy, who built one of the towers in the castle, probably not the one bearing her name. Ranulf's grandfather attacked Lincoln several times during the Anarchy, provoking the battle of 1141. For Ranulf, Lincoln resembled Mountsorrel, an obstacle to his broader ambitions.

Physical possession, however, was firmly in the hands of John's longstanding chatelaine Lady Nicola de la Haye:

> *Whom God keep body and soul,*
> *Who was lady of the castle,*
> *Defending it with all her might.*

Lady Nicola was one of those few medieval women to play an active political role. Luckier than the Countess of Leicester, pulled out of a ditch after Fornham, or the Welsh princess Gwenllian slain near Kidwelly in 1136, Nicola better resembles Countess Eleanor de Montfort, who defended Dover Castle against Henry III in 1265. Nicola's hereditary rights were as respectable as the Earl of Chester's. Having outlived her husband and son, she was defending the castle on her granddaughter's behalf, 'and she held it most loyally' (Anonymous). Appropriately, if misleadingly, the *History* termed the battle '*la bataille de Nichole*', from the French for Lincoln.

Nicola had been under spasmodic siege for nearly two years, since the Northerners briefly occupied the city in June 1215. They returned next year with the King of Scots, but once she bought them off, and once they fled the wrath of King John. The Christmas truce had interrupted a fresh investment, which was renewed in Lent 1217, and intensified when Louis returned from France:

> *It was ordered that those who were at Lincoln should vigorously press*
> *the siege. Whence, having set up engines, no respite was now given to*
> *the besieged,* [who were] *expecting nothing except only to be captured.*
> *(Barnwell)*

APPROACH

William and the king returned to the Thames Valley after the Sussex campaign, reaching Oxford on 9 May. Developments at Mountsorrel and Lincoln were unwelcome, 'the king's party thinking that if Lincoln with its garrison should fall into Louis's hands, they should suffer greater harm, besides incurring shame for not relieving the lady defending it so gallantly' (*Barnwell*). Seeking clarification, William moved to Northampton, a day's march nearer the action. There he took the single greatest decision of his life, forsaking the caution that had guided royalist strategy since John's flight from Sandwich. William's resolve to seek battle at Lincoln has been criticised as hazardous and contrary to medieval practice. Civil wars, however, demand speedy resolution. The decision was not William's alone, for it followed consultation with the legate and the hard-headed Peter des Roches. The *History* saw it as a marvel sent from God.

William issued his call to arms on Saturday 13 May, the eve of Pentecost. His words ring true, as at Gloucester, kept fresh in John of Earley's memory. William advanced a variety of reasons for action: material, chivalric, and spiritual. Henry's supporters were in arms to preserve their renown; to defend their families and win honour; to defend the peace of the Holy Church and win redemption of their sins. The enemy, like fools, had divided their forces, and Louis was elsewhere. The royalists would be soft not to seek revenge on those come from France to steal their inheritance. It was God's will, he said, in an echo of the old Crusaders' battle cry, that they defend themselves with iron and steel. Orders were despatched to castellans and knights commanding garrisons to gather at Newark the following Tuesday, to raise the siege of Lincoln. William was late, being still at Oakham in Rutlandshire on the Tuesday, then slipping between Mountsorrel and the Fens, to reach Newark on Wednesday.

Stages were long: 36 miles (58km) to Oakham and 28 miles (45km) to Newark; further if William side-stepped to meet the Earl of Chester outside Nottingham.

The host spent three days at Newark, resting horses and preparing for battle. The legate was in attendance with numerous bishops, 'to assail with prayers as well as arms these disobeyers of their king' (Wendover). Enthusiasm was at fever pitch, for William's words had set everyone's hearts afire. Factions disputed the honour of striking the first blow. Norman exiles claimed the privilege, but the Earl of Chester said he would withdraw unless given the first *bataille*. Unwilling to lose Ranulf's help, the Marshal adjudicated in his favour, saving the Normans' rights. Some commentators ascribe the squabble to Ranulf's frustrated aspirations to the regency, but Chester's grandfather made a similar claim before the first battle of Lincoln, and it may have reflected local ambitions.

Earthly disagreements resolved, the legate donned his white robes, and excommunicated Louis by name, with all his supporters, especially Lincoln's besiegers, but absolving all those fighting for the king. Everyone made confession and took communion, 'determined to conquer or die in the cause of right' (Wendover). Protracted spiritual exercises were an essential preparation for battle, building confidence and creating an exalted expectation of victory. The First Crusaders fasted for three days before their sortie from Antioch in 1098, the same period as at Newark. Victory's spiritual foundations assured, Guala took the king back to Nottingham, leaving Peter des Roches as his deputy.

The army flew to horse next morning, Friday 19 May, white crosses on every breast. Instead of heading directly for Lincoln along Fosse Way, the royalists hugged the Trent, describing a broad turning movement west of the city. Brooks and Oakley in their 1922 study of the battle describe this indirect approach as 'one of the very few pieces of tactical insight ... found in this campaign'. The Marshal and his colleagues would have been very dense indeed to have marched straight up Fosse Way. Wigford with its surrounding swamps and the lower city presented an insuperable series of obstacles on that side. Besides, the besieging rebels lay south and east of the beleaguered castle, interposed between it and the relieving army. As the Barnwell chronicler noted, 'whereas the city was perceived to be more strongly defended on the southern side, turning further off by the northern side, where the castle is situated, they drew near'. An easterly turning movement would have required a still wider detour, without addressing the communication issue. Robert of Gloucester had swum the Fossdyke within sight of the castle and fought King Stephen on West Common. William was more circumspect.

The *History* says that the royalists spent Friday night at Torksey; Roger of Wendover puts them 5 miles (8km) further on at Stowe. The Newark road certainly crosses the Fossdyke at Torksey, where the canal leaves the Trent. Described by a thirteenth-century jury as 'the key of Lindsey [part of Lincolnshire], as Dover is of England', Torksey had a castle, two monastic establishments, and a camping ground for shire levies. Three roads run thence to Lincoln: two via Saxilby, one less directly via Stowe. An episcopal manor with a fine eleventh-century minster, Stowe also had attractions for a medieval army. John stayed there twice, once in 1216 when John Marshal accompanied him on his northern campaign. William's nephew was one of several possible sources of local knowledge. Stowe lies just north of Tillbridge Lane, which the Newark road joins at Marton. Eight miles (13km) from Lincoln as the crow flies, Stowe is an easy ride to Lincoln Edge, which it climbs a safe distance from the city at North Carlton. The more direct routes from Torksey do so at Burton, dangerously near the castle's besiegers. It may be that the royalist advanced guard pressed on to Stowe, while others stayed at Torksey. Total mileage, 22 miles (36km), was undemanding by contemporary standards. Short but rapid stages avoided tiring precious destriers, while ensuring surprise. Before the rebels could absorb the royalists' departure from Newark, the latter would be approaching Lincoln from the north, forcing the besiegers to fight on the level terrain outside Newport Arch, or stay inside the walls.

William wasted no time ordering his array once within striking distance of his objective. The *History* speaks in the third person plural, but it was customary for commanders to take personal charge of forming up: Bohemund did so at Antioch, as did Simon de Montfort before Muret, and his son at Lewes in 1264. The troops fell in early on Saturday morning, arranging their *conrois* in four or five *batailles* or *eschieles*. 'Few they were, but they bore themselves well': 406 knights, 80–100 per squadron, and 317 crossbowmen. Precise and realistic numbers suggest that the poet saw a contemporary muster roll in the Marshal family archives. Later he refers to another 200 sergeants, and there may have been more. Roger of Wendover gives similar figures: 400 knights and 250 crossbows, 'besides innumerable sergeants and horsemen who could take the place of knights if necessary'. The Earl of Chester took the van, followed by the two Marshals, father and son, then William Earl of Salisbury, and finally Peter des Roches. Peter later appears in front of the army, which suggests that he delegated command of the fourth squadron. A blank line after the *History's* reference to Peter may have mentioned a fifth squadron whose existence is implied later, but it is anybody's guess. Roger of Wendover names seventeen other royalist barons, 'with many castellans experienced in war'. He also specifies 'seven dense and well drawn up squadrons', but the *History's* account is preferable, derived from eyewitnesses and reflecting the battle's tactical development.

The crossbowmen formed an advance guard, a mile (1.6km) ahead, led by Fawkes of Bréauté. Omitted from the *History's* order of battle, the *routier* for once earned Roger's approval as praiseworthy

– *laudabilis*. Wagons and pack horses followed: 'on every side the glittering banners and shields struck terror into onlookers' (Wendover). Such pageantry was customary. Richard of Hexham describes the English going to fight the Scots in 1138, 'with costly splendour, as to a royal marriage'. Unlike modern camouflage, knightly display focussed attention on the individual combatant, encouraging prowess and ensuring notoriety for slackers.

Once the troops were formed up, 'as they should be', the Marshal addressed them, 'as someone who well knew how'. He spoke more briefly in the field than at Newark. The enemy who sought to take the land by force were at their mercy, as long as hearts and courage did not fail; the slain were assured of paradise, while victory ensured everlasting renown; the enemy were fighting God and his Church, and would go straight to hell:

> *God has delivered them into our hands;*
> *Let us hasten to fall upon them,*
> *For now is the time and the hour!*

Before moving off, the Marshal made some final adjustments. Peter des Roches took command of the crossbowmen, who were drawn out in extended line opposite the enemy's right flank, with orders to pick off their horses. This oblique position kept the marksmen clear of the mounted action, shooting into the enemy's unshielded side, as Norman longbowmen did in similar circumstances at Bourg Théroulde in 1124. As a further precaution against mounted attack, 200 sergeants were told off ready to kill their own horses to form an obstacle. One imagines this was less to halt the hostile onslaught outright than to disrupt its formation, leaving it vulnerable to the counter-charge that had been William's trademark in the 1170s. The ready acceptance of such hazardous instructions indicates a remarkable confidence and discipline amongst John's old *routiers*:

All those who heard the earl, bore themselves joyfully,
As cheerfully as if it were a tournament.

Inflamed by hopes of heaven, victory, and plunder, their only concern was lest the enemy decamped before they reached the city.

CONTACT

A contemporary song says that the royalists moved off as 'the sun was touching the earth with its first beam', about 3.40 am GMT at that season and latitude. Roger of Wendover started the battle between the first and third hour. Calculating twelve hours between dawn and dusk in the medieval way, the host might have reached Lincoln between 5.00 and 7.45 am, rather less than three hours to cover the 9.5 miles (15km) from Stowe via Tillbridge Lane. They rode slowly: 3.5 miles per hour (5.7 km/h). Exactly equal to the 1914 War Office cavalry 'walk' rate, such a measured pace would preserve both horseflesh and formation, while preventing surprises. The Earl of Salisbury had done likewise at Winchester in April, when he told his men to ride prudently, well closed up, to avoid ambush.

The optimum final approach would follow the 60-metre contour along the top of Lincoln Edge. The route of today's B1398 has several tactical advantages, beside approaching Lincoln, as Roger of Wendover says, 'from the castle side'. The steep western slope protected the Marshal's right flank, the gentler eastern slope leaving space for his second and subsequent *eschieles* to deploy left of the van, which they presumably followed in an open column of squadrons. Had William followed Ermine Street directly towards Newport Arch, he would have lost the high ground, and hampered communications with Lady Nicola.

The rebels had sufficient notice of the Marshal's approach to avoid tactical surprise, though not enough to respond so effectively as some historians suggest they might have done. Not being in the castle, they lacked the extensive views available to Lady Nicola. They could have posted a lookout in a church tower, as Simon de Montfort did at Evesham in 1265, but there is no evidence for this. The alarm probably came from scouts posted on Lincoln Edge, perhaps at the viewpoint where Tillbridge Lane climbs the escarpment. Lacking telescopes, they would see only the glitter of arms as the royalists traversed the flat country east of the River Till, towards 5.00 am. Allowing twenty minutes for reports to reach Lincoln, their commanders had just over an hour to react to William's approach.

Roger of Wendover has a long rigmarole explaining how the rebels laughed at the messengers, before sending two separate reconnaissance parties, one English and one French. Robert fitz Walter and Saer of Quincy argued that the rebel army had superior numbers, so should meet the royalists at the ascent of the hill, where 'we will catch them all like larks', like limed birds. The Count de la Perche reckoned the royalist array 'in the French manner', and was misled by spare banners flying from its attendant wagons. Overestimating enemy numbers, he preferred to stay within the city and defend the walls.

The *History*'s account is simpler and more credible. The Count and Saer rode out together, and reported that, in the usual epic fashion, never had anyone anywhere seen a force better equipped for war or more resolute. On this, the rebels retreated inside the walls, saying that the royalists lacked the strength to assault the city, and were bluffing. When they were forced to withdraw, the besiegers could attack them at a disadvantage, the relieving army's horses worn out from bearing their riders all day. The *History* has no suggestion of heading off the royalists, an evolution for which there was no time. William was already nearer the crucial ascent than the rebels. The *Barnwell* and *Dunstable* chronicles both suggest that the rebels had just enough time to deploy outside the walls before retreating inside: 'The others trusting in numbers and courage, having at first drawn up their squadrons, indeed went out to meet them, but soon withdrawing, having changed their opinion, took themselves back into the city' (*Barnwell*). Roger's speeches are highly suspect, the multiplicity of banners a monkish tale to explain the battle's surprising outcome, while casting the blame on the cowardly French.

The rebel withdrawal was a setback, frustrating William's scheme for an all-arms battle. He made the best of a bad job, as a good leader should, claiming a successful first round. The French, usually foremost in a tournament, had broken their array and hidden behind walls. William was not far wrong. The rebels now occupied an ambivalent tactical position, simultaneously attacking the castle and defending the city, with the disadvantages of both forms of war. From the streets, the rebel commanders could not see what the royalists were doing, leaving themselves open to further surprises. Their mounted opponents could hardly climb walls, but they could ride round to exploit any breach. Assaulting knights entered Northampton during the Second Barons' War in 1264 in just this way. A defensive line has only to be penetrated at one point to crumble more generally.

Rebel numbers justified de la Perche's confidence: 611 French knights and a thousand foot, 'without counting the English on their side'. The latter claim appears unlikely; the poet is exaggerating enemy numbers to enhance his hero's glory. Reports of prisoners and fugitives added together indicate a total of 600 mounted rebels. Most of the named prisoners appear to have been English, suggesting that real French knights were in a minority. Again the *History*'s precision suggests a written source, such as a ransom roll.

Professor Tout's idea that the walls were too extensive for the defenders is incorrect. The Burghal Hidage, a pre-Conquest document listing contingents required to defend English *burhs*, allowed one man per 4 feet (1.2m) of wall. Given similar military technology, the rebels had quite enough infantry to defend Lincoln's northern walls. The half-mile (800m) circuit from West Gate to East Gate would absorb 660 men, leaving 300 to blockade the castle. Nobody attacked the lower city walls on the steep hillside below. Some rebel barons took charge of the gates. Others formed a mobile reserve, south of Bailgate in Castle Hill. If the royalists ever got in, however, the narrow streets would hamper efforts to control the defence, lack of space preventing the rebels exploiting their superior numbers.

RECONNAISSANCE

At this point, a pause ensues in both narrative and battle. The *History's* author found that his sources disagreed, and he could not follow both: 'for in a true story, no-one ought to lie'. A humble poet had to steer carefully between the conflicting accounts of powerful men, especially when one of them was Peter des Roches. John the Tourangeau quickly recovered his narrative poise, however, describing two successive missions to make contact with the garrison of the castle, leaving the continuity to take care of itself. Roger of Wendover mentions neither mission, saying that the garrison took the initiative in contacting its would-be rescuers. All three accounts may be true, the to-and-fro of messengers reflecting various royalist attempts to resolve their tactical impasse.

William's first move, as he closed up to the walls, was to send his nephew to clear up the situation in the castle. On the way, John Marshal met Geoffrey of Serland, one of Lady Nicola's knights. Not only was the castle still in royalist hands, Geoffrey showed John an entrance by which the host might enter – clearly the castle's West Gate, not a postern as some sources say. On his way back, John crossed some French laggards. It was a classic knightly encounter, except that they all attacked him at once. Undismayed, he met the leaders so boldly the others let him pass:

> *Well he made them see,*
> *He had come to seek them out*
> *And challenge them for his land.*

The spotlight then shifts abruptly to Peter des Roches, undermining the *History*'s chronology if not its credibility. The succession of events makes military sense, an individual patrol naturally preceding a reconnaissance in force. Seeking more information, the bishop led a party of crossbowmen down to the gate. Leaving them outside to cover his retreat, he entered the castle and met Geoffrey of Serland, 'who had been in a great fright'. The walls were shaken and tottering, rebel mangonels and perrières crushing people and buildings, smashing everything in the bailey to pieces. Urged to take cover, Peter hurried into 'the tower' to meet Lady Nicola. As the garrison's senior officer, the personal embodiment of the castle's resistance, she presumably occupied the Lucy Tower on the south-west wall, safer from bombardment than the Observatory Tower and better suited to her age and dignity. Perrières were no respecters of social status. The year after Lincoln, Simon de Montfort, the Albigensian Crusade's invincible leader, was killed by a stone shot by a group of Toulousaine women, his corpse buried without its head.

Peter des Roches enjoys mixed reviews. Roger of Wendover, no admirer of King John's servants, admits that he was 'learned in the art of war'. The *History* describes him as 'master counsellor to our people that day', on which basis modern historians anachronistically promote him to be William's chief of staff. Peter's biographer credits him with primary responsibility for the victory, a full-scale battle overtaxing the Marshal's intellectual capabilities. Brooks and Oakley are less enthusiastic, describing Peter as over-excited, dismissing his scouting exploits as invented. We might prefer to compare Peter to Brother Guérin, Bishop of Senlis, the erstwhile Hospitaller who led the French army in the opening stages of Bouvines, shaping events without diminishing Philip Augustus's overall responsibility.

Monastic sources took a dim view of the 'warrior at Winchester' – 'sharp at the accounting, slack at the scripture'. He found it hard to escape personal responsibility for the descent into civil war, the Waverley annalist styling him 'the principal agent of discord'. The *Tewkesbury Annals* punningly describe Peter as 'hard as a rock'. Militant bishops were always suspect, like Richard I's *bête noire* the Bishop of Beauvais. Roger of Howden showed little sympathy for the Bishop of Acre shot in the face at Hattin, who had placed more trust in his hauberk than divine protection. Peter's sulphurous reputation was entirely consistent with being given command of a troop of mercenary crossbowmen.

Having cheered Lincoln's chatelaine, Peter pursued his reconnaissance, sparking the battle's most vexed debate. Going out on foot through a *postiz* or postern, he spied an old gate:

> ... *of great antiquity*
> *and which joined the walls of the city*
> *with those of the castle.*
> ... *anciently closed up*
> *with stone and cement,*
> *so no-one could pass through* ...

The *History* says a merciful God showed Peter the gate. More likely somebody in the garrison pointed it out. Peter may have known already that it was there, having once been precentor at Lincoln Cathedral. Some historians, forgetting the poet's lack of archaeological training, have interpreted the words *grant antequité* as implying the gate was Roman. This is a difficult view to maintain. Archaeologists agree that the Roman West Gate had disappeared beneath the castle's western embankment years before the battle, to emerge briefly during building work in the 1830s. The Lucy Tower's south-west postern has similarly caused much confusion. Kate Norgate, a pioneering historian of Henry III's minority, thought Peter used the postern to explore the besiegers' front line in disguise, making a counter-clockwise circuit past the enemy siege engines in full swing, and so into Westgate. Professor Tout found the story so improbable he rejected it entirely.

The consensus today is that Peter found the Norman West Gate, which had been blocked up by persons unknown. Just beyond the north-west corner of the castle, West Gate would indeed connect the city walls with the castle, as the *History* says. Its location near the *Strugglers* public house at the junction of Burton Road and Westgate suits the direction of the royalists' approach. The *Dunstable Annals* specifically say that the Marshal 'approached Lincoln from the west side', the barons forming their line of battle 'outside the city on the west', while the *Barnwell Chronicle* specifies that the royalists 'broke in at the nearest gate'. Covered by archery from the castle walls, this would have been difficult for the rebels to watch closely. There is no evidence of any aperture in the city walls south-west of the castle, where the ground slopes away at an awkward angle for pedestrians, let alone horsemen. Leaving instructions to clear the barricade, Peter returned to the army with his news, laughing and joking that they should reserve him the bishop's palace, as he had found the way into Lincoln. Everyone was in an exalted humour, the troops singing, like the Crusaders at Antioch, as if they had won the battle already.

BREAK-IN

The battle narrative that follows below is a composite. Neither of our main sources tells the whole story. Roger of Wendover distinguishes two main events: a diversion created by Fawkes of Bréauté from the castle, while the royalist main body broke in through Newport Arch, and a single decisive encounter before the cathedral. The *History* adds William's entrance through the blocked gate, while downplaying the part played by Fawkes. According due prominence to the cathedral fighting, it additionally attributes the final decision to the joint defeat of a rebel counter-attack on Steep Hill by William and the Earl of Chester, who appears from nowhere on the enemy flank. Both sources then describe the defeated rebels' flight across High Bridge, and their escape to open country through the Bargate.

Our understanding of this complex battle would be greatly impoverished without the *History*. Its lucky survival in a single manuscript is a reminder of the slender basis of our knowledge, not just of this battle but of so many other medieval events. Taken with Roger of Wendover, the *History* suggests a four-stage battle: a break-in at three separate points; the melée before the cathedral; the repulse of the rebel counter-attack; their flight. The *Barnwell Chronicle's* summary is similar:

> *seeing* [the rebel withdrawal], *and thereby encouraged, [the royalists] boldly charged and broke in at the nearest gate, though not without loss.*
>
> *Meanwhile some of the king's army, having got in through the postern gate of the castle, fell on unexpectedly, and shouting came instantly to sword strokes. Astonished the other side, hardly able to move from the narrowness of the place, fought back less bravely. The royalists began to burst in on all sides. There was fighting in the city streets, and even on the cathedral porch itself; and the king's party coming off best, the others turned and fled.*

The initial attack came in three stages: the Earl of Chester's assault on Newport Arch; Fawkes' diversion; William's charge down

Westgate. Rejecting the *History*'s account of Bishop Peter's doings out of hand, Brooks and Oakley would shift the axis of the battle eastwards, so that William broke in at Newport Arch and Ranulf at East Gate. Carried away by scepticism, they ignore the additional difficulty of forcing not one but two closely defended gates, and neglect several telling pieces of evidence.

The Earl of Chester's vanguard would naturally run up against Newport Arch as it followed the retreating rebels, who had no other way of regaining the city. John Marshal's passage of arms suggests that his mission occurred before Chester's men sealed off the city's northern entrance. Modern accounts attribute Ranulf's initiative to impatience with William's cautious investigation of the defences. As in other respects, however, Chester was following family tradition. His grandfather had been repulsed from Newport Arch in 1147 with heavy loss. There is no evidence that Chester got any further. Roger of Wendover and the contemporary songster both say that the royalists broke in there, but fail to explain how. The Normans had updated the ancient Roman structure with square bastions and a new arch on the outside, creating a substantial defensive feature. This stood considerably higher than its modern remnant, which owes its squat appearance to an 8-foot (2.5m) rise in the street level. Newport was a tough nut to crack without ladders or axes.

Fawkes of Bréauté played the vital role in the battle's opening phase. While distracting attention from Lincoln's outer defences, he also inflicted significant material and moral damage on the enemy. The castle's large gates, East and West, made it the obvious way to enter the city, as Geoffrey of Serlant appreciated when he opened the castle's West Gate. The *History* gives only the briefest account of Fawkes' intervention, saying that he entered the castle immediately the bishop returned from his reconnaissance, and that his men were roughly handled. The brevity may be politic, the poet writing soon after Fawkes' disgrace in 1224. Alternatively, his informants may have been unaware of events within the walls. In any case, their purpose was to celebrate the Marshal, not rehabilitate some low-born *routier*.

Roger of Wendover is, for once, the better source, adding significant detail with none of his usual embroidery. Entering the castle's West Gate while the royalist main body was parading outside Newport, Fawkes swiftly deployed his crossbowmen on the ramparts to pick off the Franco-rebel horsemen in Castle Hill:

> *who, directing their death dealing missiles at the barons' chargers, laid horses and riders on the ground, so that in the twinkling of an eye they had reduced a great mass of knights and barons to foot soldiers.*

Seeing so many valuable prizes at their mercy, Fawkes and his companions dashed out through the East Gate, into the midst of the enemy. Surrounded by hostile 'legions', Fawkes was himself captured and dragged off, having to be rescued by his household knights and crossbowmen. One has to admire their nerve, going out to mix it with heavily armed knights who would have slaughtered their humble tormentors with no question of ransom. The *Dunstable Annals* swell the chorus of praise: 'Fawkes, like a brave knight indeed, brought in through the castle postern gate by the garrison, attacked the barons in the rear.'

Peter des Roches was unimpressed. 'They have not found the correct entrance,' he told the Marshal. 'Part of the wall is open for our use, and concealed from those inside. I will take you there; come on.' William was equally anxious to press the attack: 'God's Lance!' he said, 'Fetch my helmet.' The bishop was anxious not to fall into a trap, and insisted on sending forward ten scouts, two from each *bataille*, like the flankers thrown out by Napoleonic cavalry squadrons. The numbers conflict with the *History*'s order of battle, but the precaution belies idle stereotypes of knightly armies rushing blindfold to disaster.

Pressing on, William's men roughed up some sergeants fleeing the city, without appreciating the tactical advantage the discomfited *routiers* had bought them. While Fawkes was hogging the limelight on Castle Hill, another royalist party had been clearing the city's West Gate. Kate Norgate suggests that stones piled outside the doors were surreptitiously removed, out of sight of those within, until suddenly the gates were flung open. William now seems to have lost patience with the bishop's prudence. 'Errez!' he cried, 'Charge … you'll see them, they will soon be beaten. Shame upon anyone who hangs back any longer!' Bishop Peter continued to advocate cohesion over speed: 'Await your men,' he said, 'our enemies will fear us the more when they see us all together.' William spurred on, 'quicker than a falcon', his boldness infectious. A valet had to remind him about his helmet. An enemy at his lance point for the first time in fifteen years, William could hardly be expected to resist this God-given opportunity to relive the excitements of his youth.

Helmet laced on, William looked the finest of them all, as swift as a bird, a sparrowhawk or eagle. A famished lion, the same image the *History* uses for Richard at Gisors, could not have fallen upon his prey more quickly than the Marshal charging his enemies. Striking in with his spurs, he thrust three lance lengths into the opposing ranks, disrupting their formation, driving the press before him: *espresse* and *empresse* – dense and unyielding – a play on words that the *History* uses more than once. The bishop rode behind him, raising the old tournament cry: *Ça! Dex aïe al Marechal* – 'Here! God help the Marshal!' One casualty of the sudden irruption was the French perrière master. Mistaking royalists for his own people, he calmly loaded a stone into his machine:

> And someone who was behind him,
> Just as he said 'é!' twice made him miss another 'é!'
> For he cut his head off, without further ceremony.

The poet's sponsor has his own moment of glory, young William leading his men through the breach while his father was donning his helmet, his banner foremost in the melée. Together, the Marshals and the Earl of Salisbury drove the enemy before them, roughly down the line of today's Westgate street, past the castle's north wall towards St Paul's Church. Established on the site of the Roman forum, St Paul's stood near the southern end of Bailgate until its demolition in 1786. It was the logical place for the royalist main body to turn right to reach the upper city centre, between the cathedral and Castle Hill. The perrière master's immediately preceding death implies a Franco-rebel artillery position nearby, opposite the castle's north-east corner. As yet the area was unswept by the arrow slots of Cobb Hall, built after the war, perhaps in response to the sector's proven vulnerability. Archaeologists may have found the attackers' exact route, a curved lane which shadows the castle's northern embankment, passing either side of St Paul's before turning south-east towards St Mary's Cathedral.

As the royalists wheeled right, they passed *un moustier* or minster on their left. Kate Norgate believed that this was All Saints Church, described in 1114 as a *monasterium*, meaning minster. Brooks and Oakley denied this, claiming that other buildings blocked the view and 'a minster' must mean the cathedral, a fatal blow they thought for a Westgate entry point. The upper city was still relatively empty, however; All Saints and the newly discovered lane were adjacent, and if the poet meant the cathedral, he would surely have used the definite article, as he did unambiguously twenty-two lines later. We do better to accept the consensus, and imagine the Marshal clattering into Bailgate between St Paul's and All Saints with 200–300 knights, to confront the rebel's main body before the cathedral.

Dogfight

The Franco-rebel army appeared paralysed, 'in great fear and dismay'. Attacked from several directions, they were caught under a deadly hail of crossbow bolts, to which slow-acting perrières were no answer. Not every rebel remained spellbound. Robert of Ropelai, one of King John's witnesses at Runnymede, had turned traitor. Now Gilbert of Ghent's second-in-command, he counter-charged with such force that he broke his lance upon the Earl of Salisbury. William in turn struck him a sword blow between the shoulders that almost knocked him from his saddle. Fearing worse treatment to come, Robert slipped into a nearby house and hid upstairs as the cavalcade swept past.

As often happens, the attack became bogged down once the initial impetus was spent. The royalists were probably in full strength now, the Earl of Chester forcing Newport Arch as rebels nervous of being outflanked abandoned their positions. Fawkes was still in action, one of his household knights featuring in the melée's savage denouement. It was a struggle in slow motion, horses at a standstill while riders laid about them in fury:

> *They defended themselves most stoutly,*
> *While our people sought to injure them with all their might*
> *For they hated the men of France*

Many on both sides were wounded, bruised, crushed, or captured, for nobody looked for quarter: 'Everybody meant to fight'.

The melée's epicentre was unequivocally *devant le moustier* – before the cathedral – between its West Front and the later Exchequer Gate. The area had been a burial ground before the Norman Conquest, the Dunstable annalist confirming that the Count de la Perche defended himself in 'a certain cemetery'. The *Barnwell*

Chronicle places the fighting *in ipso atrio matricis ecclesiae* – on the very cathedral porch itself. Franco-rebel numbers should have proved superior to royalist fury. Roger of Wendover, however, seems to have discussed the battle with one of Fawkes' veterans. He accorded rare praise to the plebeian crossbowmen: 'by whose skill the horses on which the barons were sitting were mown down and slaughtered like pigs'. Unlike their noble riders, safe in their hauberks, the rebel horses were terribly vulnerable to crossbow bolts raining down from above.

Killing horses was common in battle, as opposed to tournaments, but it took time. Joinville's horse remained operational at Mansourah in 1250 after fifteen hits. William's pincer movement through the castle and down Bailgate, however, had trapped the rebels in a killing ground from which they could only escape by flight. Fawkes' crossbowmen on the castle ramparts could safely support William's charge from the flank without hitting their own people. The combination of missile and shock action had featured in the Marshal's deployment at Stowe, and in more than one of Richard I's battles; its reappearance at Lincoln suggests tactical foresight rather than a topographical fluke. For Roger, or his informant, it was the crossfire from the castle that wore down the barons' resistance, 'for when the horses fell ... their riders were taken prisoner, as there was no-one to rescue them'. Stunned from the fall, they were easy meat for royalist squires whose job it was to follow their lords into action to finish off disabled enemies or drag them off in chains, depending on their commercial value. Charles of Anjou detailed two varlets to mop up behind each mounted man at the battle of Benevento in 1266. Richard I made similar arrangements during his attack on a Saracen caravan in 1192.

The Marshal watched rebel resistance ebbing away. As his men pushed the enemy off the high ground to surround the French commander, he seized the count's bridle to take him prisoner:

… as seemed right
Because he was the most eminent man
Who was there among the French …

It would have been the crowning catch of William's career: the commander of a hostile army, representing the heir to the French throne, taken on the field of battle:

But first he was wounded
Through the eye-holes mortally
By a straight cruel sword thrust.

Reginald Croc, one of Fawkes' knights, had rudely interrupted the chivalric niceties. Offered quarter, Thomas refused to surrender to English traitors, and was neatly stabbed through the *oiliére* of his helmet. Thrust through the brain, the dying count dropped his reins, took his sword in both hands, and dealt William three great blows so powerful they left marks on his helmet, before falling backwards off his horse.

Everyone thought the count had fainted. William asked a knight to dismount and remove his helmet to give him air. Great was the distress when, on removing the helmet, Thomas was found stone dead. The grief may have been as insincere as William's for his brother in 1194. Thomas was related to the Marshals via an aunt who married a de la Perche in the 1140s. He left English estates to which the Earls of Pembroke and Salisbury would soon lay claim. As George Duby remarked, grief was a sentiment only indulged in by those due to inherit.

The moral ambiguity of de la Perche's death, liquidated by a mercenary while the Marshal tried to take him prisoner, once more reveals the clash between competing styles of war: professional ruthlessness against chivalric cupidity. The word *leidement*, used to qualify the fatal blow, means shabby and outrageous as well as cruel. Unlike Reginald who used the point or *estoc*, William is usually described as delivering great sweeping blows with the edge of his sword, no doubt hoping to disable his opponent, like the constable at Milli, while leaving them in a saleable condition. Croc's initiative could have had disastrous repercussions for the Marshal. Henry I survived a series of blows to the head at the battle of Brémule thanks to his helmet, but a similar onslaught in 1106 left Robert fitz Hamon with permanent brain damage. William remained clearheaded, however, directing operations and finding time to discuss the course of the battle with his son.

The count's death convinced the rebels they could no longer defend the graveyard, and they filed away towards Wigford down a street on their left, i.e. Steep Hill. A commander's elimination was usually decisive, as Bouvines and Muret demonstrated, but the rebels had other leaders. Men as inured to treason as Robert fitz Walter and Saer of Quincy were unlikely to give up prematurely. Part way down the slope, they found some more of their supporters, upon whom they rallied, though, as the *History* comments, they might have done better to keep moving.

The exact spot where the rebels reformed is debatable. Roger of Wendover is no help, omitting the episode entirely. Some historians put it beyond the Strait outside St Peter at Arches, at the bottom of the lower city just inside Stonebow. Others, led by Brooks and Oakley, prefer the relatively level junction of Christ's Hospital Terrace and Steep Hill, just beneath the Norman House attributed sometimes to Aaron of Lincoln, the prince of usurers. This would save the rebels remounting the slope, a challenge for unencumbered pedestrians let alone armoured men on jaded horses. It also agrees with the *History*'s statement that the rebel counter-attack was defeated near the top of the hill, as the royalists emerged between the church and castle.

The rebel advance began in good order, *serré & bataillé*, but soon ran into trouble. The Earl of Chester re-enters the *History*'s narrative on the rebel right flank, implying that he had found the breach in the city walls created to extend the cathedral eastwards, and was picking his way across the site of the unfinished Bishop's Palace. If the encounter took place near Stonebow, he must have got in through Clasketgate, raising similar access problems to the upper city gates. It is a pity we do not have Ranulf's commemorative poem, if one existed, to elucidate his part in the battle.

Outflanked by Chester's gallant band, the remaining French and their English associates were met frontally by the Marshal:

> *Our people charged them*
> *So vigorously they threw them*
> *Back down the hill by force*
> *Without caring which way they went.*

At this psychological moment, another royalist party led by Sir Alan Basset charged the rebels in rear. One of John's familiars, Alan had accompanied the Marshal to Flanders in 1197, and proposed the regency shortlist in November 1216. Now he decided the battle of Lincoln, sending the rebels tumbling down the hill in irremediable disarray.

DECISION

The rebels did not stop until High Bridge, where Ermine Street crosses the Witham and becomes High Street. Here they were outside the city, on soft ground rather than paved streets. So suddenly did they halt at the obstacle that the younger Marshal's standard bearer overshot and went into the river, horse and all. Pinned against the stream, the rebels expended their last reserves of strength. No-one had to look about for feats of arms, for everyone had their hands full. There was no time for the alehouse challenges of an evening. Even the strongest were exhausted with giving and taking blows.

This final passage of arms, on the point of victory, is the poem's dramatic climax, an opportunity for the poet to interrupt the narrative and ponder the nature of chivalry, justifying the pampered life style of its exponents, compared with the peasant's humdrum existence:

> *What is it to bear arms? Are they handled*
> *Like a sieve or riddle*
> *Or a mallet or an axe?*
> *No, it is much harder work,*
> *For he who labours takes a rest*
> *When he has worked a while.*
> *What then is chivalry?*
> *So rough and bold a thing*
> *And so very painful to learn*
> *That no-one unworthy dare undertake it.*

To emphasise the knightly calling's uniquely fearsome nature, the poet evokes the final struggle in all its sound and fury:

> *There might be seen great blows struck,*
> *Helmets ringing and echoing*
> *And lances flying in pieces,*
> *Knights captured and saddles emptied.*
> *There might be heard among the courtyards*
> *Great blows of swords and maces*
> *On helmets and arms,*
> *And knives and daggers drawn*
> *To stab horses to death:*
> *Horse covers were not worth a monk's habit.*

There might be seen hands stretched out
On many sides to seize bridles.
Some spurred on to help
Their companions and to rescue
Those they saw coming to grief,
But safety there was none.
There was the noise so very great
God's thunder might not be heard ...
When they cried, 'Royals, Royals!'

The struggle did not last long before the rebels turned and fled. The fugitives would not rally again. Among those taken were Saer of Quincy and Robert fitz Walter, leaving the rebels definitively leaderless.

The survivors' difficulties were not over. Their flight down High Street soon brought them to what the *History* called *la dererene porte* – Lincoln's back door – the only exit from the cul-de-sac formed by the Witham and Sincil Dyke. There were two gates, West Bargate on the main road and East Bargate off to one side. Primarily a commercial barrier, they were lightly fortified. The king allowed £20 from Lincoln's tax bill in 1228 against repairs to the walls and little towers of 'Vicford', near St Katherine's Hospital, which like modern hospitals lay just beyond urban limits. None of these structures survive, except the bridges, the Dyke itself, and the streetname 'Bargate'.

Our sources do not specify which Bargate the fleeing rebels sought to pass. One can imagine the leaders arriving directly at West Bargate, later arrivals forking left to avoid the tailback. This was aggravated by a circumstance so ridiculous that Brooks and Oakley claimed it was invented. Both the *History* and Roger of Wendover refer to the incident, however, and it is too bizarre to suppress. Both sources describe the gate as a flail, *fleel porte* or *flagellum* respectively. Sometimes translated as 'drawbridge' or 'portcullis', this term also suggests a vertical swing barrier, with an up and down action like a counter-weight stone thrower. Easier to raise than a portcullis, it allowed just one rider through at a time. Not only did individuals have to dismount to activate the mechanism, the *History* claims that a luckless cow had trapped herself in the gate, blocking the passage, and a great haul of knights was taken. One chivalric deed shone out amidst the rush to escape. A rebel knight was lifting his wife onto his saddle to get away, when a royalist told him to leave her behind. Putting her down, the knight dismounted his challenger with a well-directed lance blow to the chest, recovered the lady, and rode off.

Roger of Wendover reckoned that 200 rebel knights escaped to London, led by the Castellan of Arras, whom the *History* made the butt of a rude joke about rats. So frightened were the fugitives, they stopped neither by night nor day, nor in town nor house. Thinking every bush full of Marshals, they threw away everything that might slow them down. Where Holland Bridge was broken, they killed their horses to make a way across, as defeated English men-at-arms did after Bannockburn a century later. Holland Bridge was the causeway at Bridgend near Horbling, now the A52 Sleaford–Boston road. Its eastwards direction suggests that some rebels took King's Street, a Roman road that forks left off Ermine Street, heading for Peterborough. That they were still running, 25 miles (40km) south of Lincoln, indicates the complete moral dislocation of the defeated army.

AFTERMATH

The battle was all over by the 'ninth hour' – almost 4.00 pm. If the royalists spent all morning probing the defences, the fighting had lasted about four hours. This seems a long time for the small numbers engaged. Battles in the open, like First Lincoln, were often resolved 'in the twinkling of an eye'. The confined space at Second Lincoln, and the succession of partial engagements with pauses to regroup, ensured a more protracted affair.

Fatalities among the chivalry were absurdly low: Thomas de la Perche, Reginald Croc, and an unknown rebel sergeant. Matthew Paris added two more French knights, but he is late and unreliable. Neither of the baronial party's casualties could be buried on consecrated ground being excommunicate, so the count was laid in the hospital orchard near the scene of his army's final trial; the sergeant at a crossroads outside the city. The moral ambiguity of the count's death was underlined by Reginald's own killing, the only royalist casualty of note. The historical novelist Alfred Duggan suggests foul play spiced with class prejudice, William's retinue permitting the count's men to take revenge on the mercenary intruder.

The rebel foot did not get off so lightly, 'for the inhabitants of the towns through which they passed in their flight, went to meet them with swords and bludgeons, and, laying snares for them, killed numbers' (Wendover). The *Barnwell Chronicle* confirms Roger's account, referring to the fugitives' sufferings along the road, 'which was long and exceedingly dangerous, [being] either spoiled or indeed killed'. Enraged peasants exacted a terrible revenge on their demoralised tormentors, as they had after Northallerton, Fornham, and Alnwick.

Roger of Wendover said that the royalists restricted their pursuit for reasons of kinship. Prisoner lists do not support him. Gervase of Canterbury, the most extensive, named forty-six magnates, among them 'those who had most actively promoted the war' (*Waverley*). Eight were members of the committee of Twenty-Five, now reduced to half strength following the earlier deaths of Eustace of Vesci and Geoffrey of Mandeville. The rebel cause had been decapitated. Anonymous of Béthune commented that nearly all the great men of England had been taken. John Marshal did especially well, capturing seven barons flying banners. Most sources claimed that 300 unnamed knights were taken, a figure that the Barnwell chronicler inflated to 380, 'though of sergeants, burgesses and the middling sort of men there was no count'. About 200 knights reached London. To eliminate over half the enemy's mounted strength and most of their foot in a single day was not bad going.

Record evidence reveals no inhibitions about extorting ransoms. Some prisoners were held into the 1220s, compelled to pay such high ransoms they could no longer fulfil their social duties as knights. This was not just the behaviour of hard-faced castellans with garrisons to pay. Nicolas of Stuteville, one of Gervase of Canterbury's list, paid the Marshal 1,000 marks. Among the hardest bargainers was John Marshal. The *History* made no bones about the material advantages of victory:

> *No knight intent*
> *On gain or taking knights*
> *Could miss doing so that day.*

Lincoln was given over to plunder. The citizens had backed the wrong side, as in 1141, and were 'pillaged to the last farthing' (Wendover). The *History* says little about this. The deliberate sack of one of England's most prosperous cities would not enhance its hero's image. Roger of Wendover covered the episode at some length, and other sources confirm his story. Churches, including the cathedral, were a particular target, partly as traditional depositories of treasure, and also 'because the clergy of the city had sided with the rebels, and [were] hence excommunicate and their churches defiled' (*Barnwell*). The royalists came prepared with axes and hammers to break open chests and store rooms, 'seizing the gold and silver in them, clothes of all colours, women's ornaments, gold rings, goblets, and jewels' (Wendover). Bishop Peter's successor as precentor lost 11,000 marks in silver ingots, an immense sum.

The disorder was soon over, compared with the two days and nights when Wellington's army ran riot in Badajoz in 1811. After six hours, King Henry's peace was declared, and everyone 'ate and drank amidst mirth and jollity' (Wendover). The worst aspect of the sack was the accidental loss of life when a large number of townswomen took to the boats in Brayford Pool with their children, servants, and property, and capsized the over-loaded craft. The disaster was a sad conclusion to what became known as *Nundinae Lincolniae* – Lincoln Fair. Roger of Wendover said it was named in derision of Louis and the barons, but the term was commonly associated with tournaments and other military gatherings. Stephen banned *militares nundinas* at York at Easter 1142 as a distraction from fighting Matilda. When Richard beat the French at Gisors, the poet compared the press to a market or fair. William the regent could not stay to enjoy the festivities. Once the prisoners were secured, he rode straight back to Nottingham without eating, to carry news of the victory to the king and legate. This final 36-mile (58km) ride would have taken him seven hours at a regulation 'trot and walk', not arriving before 11.00 pm at the earliest. For a septuagenarian who had been in the saddle for nineteen hours and led a cavalry charge, it had been a long if satisfactory day.

VII

THE BATTLE OF SANDWICH AND THE TREATY OF KINGSTON

The Fair at Lincoln did not end the war. Some deny that it changed anything, claiming that the Dauphin's diplomatic difficulties guaranteed the eventual ruin of his cause. Strategic decisions, however, follow tactical outcomes on the ground: loss of personnel, the exchange of territory, the destruction of material resources. At the very least, Lincoln confirmed Louis's weakness. More realistically, it represented a decisive shift. Before Lincoln, the royalists had never risked confronting Louis in the open; afterwards he dared not face them again.

The only land battle in a war of raids and sieges, Lincoln was a triumph following the disappointments of the winter and spring. It vindicated the Marshal's strategy and consolidated his authority. William had appealed to the Almighty, and God had declared in his favour. Roger of Wendover shared the *History*'s providential view of the Franco-rebel defeat: 'unless they were corrected … men would say, "There is no God".' Popular songs confirm the battle's electric effect upon public opinion. Rebel defections shot up from almost zero in May to 150 in June and July, including the Earls of Warenne and Arundel. As long as Louis controlled London, however, he remained a menace.

A new stalemate set in for a brief period, but the equilibrium was deceptive, soon upset by another startling victory, fought beyond all precedent on the open sea. The battle of Sandwich on St Bartholomew's Day, Thursday 24 August, was decisive in every sense. William was less directly involved than at Lincoln, but he was no less responsible for the outcome, steering to victory in the face of opposition from enemies and friends. The Treaty of Kingston in September embodied his achievement of the war's central aim, the expulsion of the French and the establishment of Henry III's authority across the realm.

AFTER THE FAIR

The morning after a battle is no time for renewed efforts, as the most energetic commanders have discovered. Physical exhaustion, emotional reaction, the disruption of tactical units – all conspire to hinder immediate exploitation. The ruthless pursuit following Napoleon's victory at Jena was a unique event in the emperor's career. Inertia was more usual. Medieval armies with their informal command structures were especially prone to such checks.

William himself wasted no time. Despite his exertions, he was back in Lincoln on Sunday 21 May, to discuss the next move. Some wanted to march on London, others to bypass the capital and raise the siege of Dover. The Earl of Chester rode to Mountsorrel to fulfil his personal victory conditions by razing the castle to the ground. In the absence of agreement, the Marshal, 'who knew more about war, and had seen more of it' (*History*), suggested a pause to secure the profits of victory. Everyone should lodge their prisoners in safety, and present themselves refreshed at Chertsey, at an agreed date. With access to either bank of the Thames via the Roman bridge at Staines, Chertsey made a good jumping-off point for further operations. Occupying a central position on London's western approaches, just south of the river, it covered Angevin positions in the Thames Valley, isolated French garrisons in Hampshire, and menaced the capital. The pause to secure prisoners was no chivalric nicety, but good business practice. A knight's first duty, as William knew from Drincourt, was to make a profit.

The Dauphin had returned to Dover on Friday 12 May, setting up his trébuchet on the high ground north-west of the castle. Progress was slow, however. His siege engines caused little damage, and reinforcements from Calais were driven back by bad weather, or intercepted by English vessels sailing from Romney, 'four score *nefs* [ships] large and small including twenty great ships all embattled and rigged for fighting'. The Monday following, the English captured eight French ships, and massacred their crews. The knights were clapped in the bilges, 'where they suffered pains enough' (Anonymous). The English then anchored off Dover to prevent food or other help from reaching the Dauphin.

Thursday 25th brought news of Lincoln. Once more, Anonymous of Béthune allows us to look over the hill, fleshing out imaginary English accounts of Louis's reaction. Advised to withdraw to London and summon help, he dismantled his trébuchet, but awaited confirmation before moving further away from home. Six score French ships fought their way past the English next Monday, 'but all were sergeants, merchants, or seamen: of knights there were only eighteen'. Vexed at this meagre assistance, Louis despatched letters home requesting help, and retreated to London, having burnt the rest of his ships:

> For he greatly feared and suspected
> Lest the Royals surprised it,
> Or took it by force
> Or that they should come and attack him.

Louis reached London on 1 June, lodging in the Archbishop of Canterbury's vacant Palace at Lambeth, 'not venturing forth in any direction, nor launching any risky attacks' (*Barnwell*). All but one of the city gates were blocked for added security.

The *History* savoured the imagined despair of Philip Augustus on learning of John's death and the Marshal's taking charge: 'nothing is to be gained in England, for the land will be well defended by the wisdom of that *prud'homme*'. Louis would soon be chased out, since the Marshal had taken the matter in hand. Philip Augustus had his own problems. Recently reconciled to the Pope after a protracted dispute over his matrimonial entanglements, he was unwilling to court renewed papal displeasure by openly supporting his son.

The prime mover in French rescue attempts was the Dauphin's wife. Blanche of Castile, mother of Saint Louis, was the most impressive of Henry II's grandchildren. Like the Marshal's countess in Leinster, Blanche took the lead in her husband's absence, attracting a barbed tribute from Matthew Paris who compared her to the Babylonian Queen Semiramis: 'a woman in sex but a man in counsel'. The *History* describes Blanche scouring the cities of France for men and money, which she did so effectively that had all the troops raised come to London, they would have conquered the entire kingdom. Her efforts were confined largely to Louis's County of Artois, however. Despite covert subsidies from her father-in-law, money was short. Merchants and seamen were unpaid from the expedition of May 1216. Some were still awaiting their money in the 1230s, four years after Louis's death. Nobles who had accompanied Louis complained of their poor reward. The disappointing reinforcements of 29 May were a clear reflection of this lack of means.

The royalists approached Chertsey on 6 June, billeting their troops in the country roundabout, 'for they well thought that Louis and his people, who little trusted the people of London, would not dare leave the city alone' (Anonymous). The royalists, however:

> ... rising up everywhere, grew stronger beyond all measure. Having occupied, captured and fortified its approaches on all sides, they approached London with a strong force, as if to besiege Louis in the city. And while those with Louis were preparing to defend themselves, some having interceded that there might be peace between the parties, set off by turns and met in hope of peace. Louis, however, put it off, on account of the assistance he was expecting from overseas, and the royalists so they might more freely ravage the possessions of those who were on the other side.
>
> (Barnwell)

The motivation behind the deadlock was not entirely cynical. The Archbishop of Tyre led a delegation of abbots to Chertsey on 12 June, negotiating terms not dissimilar to those agreed three months later. Louis, however, would not abandon his clerical allies to the legate's vengeance. Exploratory talks with the Londoners also collapsed, the citizens fearing to be pillaged like Lincoln. Egged on by inflammatory sermons, they renewed homage to Louis, and remained obdurate. Vexed at the legate's intransigence, the royalist host dispersed, William returning to Oxford with the king. To maintain political pressure, he instructed sheriffs to have the Charter read out in public, and look to its implementation. Louis moved into the Tower for safety. Post-Lincoln defections proved a mixed blessing in the west, the Welsh reacting violently to Reginald of Braose's changing sides. Llewelyn ravaged Brecon and Gower, and besieged William's Flemish tenants in Haverfordwest, extracting hostages and the promise of 1,000 marks come Michaelmas. William visited Goodrich and Chepstow, but had little time to do more.

Meanwhile, Blanche gathered her forces: 100 knights said the Anonymous; 300 said Roger of Wendover, enough to replace the losses at Lincoln. The Marshal was greatly distressed, pondering deeply how he might save the kingdom. The king was young and lacked money; most of the magnates sided with Louis, and now the choice barons of France were coming all equipped to take the land. Later generations of strategists might have hoped to intercept the enemy at sea. In 1217, however, a naval solution was an unprecedented and risky option.

THE WAR AT SEA

The Anglo-Danish kings of England had maintained powerful fleets, which their post-Conquest successors allowed to decay. When threatened by Viking raiders, they massed troops on the beach, or fortified estuaries. During the Anarchy, invaders came and went as they pleased. Navies require a buoyant economy and strong central government, the antithesis of Anglo-Norman feudalism. As Scandinavia lapsed into chaos, however, no obvious threat demanded an English navy. Normandy and its Flemish allies controlled both sides of the Channel, while poor communications hindered the interception of invasion fleets. It was better to catch invaders on dry land, like Harald Hardrada at Stamford Bridge in 1066, or the Flemings at Fornham. Bad weather was a more certain deterrent to overseas adventures than warships. Memories of the contrary winds that frustrated the Young King in 1174 may have comforted William in 1217.

What Anglo-Norman kings needed was a cross-Channel ferry service. This was assured by the king's *snecca*, an updated Viking longship, or by hired merchantmen. The preferred route, before the loss of Normandy, was between Barfleur and either Southampton or Portsmouth – originally Portchester, the Roman fortress at the head of Portsmouth harbour. Henry II had sailed from Barfleur to Southampton in 1174 at the height of the Young King's Revolt. Portsmouth, as modern ferry operators know, is nearer France than Southampton, a powerful tide carrying ships in and out of the land-locked harbour twice daily. Richard I and William sailed thence to Barfleur in 1194. When John left Normandy for the last time, he did so from Barfleur, reaching Portsmouth two days later.

The *grant navie* assembled by Richard I for the Third Crusade was a new departure in English naval affairs. The greatest royal expedition since the Norman Conquest, it comprised 170 sailing ships and thirty-six oared galleys. More significant for the long-term recovery of English naval power was the charter that Richard granted Portsmouth, a fishing village by the harbour entrance. Like Richard, John kept his galleys and other naval stores there, probably near the future Gunwharf, convenient for Richard's royal palace at the top of the High Street. John ordered a strong wall for his *exclusa* at Portsmouth in 1212, usually interpreted as a sluice gate, implying a wet dock or basin. The following year it was to Portsmouth that John directed shipping mobilised against the French invasion threat. Besides impressing civilian ships, John built a fleet of galleys. He had fifty-two in 1205, distributed around the southern coast from East Anglia to Ireland. Among the squadron commanders was William of Wrotham, 'keeper of the sea ports', a prototype Lord of the Admiralty.

We may gauge William's opinion of naval operations from his comparison of the problems of regency with being embarked on the open sea, unable to find shore or bottom. His active career ended before John recreated English naval power. William's maritime experience as a passenger suggests some of the risks involved. Hurrying to meet his new bride in 1189, he suffered a painful leg injury when the ship's deck collapsed, leaving him clinging onto a cross timber. Maintenance was low priority. Roger of Howden explained one shipwreck by the drying out of the ship's timbers, which let in the sea. We know of William's first visit to Ireland in 1201 from his foundation of a monastery in gratitude for not being drowned on the way. Four years later, Portsmouth provided a backdrop for political shipwreck, when William refused to accompany John to Poitou. Documentary evidence shows them in residence at Portchester, but the *History* specifies the location of their confrontation as *Portesmue*, beside the harbour and the open sea, perhaps during an official visit to the nascent royal dockyard.

John's naval build-up suffered two major constraints. No medieval government had the administrative and financial resources to maintain a permanent navy, and the necessary infrastructure. John's ships and facilities disappeared under his impoverished successor. Secondly, most shipping came from private sources. There were three main ship types.

The most significant was the great ship or *nef*, from the Latin *navis*. Sometimes known as cogs, they were Europe's standard ocean-going vessel, capable of transporting horses and even a royal elephant. Possessing a deep hull and high freeboard, such vessels were stable enough to mount castellated fighting platforms fore and aft. F.W. Brooks, in his study of Angevin naval forces, reckoned that English examples ran to 47 feet (14m) long and 15 feet (4.5m) abeam, with a master, twenty men, and a boy or two to send aloft. They stood high out of the water with several decks and a three-storey after castle, a great advantage in a sea fight, allowing their crew to shoot or leap down onto the decks of lower craft. Flat-bottomed and driven by a large square sail on a single mast stepped well forward, *nefs* steered with difficulty and went rapidly to leeward, i.e. downwind. Masts were massive structures, 100 feet (30m) high, stout enough to carry the heavy sail and its supporting yard, as well as a round fighting top for several men armed with rocks and other projectiles. The 1217 Channel fighting suggests such that vessels could tack, but had little capacity for beating into the wind. Foul winds were ridden out at anchor, of which a dozen might be carried. The *History* makes particular reference to anchors, 'for lying off harbour', in the prelude to Sandwich.

King John had some great ships, but most royal ships were galleys, also described as *sneccas* or snakes. They were distinct from the Mediterranean galley, up to 130 feet (40m) long, built for speed with one row of 16–30 oars a side, each pulled by a single oarsman. Galleys were low in the water, incapable of attacking a *nef*, as the *History*'s description of Richard's fleet shows:

> *Many great ships there were embattled with castles*
> *And richly equipped,*
> *Manned by such fine crews*
> *They feared no galleys*
> *Nor hostile people who might come against them …*

Tactical inferiority was confirmed by the lack of an iron beak. Classically influenced chroniclers thought galleys should have one, but there is no financial or physical evidence for such items. The best a galley could do in a melée was to smash the rail along an opponent's side that supported his oars. When Richard's galleys encountered a large Muslim ship off Acre, they allegedly employed a diver to bore holes below her waterline, a tactic more appropriate to a folksong than a naval battle.

Galleys usually operated under sail, their faster lines making them invaluable for reconnaissance, explaining their dispersal around the coast as an early-warning screen. John despatched Geoffrey de Lacy with six galleys to hunt pirates off the Irish coast in 1210. Independence of the wind when under oars suited them to amphibious and coastal operations. John sent twenty to ravage the Gwynedd coast in 1213. The task force that recovered the Channel Islands from the French in 1205 included five, accompanied by three great ships. The Marshals operated their own galleys, presumably from the Wye at Chepstow. William's son Richard used his to rescue a fugitive Hubert de Burgh in 1233. The Marshals' successor, Gilbert of Clare, dominated the Bristol Channel in the 1260s with three *naves piracticas*, 'which in the vernacular are called *galyas*' (Thomas Wykes).

The least significant craft in size though not numbers were known as *bastiaux* or boats. Great ships towed or carried several, as suggested by the presence of two with a great ship and four galleys at Portsmouth in 1228. Of uncertain fighting power, they acted as auxiliaries, carrying English boarding parties across the shallows at Dam in 1213. Some may have been significant fighting units: the loss of a *lonc batiel* or longboat off Rye in February 1217 shook the English fleet enough to let the French lift the blockade. Anonymous of Béthune included several such craft in the English order of battle at Sandwich.

Arms and weapons at sea were generally the same as ashore. The absence of horses levelled the playing field between knights and sergeants, the latter's less elaborate armour enabling them to move more easily around decks. Men owning a twelfth of a ship at Bayonne were expected to have iron mail, other seamen a gambeson and iron cap. The absence of horsemen favoured missile weapons, 'bows, arbalests and quarrels, sharp pointed and swift', says the *History* apropos of Richard's fleet. The thirteenth-century *Romance of Eustace the Monk* describes the English at Sandwich using 'great bows and arbalests', while Roger of Wendover refers to the death-dealing missiles of the archers and crossbowmen, echoing his earlier recognition of the common soldier's role at Lincoln. Matthew Paris's illustration of Sandwich shows a longbow, drawn to the ear, and a staff sling. Maritime contracts confirm the importance of missile weapons, particularly crossbows whose operators could shelter behind bulwarks to reload. Some ships carried the more powerful two-footed variety of crossbow, whose extra range would have been useful at sea. Numbers specified vary from a couple to twenty per ship, with thousands of quarrels.

Naval specialities included *rochets* or hooks to cut the enemy rigging, and *triboli* – triple pointed iron booby traps – to scatter on his decks. Financial records for 1213 show soap being issued to render enemy decks slippery, but no payments for the quick lime reported at Sandwich. Siege engines sometimes appear during naval actions in confined waters during siege operations, as at Rye, never on the open sea where target and platform were in constant motion. The trébuchet featured at Sandwich was cargo. None of the weapons available to thirteenth-century seamen could sink an enemy ship. Battles were resolved by hand-to-hand combat following a preparatory barrage to sow confusion across the enemy decks. As in Nelson's day, ships were valuable prizes, to be captured not sunk.

John's naval renaissance was made necessary by the French eruption along the Channel's far coast. The loss of Normandy and the French acquisition of Flanders shifted the maritime focus to the Dover–Calais narrows, the shortest route between England and the continent, and the traditional route for foreign invasions, from Julius Caesar to William the Conqueror. When the Marshal emerged from internal exile in 1213, he found King John awaiting the French at Barham Down, near Dover. The maritime struggle, of which Sandwich formed the last act, was more amphibious than naval. Troop movements by sea were common, but encounters between hostile squadrons a rarity. Ships struggled to beat to windward or ride out a storm. John's precocious attempt to intercept the Dauphin's fleet in April 1216 fell victim to the weather. It was easier to destroy enemy ships in harbour, as the Earl of Salisbury did in the first major action of the war. Dam was an old-style coastal battle, a surprise attack on a fleet drawn up along the beach. It was the sort of blow Harold's ships might have delivered against William the Conqueror, had the latter not won a swift victory ashore.

The *History*'s enthusiastic reaction to the plunder at Dam is a reminder of thirteenth-century frugality. Standard naval stores – corn, bacon, and wine – drew the comment that 'never before came such booty from France to England, since King Arthur went to conquer it'. Not content with his partial destruction of the French invasion fleet, Salisbury lay off Walcheren until Philip Augustus completed the job by burning the rest and walking home. Philip's official biographer commented, 'The ways of the sea were not well known to our Frenchmen', which seems hard on seamen from the Biscay coast. The English return voyage was no pleasure cruise, fierce gales scattering Salisbury's ships as far as Northumberland and Scotland.

Raids and transportation escalated into deliberate attempts to assert command of the Channel. John's bad luck in April 1216 was compounded by the subsequent loss of dockyards, the collapse of royal finances, and defections of key personnel, as William of Wrotham joined the rebels. Louis, or rather Eustace the Monk, controlled the seaways for nine months, allowing French reinforcements to come and go at will. Not until February 1217 did the Cinque Ports return to the Angevin camp, perhaps resenting the Monk's depredations, allowing royalist shipping to contest command of the narrow seas.

Maritime forces were central to William's Sussex campaign. While the Marshal was away at Lincoln, Philip of Aubigny continued to dispute the straits, hampering Louis's renewed siege of Dover, not just by blockading the port, but twice offering battle in mid-Channel, on 15 and 29 May. The latter occasion saw a two-phase chase action, resembling the tactics used three months later at Sandwich. Menaced by superior numbers of French ships, the English retreated until the French gave up, whereupon the English went about and fell upon the enemy rear, taking eight stragglers before they reached Dover. Not only was sea power a crucial element in the four-year cross-Channel confrontation, naval warfare had evolved a new tactical form which at Sandwich would prove decisive.

SANDWICH

The Marshal was not unaware of Blanche's preparations. Sometimes English ships sailed close enough to Calais to shoot at the French sailors as they made ready. Once the French came out, compelling the lightly manned English ships to scuttle home. English monastic sources put the French fleet between sixty and 100 ships. The Anonymous splits the difference with eight score *nefs* great and small, including ten large ones, four manned by knights and six by sergeants, 'and in the other small ones were the harness [i.e. armour] and merchandise'. The *History*'s claim that there were 300 French ships is exaggerated. We may imagine the fleet as ten capital units convoying seventy smaller supply ships.

Orders of battle are easily confounded with total casualties. The *Melrose Chronicle* may reproduce the expedition's military complement in its statement of French 'losses': 125 knights, thirty-three crossbows, 146 mounted sergeants, and 833 foot sergeants. The total force bears comparison with the Franco-rebel army at

Lincoln. Mounted numbers (271) resemble those given by the Anonymous and Roger of Wendover (100 and 300 respectively), assuming that Roger conflated knights and mounted sergeants. Either thirty-two or thirty-six knights were captured in the flagship, leaving thirty in each of the other three knightly manned vessels. Knights sailed together to escape the insolence of ship masters. Wendover boasted that the French were unused to fighting at sea, but this is jingoistic bravado. French national sea power was of recent growth, but the sailors were heirs to centuries of cross-Channel bickering, and recently encouraged by the English setback off Calais.

Military command was in the hands of Robert of Courtenay. Castellan of Reigate Castle, Robert was a close associate of Louis, becoming royal butler on the Dauphin's accession and accompanying him on the Albigensian Crusade. Also in the flagship was the younger William des Barres, a veteran of Muret, often confused with his father of the same name. Navigation was entrusted to Eustace the Monk, who 'had taken much trouble over this business; many times had crossed the sea, as one who knew all about it' (Anonymous). English sources were less enthusiastic, describing him as a frightful pirate and turncoat to both sides (*Dunstable*). Matthew Paris called him *viro flagitiosissimo*, an utter villain:

> *Who never missed any chance*
> *To do all the harm in his power ...*
> *No worse trickster could be.*

> *(History)*

The Barnwell chronicler summed up Eustace's career as 'inclining sometimes to one side or the other, as fortune willed, [he] had for many days previously caused much trouble on the sea and coast, as much this side of the sea as the other, and also seized certain islands by force'. English records and the *Romance* expand the monastic epitome, sometimes straying into fairy tale.

Eustace was born about 1170, the son of a Boulonnais knight, inheriting the family name *le Moine*. He did pursue a monastic career at first, the *Romance* alleging that Eustace had gambled away abbey funds in the alehouse. A Laon chronicler described his progress 'from black monk to blacker demoniac'. Medieval humour enjoyed ascribing clerical connections to doubtful characters. One of the knights who praised William's prowess at the St Brice tournament in 1166 was nicknamed Bon-Abbé de Rougé; he once spent a period as an outlaw, much as Eustace would do. Eustace's education also included a spell at Toledo, a focus of Arab scholarship and notorious hotbed of necromancy. Here he is said to have acquired the magical skills behind his naval expertise, studying the zodiac and learning to foretell the future. It is easy to see how puzzled landsmen might interpret an ability to forecast the Channel's ever shifting tidal flows as a black art.

Unjustly driven into outlawry, Eustace became the anti-hero of a series of Robin Hood-style adventures, blinding and mutilating his enemies, reversing his horse shoes to baffle pursuers, and being offered a groat (4d) for sexual favours while disguised as a woman. Clerical transvestism is a typical feature of medieval humour, previously occurring in William Longchamps's misadventures. Having made the Boulonnais too hot for himself, Eustace took service with King John, becoming another of his alien mercenaries. Eustace recovered the Channel Islands for the Crown, 'leaving nothing to burn either in castle or manor' (*Romance*), being rewarded with estates in Norfolk. Adept at helping himself at others' expense, he made Sark a pirate nest, and built up connections with Winchelsea, which returned to haunt him. John's rapprochement with the Count of Boulogne before Bouvines drove Eustace into the arms of Philip Augustus, now in need of naval experts. The *Romance* describes his escape disguised as a minstrel, but the Dunstable chronicler said that Eustace left in style, taking five galleys with him. He also suffered from John's hostage-taking, his daughter being held at Wilton Abbey, where she may have died.

Perhaps for this reason, Eustace took a leading role in the naval war against England, gaining such an ascendancy over the popular imagination that his imaginary exploits eclipsed those of the strait-laced Dauphin. Eustace features significantly on at least six occasions: guiding the French fleet to Dam, ferrying military aid to English rebels, retaking the Channel Islands for the French, twice transporting Louis across the Channel, and helping rescue him from Rye.

The French could hardly disguise their preparations to rescue the Dauphin. The Angevins had a tradition of intelligence-gathering. John's spies, 'of whom he had the best' (Wendover), had warned him of previous French expeditions, and helped him evade pursuit in East Anglia in 1216. William, said the Anonymous, was well aware of Blanche's preparations at Calais. On his advice, the king deputed Philip of Aubigny and John Marshal to guard the maritime approaches with seamen of the Cinque Ports and other forces. William moved closer to the scene in mid-August. Leaving Reading on the 14th, he marched via Farnham, back in English hands, and Lewes, reaching Romney on the 19th. Command was shared, as at Lincoln, leading to similar disputes over responsibility for the success. The debate has been fuelled by naval historians' failure to utilise the extensive range of contemporary material. Few medieval sea battles are so well documented, including three independent accounts based on eyewitness testimony. Their duplication suggests an underlying accuracy. The battle was clearly perceived as a major event, a providential deliverance from foreign invasion, comparable from our point of view with the Spanish Armada, Trafalgar, and the Battle of Britain.

The usual port of call is Roger of Wendover, supplemented by Matthew Paris, who for once provides genuine additional information, based on Hubert de Burgh's reminiscences. Available before the *History* was rediscovered, Paris has dominated naval historiography of the battle ever since he formed the basis of the account of the battle in the Victorian *Dictionary of National Biography*. Paris, with his customary anti-Marshal bias, suppressed the part played by William and others of greater contemporary significance than Hubert de Burgh, whom Matthew hailed as *victor miraculosus*. The new edition of the *Dictionary of National Biography* casts doubt on de Burgh's central role as retailed by Wendover and Paris, but the latter's partial account appears in the *Navy Records Society* collection of *British Naval Documents*, and continues to form the basis of recent discussions of the action.

The *History's* author, as at Lincoln, struggled to reconcile his several informants' accounts, providing a bumpy but invaluable narrative. Replete with new information, it corrects Paris and enriches our understanding of the battle. Anonymous of Béthune, changing sides as often as Eustace, contrived a ringside seat in the entourage of the Earl of Warenne, who had abandoned Louis in June. As well informed as ever, Anonymous confirms much of the *History's* account while avoiding its excessive focus on the fate of Eustace. Monastic notices of the battle share that weakness, as does the *Romance*, of which Sandwich provides the dramatic conclusion.

The true hero of Sandwich, apart from Eustace, was the Marshal. Without him there would have been nobody to fight the battle. Hastening to the coast, William summoned mariners from the Cinque Ports and elsewhere, winning them over with gifts and promises of political and financial advantage. Trusting his word, they went straight to Sandwich to refit their ships with new rigging, good anchors, and strong cables, to fight the French and bring down their pride. Two factors complicated the Marshal's task. The mariners still resented the wrongs King John had done them, and they were shaken from their recent mishandling off Calais. The *History* recounts this setback as if it occurred on the morning of the 24th, immediately before the battle, throwing the narrative into confusion. It makes more sense as a misplaced reference to the earlier defeat mentioned above. Leaderless and fearing the enemy's superior numbers, the English shipmen had shamelessly taken to their boats and fled, leaving their ships under full sail. William restored the mariners' spirits, saying they would have knights and sergeants, 'valiant, daring, and bold', and promising to restore their *franchices* – the privileges John had slighted. William offered persuasive material inducements besides. The king would replace any ships lost in action, while prizes would be the property of their captors. In return the seamen pledged that there would be no slacking on their side, whether they were taken or killed.

William did not take command at sea. His men insisted he remain ashore, for who would defend the country if he were taken or killed? Matthew Paris claims that Hubert de Burgh took the lead. William and the Bishop of Winchester, two of Matthew's least favourite people, had both declined, making the improbable reply, 'We are not sea soldiers, nor pirates, nor fishermen, go yourself and die'. The secular narratives show that Hubert was just one among several captains. Philip of Aubigny had held the king's commission in the Channel, while Hubert was confined to Dover Castle, and carried news of the victory to Henry after Sandwich, an operational commander's customary responsibility. He disappears from subsequent accounts, overshadowed by the justiciar. Richard of Chilham, King John's bastard son by the Earl of Warenne's sister, also commanded a ship full of knights and sergeants, flying his uncle's banner, who, like the Marshal, remained ashore. Sea warfare was a young man's sport. Philip and Richard played the leading role in the day's decisive moment, the capture of the French flagship. Several authorities make Richard responsible for the death of Eustace. Hubert reappears with his prizes, when the fighting was over. Justiciar of England and William's successor as secular head of the minority government, Hubert's naval exploits have attracted natural but unjustified attention.

Estimates of English numbers show rare consensus. The *History* says that William assembled twenty-two *nefs*, great and small, chosen for strength, richly furnished with both arms and good men. Besides the three ships whose captains appear above, the Marshal's sergeants manned a cog, whose height proved decisive. Everyone else made what shift they could. Whether this indicates inadequate material resources or defective poetic memory is unclear. Other estimates range from 'sixteen well armed ships with twenty accompanying *naviculi* – lesser ships' (Paris), via 'xviii large nefs and several boats' (Anonymous), to 'twenty ships and four galleys and two great ships' (*Worcester*). Roger of Wendover spoke of a few English ships, 'which between galleys and ships did not exceed forty'. Total numbers favoured the French, while the English had more major units. The idea of an inferior English fleet resurfaced in the nineteenth century, as part of the Royal Navy's evolving foundation myth. Seamanship and fighting spirit were supposed to have compensated for numbers, just as they would in the Armada's defeat 371 years later. Vice-Admiral Rodgers of the US Navy suggests that in combat power the English fleet at Sandwich outclassed the French, with odds in capital ships of three-to-two or even two-to-one.

William spent the eve of battle at Canterbury, safer for the king than the coast, enjoying good roads to Dover and Sandwich. There was little sleep. Everyone was ready at day break (about 5.00 am) to ride the 12 miles (19km) down to Sandwich. The Marshal travelled with Philip of Aubigny, Richard fitz John, and the Earl of Warenne, besides the younger Marshal, and too many valiant bachelors to name. The rank and file were already on board, William's sergeants taking over their cog the evening before. Maintaining a brisk War Office trot of 7m/h (11.5km/h), the top brass would arrive before 8.00 am, supporting the Worcester annalist's statement that the struggle lasted from early morning nearly to vespers.

Some modern historians talk of the battle of Dover, perhaps misled by Matthew Paris' partiality for Hubert de Burgh, the constable there. William Laird Clowes in his pioneering history of the Royal Navy places the action off the South Foreland, between Dover and Deal. The *History's* repeated references to *Sanwiz*, however, are supported by copious literary and circumstantial evidence. Sandwich was the victor's headquarters, the conventional source of a battle's name, hence Waterloo rather than La Belle Alliance. The Anonymous and *History* both describe the royalists embarking there, as do the *Worcester Annals*. Gervase of Canterbury, an eminently local source, says that 'many French nobles with a great army were defeated and captured by our people at sea near Sandwich – *juxta Sandwicum*'. That careful historian, the Barnwell chronicler, states that 'the royalists gave battle to Eustace the Monk, coming with all his fleet, not far from the Isle of Thanet', i.e. beyond Sandwich when heading northwards from Dover. It was to Sandwich that the victors returned after the battle, using their prize money to endow a hospital there that is still extant.

Medieval Sandwich lay at the southern end of the Wantsum Channel which once separated the Isle of Thanet from mainland Kent. The emergence of Stonar bank diverted traffic from the Roman entrepôt at Richborough down to Sandwich, which lay on a triangular peninsula between the River Stour and the embankments that mark the southern boundaries of the medieval borough. Domesday Book recorded 383 households, implying a population of nearly 2,000, a third of Lincoln's. The Stour provided access to the open sea from Sandwich Haven, a landlocked harbour west and northwest of the town, providing ample space for the Marshal's modest fleet. Sandwich Haven could shelter 600 coastal craft in Tudor times, with the necessary quays. Since then, material eroded from the cliffs north of Sandwich has choked the river. Today the Stour estuary winds between industrial estates, wheat fields, and golf courses, drying out at low tide. *Reed's Channel Almanac* recommends seeking local advice before entering. The Haven, like the rest of the Wantsum Channel, has vanished under agricultural land, ending Sandwich's maritime glory.

Dover may seem more significant than Sandwich now, but it was not so in 1217. The Romans preferred Sandwich, as did Hengist and Horsa. One of Alfred the Great's brothers fought Vikings off Bloody Point in 851, now the Prince's Golf Links. Kings and invaders frequented Sandwich Bay throughout the later Anglo-Saxon period, from Aethelred to Harold, from Olaf Tryggvason to Earl Godwin. Becket and Richard I both landed there, as did Louis. Sandwich was not a maritime cross-roads by accident. It was the natural consequence of the area's physical attributes, supplemented by the prevailing south-westerly winds and the alternating pattern of tidal flows up and down the Channel. These follow the opposing coasts, flowing south-west through the Straits of Dover on a rising tide, and north-east, back into the North Sea, following high water at Dover. Like a modern yacht, a medieval ship would leave Calais on a rising tide to be carried out from the French coast. Making four or five knots with a southerly wind on her port beam, she might cross the Channel within a single six-hour tide, counting from the ebb to high water. Once off the Kentish coast, she could catch the flow as it set north-eastwards, running downwind past Dover, towards Julius Caesar's 'soft landing' near Sandwich. Modern tide tables suggest that a canny skipper might gain up to 2.6 knots (4.8km/h) by thus working the tide.

Eustace usually sailed overnight, like Caesar and William the Conqueror, to approach England around dawn. Trumpets had signalled the Dauphin's departure for England in 1216 at 9.00 pm. The Anonymous says that in August 1217 Eustace sailed for the Thames on St Bartholomew's morning, implying some time after midnight. He reached Sandwich about the same time as the Marshal. The day was fine and clear, allowing visibility far out to sea, the French fleet heaving into sight on a gentle wind, 'so closely arrayed in ranks, there was nothing like it except a field of battle'. The tide was setting up-Channel to carry them clear of the North Foreland, the *History* describing how the English 'steered straight out, though very close – *estroit* – to the wind, borne on the rising tide'. Wendover says that the French made a quick crossing with 'a fresh stern wind which drove them vigorously on towards England'. No contemporary gives the quarter, but the wind was presumably a southerly, as a south-westerly would have been foul at the start of the French voyage. As the fleets headed up-Channel, the ever-narrowing coasts would exert a funnel effect, strengthening the wind as they went, amplifying the effect of the tide.

The imminent confrontation was a unique event for its day, a ship-to-ship action under sail on the high seas. It may have benefited from the shelter of the Goodwin Sands, 4 miles (6km) east of the Kent coast, but as the English probably passed north of the Goodwins there is no particular reason to assume the action took place within the Downs anchorage, especially as Wendover specifically says the English traversed a considerable extent of sea before they met the French. Contemporaries queue up to emphasise the unusual mid-sea location. The *Romance* places the action *en haute mer*. William the Breton says the French were 'in the middle of the sea'. The *Melrose Chronicle* uses the expression *in medio mari* twice.

The Marshal spoke briefly as his men hurried on board. The enemy had returned to dispute the land, against God's will as expressed at Lincoln. God, however, had the power to help the righteous on both land and sea: 'You have the better hand in the game; you will vanquish the enemies of God.' The French, nevertheless, were unmoved by their earlier defeat, which had mainly affected their English allies. When they saw the royalist ships leave harbour, they underestimated their numbers and shortened sail, thinking it would be easy to capture them: 'It's only foot, not a knight among them. Chance has delivered them to us. They will cover our expenses; we shall carry them off to London, or they will stay here fishing for flounders.' William the Breton, the official Capetian chronicler, confirmed the French mood, without which the *History*'s words might be dismissed as a rhetorical device designed to emphasise the imminent change in French fortunes.

Matthew Paris has Hubert de Burgh join the Marshal at Sandwich after swearing his knights to defend Dover Castle, even if he was captured and threatened with hanging. So far, Matthew's account seems plausible. His further claim that Hubert brought thirty-six ships is plainly wrong, representing the whole English fleet. It is more likely that Hubert rode along to Sandwich, where he boarded 'a rich *nef*, with a splendid complement, an abundance of arms and magnificent fittings' (*History*). Sadly, the Haven's reclamation makes it impossible to guess where. As justiciar, the senior royal official from the previous reign, Hubert naturally took the lead. The *History*, however, makes great play with his feigning to close, passing outside the enemy line under full sail, letting both sides see that he was only pretending to fight. The French ribalds, full of bravado, shouted, 'The noose! The noose', but they themselves were soon to be choked with salt water.

Roger of Wendover attributes English slowness to engage to their earlier defeat. Paris shows it was less hesitation than skill. Victorian naval historians saw his account as evidence of some innate English gift for naval tactics. For the first time, a fleet sought the weather gauge to attack an enemy to leeward, an innovation that like Paris they attributed to de Burgh. English ships, however, had performed a similar manoeuvre on 25 May, under Philip of Aubigny's command, suggesting that the tactic evolved organically, independently of any single individual.

The manoeuvre as executed at Sandwich consisted of two parts. First the English sailed eastwards across the French stern, the wind on their starboard beam: 'thus they boldly reached across, inclining their helm at an angle – *obliquando* – that is luffing, as if they wanted to fetch Calais' (Paris). A luff was a spar used to help a sail catch the wind, but it is also a verb. In this case 'to luff' means to put the helm to leeward in order to sail nearer the wind, which the English needed to do to pass astern of the French. Eustace was glad to see them go. His orders were to relieve the Dauphin, not dispute command of the Channel: 'I know these wretches mean to fall upon Calais like brigands,' he is supposed to have said, 'but in vain, for it is well defended' (ibid.). William the Breton confirms the sense if not content of Matthew's imaginary speech. Robert of Courtenay, the expedition's military commander, however, overrode Eustace's professional caution and gave the order to engage. No doubt Robert, a landsman, expected the other French capital ships to support him, not realising that the wind and tide would soon carry them out of reach. The English now implemented the second part of their manoeuvre: 'suddenly, when they realised the wind had failed, having put over their helm, with the wind now behind them, the English fell promptly upon the enemy …' (ibid.).

The French flagship was a great *nef* from Bayonne on the Biscay coast. Deeply laden with King Philip's treasure, destriers, and a new trébuchet, she was in poor fighting trim, the waves nearly washing across her decks. Eustace had originally been ahead. As the *nef* fell out of line, she dropped astern, coming under attack from a succession of English ships. 'More than twenty ships passed before him', says the *Romance*, 'and vigorously assailed him with many great bows and crossbows, for such they had placed in their *sneccas*'. Roger of Wendover attributes the barrage to Philip of Aubigny, his archers and crossbowmen causing great slaughter among the enemy. According to the *Romance* Eustace shot back, defending himself as well as any baron.

The first ship to close was the Earl of Warenne's, sailing second in the English line, as befitted Richard fitz John's semi-royal status. The Anonymous and *History* agree that Richard was first to engage, Hubert de Burgh vanishing from the narrative. Richard made little progress, however, until the Marshal's sergeants joined him in their cog. Standing high out of the water, its crew used their height to hurl down great pots of quick lime, 'which deprived them [the French] of their sight, so they could see nothing' (*History*). Finely ground calcium oxide flew about in blinding clouds, combining violently with the water in eyes and skin to form slaked lime (calcium hydroxide), burning and blinding its victims, like a medieval version of mustard gas. Modern commentators doubt this stratagem because it appears in contemporary military textbooks, and is supposed to have been plagiarised. All three secular accounts of the battle mention it, however. Roger of Wendover and the *Romance* add the telling detail that the dust was carried downwind, away from the English, an essential pre-requisite for successful chemical attacks: 'From which they [the French] could no longer defend themselves; for their eyes were full of hot dust' (*Romance*).

A gallant sergeant from Guernsey took advantage of the confusion to leap down onto the French flagship's deck, knocking over William des Barres and Robert of Courtenay, and sending another knight flying. More sergeants followed, 'as eager as any hunting dog' (*History*). Eustace laid about him with an oar, breaking arms, heads, and collarbones, but enemy ships assailed him on all sides, overwhelming the French knights with numbers. Eustace hid in the bilges, to be found by a Winchelsea man, named Stephen Crabbe or Crave, 'who had long been with him' (Anonymous). Eustace offered 10,000 marks for his life, but he had met his master in cruelty. Stephen dwelt at length upon the undeserved and unspecified wrongs Eustace had done him. The only choice Stephen offered his old associate was to have his head cut off on the trébuchet or on the side of the ship. Eustace showed little appetite for either, so was executed on the spot, to general satisfaction: 'the predator become the prey,' wrote Paris.

The tactical obsession with Eustace was matched by popular mythology. Walter of Guisborough, who died in 1313, recounted the lucky defeat of a Spanish tyrant called *Monachus* who menaced the English coast with a great fleet in 1217. John of Canterbury's *Polihistorie*, of similar date, claimed that Eustace made his flagship invisible, until Stephen Crabbe, whom Eustace had initiated into the black arts, jumped aboard and killed him while he apparently stood on thin air. A great storm then blew up and sank the French fleet, as St Bartholomew hovered overhead to reassure the English. Like other mythical saviours of their country, such as Arnold von Winkelried at Sempach in 1386, the legendary Stephen perished in the moment of victory. The historical Crabbe survived to receive 20 shillings for new robes in 1225, with other royal shipmasters. Eustace's head last appears stuck on a spear, carried round coastal districts to prove the bogeyman was dead.

The Monk's death was decisive. Leaderless and swept along by wind and tide, the other French capital ships ran for home:

> *As soon as the great ship was taken*
> *By valour and great hardihood,*
> *So boldly our people bore themselves*
> *The French would not stand or await them,*
> *But fled away as quickly as they could.*
>
> *(History)*

Barnwell agrees: 'some of the leaders of their party having been captured, the rest sought safety in flight, and many of the smaller fry having been killed, alternately disordered and scattered, they put up no further resistance.' No more great ships were taken, but for the transports the day was a disaster. The Waverley annalist reckons that just fifteen escaped, while the Worcester annalist said that fifty-five were captured, accounting between them for all seventy. The high loss rate is our only evidence for better English seamanship, as superior ship handling would be decisive in a race for safety between broadly similar vessels.

Human casualties were in proportion. The *History*'s author took no responsibility for an outsize estimate of 4,000 French dead, but different rules applied at sea. As Chaucer said of his Shipman, whose ancestors may have been present:

> *When as he foughte and had the upper hande,*
> *By sea he sent them home to every lande.*

The French joke about fishing for flounders, a bottom feeder, rebounded horribly upon their auxiliaries. While monastic sources describe panic-stricken French sailors jumping overboard, the *History* confessed:

> *When they caught up with a ship,*
> *... they made no bones*
> *About killing those they found on board:*
> *But threw them as food to the fishes.*

One or two were saved per ship, 'no more; all the rest were killed'. In the flagship only the knights escaped death. A grisly pen sketch describes a fortune hunter fishing a red cloak from the sea, only to find it soaked with blood. Just thirty-two prisoners were taken, says the poet. If the defeated fleet lost fifty-five ships with twenty men on each, some 1,100 Frenchmen may have perished, plus 100 in the flagship.

Roger of Wendover's claim that English galleys dashed about perforating French ships with imaginary iron beaks is impossible. Admiral Rodgers, a student of galley warfare, points out that ramming from astern is ineffectual. Besides, northern hulls were too solid, as Julius Caesar discovered when he fought the Veneti. A more plausible aspect of the Wendover/Paris narrative is the English use of grappling hooks and axes to cut through hostile ships' halyards and bring their sails down, catching the crew like birds in a net. Some historians cast doubt on all this, but continental regulations required ships to be equipped with *rochets* or hooked blades to cut rigging, and the *Romance* mentions the use of great axes against the Bayonne *nef*.

Hubert de Burgh was among those winning prizes: 'not in truth the first to engage, but he took two ships, which he kept when he returned' (*History*). The Marshal clan was clearly irked by Hubert's arrogation of the leading role in the battle. So much money was captured that the sailors dished out *deniers* in bowlfuls. Others swaggered about in silks and furs, squabbling over who had the finest. William, as commander-in-chief, divided the spoils: robes, horses, arms, and armour. Much of the plunder was surprisingly ordinary: meat, wine, corn, iron, and steel dishes, a boost to an over-stretched wartime economy.

The *remanant* of the plunder, the proportion saved for the Crown, William devoted to a chapel dedicated to St Bartholomew and sixteen almshouses. No record evidence links the establishment directly with the battle, but there seems little reason to reject the literary sources. The earliest documentary reference dates from 1225, and a custumal of 1301 supports the independent evidence of the *History* and John of Canterbury. The Marshal himself ascribed the victory to the saint's intervention, and his other monastic foundations evince a punctilious attitude towards religious obligations. The institution retains its original site just outside the medieval borough's southern boundary beside the Dover Road. Sandwich children still race round the chapel for currant buns, every Patronal Day (24 August), while elderly couples from Sandwich occupy the almshouses, distant beneficiaries of the medieval advantages of war. Ralph of Coggeshall's judgement on the battle was suitably biblical:

> *And thus the Lord smote the head of his enemies coming to annihilate the English race, and many were captured in other ships, and the Lord drew the waters of the sea over certain of them as they fled, and they were sunk like lead in the stormy waters.*

KINGSTON

Even sceptical commentators accept that Sandwich was decisive. Victorian naval historians saw it as England's first great sea victory, a precursor of subsequent triumphs. It left the Dauphin unable to replace the losses at Lincoln, definitively ending his cross-Channel adventure:

> *From this day the king's party plainly began to prevail, and that of Prince Louis to fall behind. Hence, the king's forces having once more beset London, Louis did not delay making peace, whatever destiny offered.*
>
> *(Barnwell)*

> *... destitute of present help, and despairing for the future, and reduced by want to utter famine, [Louis] sought peace with the legate and the king's men, for himself and all his lay supporters ...*
>
> *(Dunstable)*

The Northerners, who had started the whole business, were also hard pressed, with reports from Northumberland and Yorkshire of the defeat and capture of many nobles hostile to the king. The Earls of Chester and Derby took Bolsover and Peak Castles, 'and thus the hand of God was arranging universal good fortune for the king and his supporters' (*Dunstable*).

News of Sandwich reached Louis on Saturday 26th. He acted swiftly, sending his cousin Robert of Dreux, whose father had served with William at Lagny thirty-seven years before, to open negotiations at Rochester. While Robert was held surety, the luckless Robert of Courtenay was released from Dover Castle, and packed off to London to explain his defeat. Both sides' leading men, Louis, William, and Hubert de Burgh, met near London on Tuesday 29th, and agreed in principle to make peace. Not every royalist accepted the need for talks, haughtily demanding that London should be besieged without further parleys. They had kept a lower profile in the hour of greatest need, said the *History*, staying well away from the seaside. Wiser heads, anxious to end the troubles quickly, begged William to get the French out of the country at any price, offering to assist the public purse from their own resources. Roger of Wendover confirms the war-weary mood, royalist chiefs desiring 'beyond measure' to be rid of Louis.

Agreement proved difficult, requiring more than one meeting. William tightened his grip on London, ordering the Cinque Ports to blockade the Thames with their own ships and those taken at Sandwich. He was right to avoid more direct action. London would not fall easily, and the sack of the kingdom's chief commercial centre was not to be entertained. French knights, alarmed by William's slow response, planned a last death-defying sortie, preferring to place themselves *en aventure* than be shut up any longer. As they were arming themselves on the night of Saturday 9 September, letters came from William greeting Louis amorously – *comme son demoiselle* – and requesting an extension of the truce. Final terms were agreed on the Monday, to be confirmed next day, Tuesday 12th. The meeting took place on an unidentified island in the Thames near Kingston, the Dauphin's safety guaranteed by the Earls of Pembroke, Salisbury, Warenne, and Arundel. As when Edmund Ironside and Cnut made peace at Ola's Island in the Severn in 1016, the armies remained on opposite banks to prevent accidents.

Conditions were similar to those agreed in June. Louis and his foreign adventurers were to leave England immediately, never to return, restoring any castles and lands they had seized, as should his Scots and Welsh allies. Prisoners were to be released without further ransom. Louis's excommunicated supporters should be absolved and get back their confiscated estates: 'For it was expressly stated … that none should be disinherited on account of the war, but everyone should be in the same state as they were at the beginning.' They should also share the liberties granted by the reissued Charter, the evil customs, 'which had as it were been the cause of this war', being abolished (*Barnwell*). In token of the transfer of power, Louis returned the captured Chancery and Exchequer records.

Louis received a pay-off as in previous Angevin-Capetian treaties: an indemnity of 15,000 marks – *grand plenté d'aveir* said the *History* – a great deal of money. Nominally to cover expenses, it was more a golden handshake, to sweeten his departure. Louis was said off the record to have promised to persuade Philip Augustus to restore the lost Angevin lands in exchange. The main difference from June was the treatment of the Dauphin's clerical adherents, who were abandoned to the Legate's wrath, 'so that elsewhere the clergy should hold themselves more aloof from lay conflicts' (*Dunstable*). Individual clerics were 'degraded' or translated to less profitable 'upland benefices'. Altars and chalices defiled by excommunicate priests' celebration of Mass were destroyed.

Some thought the terms too easy. William stands accused of letting Louis slip off the hook to avoid an embarrassing showdown with the son of his own feudal lord, the King of France, endangering his wife's Norman estates. In exchange for vague promises William provided the Dauphin with a golden bridge at the taxpayer's expense. Henry III, never the sharpest political operator, upbraided the Marshal's son Walter for his father's generosity, an accusation echoed by Nicholas Vincent, the modern biographer of Peter des Roches. The bishop, whose abrogation of the Charter had precipitated the country into civil war, presumably wanted harsher terms. He refused to contribute to taxes levied to pay the indemnity, alleging lack of consultation. A stranger to moderation, Peter pursued his absolutist line into the 1230s, until dismissed for allegedly procuring Richard Marshal's death.

Sidney Painter's view that the treaty was generous and statesmanlike seems more appropriate to the circumstances of September 1217. The settlement was a triumph for the Marshal, over his supporters as well as the enemy. The indemnity was well worth paying if it ended the war. London remained loyal to the Dauphin, with a powerful garrison of French knights, who continued to launch *chevauchées* into the countryside, returning with much booty. Military outcomes are always doubtful, and William was no lover of fighting for its own sake. Like Henry II, who 'oiled the palms' of the Young King's French supporters, William bought off his opponents, a subtlety beyond Henry III or Matthew Paris. A fairer criticism of the indemnity is that any more was paid after the first instalment, with no surety for the Dauphin's fulfilling his promise. Many, however, found the sudden reversal of fortune simply astonishing:

> *And this was as a miracle that the eldest son of the king of the French, having got deep inside the kingdom with such a mass of*

*troops, having occupied so much of the kingdom, so many of the
magnates having joined his party, was so swiftly removed, not to
say expelled from the kingdom, with all his people, without hope of
recovery.*

(Barnwell)

Once terms were agreed, matters moved swiftly. Louis and his
French followers were absolved on Wednesday 13th, barefoot and
shirtless in their woollen drawers, a humiliation that only the *History*
records. Louis kept his tunic as a special concession. Before the
month was out, regent and legate had escorted Louis to the coast,
and seen him safely on his way. On 29 October, a year and a day after
his coronation, Henry III re-entered his capital.

VIII

NUNC DIMITTIS

he end of hostilities is not the same as the restoration of peace. The Dauphin's departure ensured England's dynastic continuity, but left many other problems. Country and government were impoverished, royal administration at a standstill, the ruling elite divided. For the last eighteen months of his life, William sought to revive government and restore national unity, his greatest and least known public service. But he was lost too soon: to the country's continuing detriment malice overpowered prowess.

PICKING UP THE PIECES

William's peace-time regency was inevitably an anti-climax. The *History* says little about the period. Record evidence, however, suggests a punishing work rate. Paul Meyer's reconstruction of the regent's movements, in his 1890s edition of the *History*, reveals that William visited sixty-three locations in twenty-two counties during the year from October 1217. William of Newburgh's continuator might think: 'Pharaoh having been defeated and the enemies fled, truth and peace was restored in our land', but much remained to be done.

Demobilised knights promptly revived the tournament circuit, 'an outlet for the relics of discord', thought Anonymous of Béthune. In government, their erstwhile champion banned them, 'until the state of peace of the kingdom ... has been made firmer'. Politics had come full circle. Central administration had collapsed, as in Stephen's reign. The Court of King's Bench had not sat since 1209. No regular taxation had been collected since 1214. Devoid of money and troops, the government struggled to regain control of royal castles, despite the *History*'s assertion that William installed his own castellans as soon as Louis had gone. The recovery of Carlisle from the Scots was a rare success, exchanged for the Earldom of Huntingdon, traditionally held by the Scottish royal family. Reluctance to supplant John's appointees until his heir came of age reinforced practical obstacles to the reassertion of royal power. William's colleagues were torn between their curialist urges to restore the king's government, and a baronial instinct to hang onto royal assets acquired during the civil war. William feathered his own nest, dividing the Berkshire estates of Lincoln's most notable casualty with the Earl of Salisbury. The Earls of Chester, Derby, and Aumale never sealed the Treaty of Kingston, suggesting disagreement between Northern royalists and the southerners who made the agreement, many of them recently defected rebels. At the heart of the regency lay tension between William, Peter des Roches, and Hubert de Burgh.

A second reissue of Magna Carta in the autumn of 1217 provided a degree of common ground between curialists and magnates. Sealed by William and the legate, it was in principle a temporary grant, because non-royal. However, it claimed to be *in perpetuum*, and in practice became so. The charter's second reissue reflected its evolution from political wish list to practical tool of government. With coffers to be filled, restraints on the Crown's ability to raise revenue were dropped. A new clause ordering the demolition of private castles built during the war reflected problems similar to those Henry II had faced after the Anarchy. The most abiding change was separation of the vexed issues of Forest Law into a lesser document, or Little Charter, the parent document acquiring the title of Great Charter by which it is still known. Limits on royal exploitation of forests and fresh curbs on sheriffs further diminished royal authority, a political victory for militarily defeated rebels.

The Marshal's most pressing concern was lack of money. In November 1217, he wrote to the Pope, excusing his inability to pay the 1,000 marks tribute that John had promised. Georges Duby, the distinguished French medievalist, thought that William lacked financial acumen, but the Marshal was well aware of the economic realities behind political power. The *History* saw the failure of the Young King's Revolt in 1174 in strictly financial terms:

> ... *when the money runs out,*
> *pride declines and falls:*
> *Whoever rises through great wealth*
> *By poverty is reduced to shame.*

Long before he had lands or rents of his own William was a man of credit. When funds were wanting to pay the Young King's tournament debts, the anxious merchants turned to the Marshal for reassurance. As a landlord, he founded markets to supplement his feudal revenues, and even had a lighthouse built at Hook Head to guide ships to his settlement at New Ross.

Even before the Dauphin left England, William initiated inquiries into debts owing to the Crown and lands gone astray in the civil war. The Great Council at Westminster in October granted a scutage of 2 marks on every knight's fee to pay the indemnity.

Only three-eighths was ever collected, the most prominent defaulters being Peter des Roches and Fawkes of Bréauté. William took a close interest in its collection. He supervised the tallaging (levying of tax) of royal estates, and sought feudal aids from Ireland. He lent money and pledged his own lands to meet the indemnity. His most important step was to reintroduce the Exchequer in November to supervise revenue collection. New chequered cloths, thirteenth-century adding machines, were bought to assist the judges' calculations. William himself presided over proceedings in January 1218, evidence of concern if not expertise.

The regent's last significant administrative act was to announce the first judicial visitation of the new reign on 4 November 1218. It was an appropriate measure for an erstwhile servant of Henry II, the father of England's judicial system. Groups of itinerant justices would tour the counties to administer oaths of loyalty, clear the legal backlog, review sheriffs' judicial activities, and collect outstanding revenue. Bringing government to the localities, they asserted royal rights, settled property disputes, and prosecuted burglars and builders of illegal castles. Documentary evidence leaves no doubt of William's central role, clarifying instructions and deciding appeals. A symptom of the return to normality was the appearance of ex-rebels, such as the Earl of Arundel, on the judges' bench, and successful cases brought against royalist grandees by erstwhile traitors such as Gilbert of Ghent: 'in this year peace returned and was established in England, and the justices ... went through all England after Christmas, reviving the laws and causing them to be observed' (*Waverley*).

The *History* says nothing of these mundane matters, to the detriment of William's reputation as a man of affairs. Instead it details an episode hardly mentioned elsewhere but indicative of his problems as a Marcher lord and the regency's factional undercurrents. In accordance with the Treaty of Kingston Llewelyn of Gwynedd laid down his arms and did homage to Henry III. His cousin, Morgan ap Hywel, the last Welsh lord in South Wales, refused to make peace, however. He had taken advantage of the Marshal's distractions elsewhere to seize Caerleon-upon-Usk, which William's father-in-law had taken half a century before. When Llewelyn called on his supporters to cease hostilities, Morgan refused to comply, declaring his intention of fighting on as long as the Marshal held a foot of his land. William's bailiff, John of Earley, summoned friends and retainers to storm Caerleon, an incident confirmed by Welsh sources. Ten of William's better class of tenants were killed in a single day's fighting, whether in an ambush or during the assault is unclear.

The conflict dragged on into March 1218, when a parliament was summoned to Worcester to resolve the issue. Llewelyn appealed to the king to return Caerleon to Morgan, supported by William's usual opponents, the Earl of Chester and Peter des Roches. Llewelyn was well briefed, appealing to the 'form of peace' agreed at Kingston, by which everyone should have his land as he had done before the war. Rather than defend his bailiff's action in retaking Caerleon, William sought counsel of his men, asking their opinion and allowing the 'best at speaking' to present the agreed Marshal position. The *History* claims that William was inclined to compromise. His men were not. Morgan had chosen to ignore the truce, killing William's knights and other people, burning twenty-two churches and devastating the land, for which he had been excommunicated. All of this the Marshal's spokesman offered to prove, implicitly by combat. Perhaps unsurprisingly the assembly found in William's favour, leaving him in possession of Caerleon Castle and its appurtenances. The *History's* chronology is confused, and the final discussions probably took place at Westminster, but like the regency debates at Gloucester, the episode illustrates the subtleties of a lord's relations with his men; the collective nature of medieval decision-making; the desire of men to cloak their actions in legality, however dubious.

Faced with obstruction and hostility from his closest colleagues, William made little progress in regaining control of the government's key military assets: its castles. Most were held by King John's castellans, who lived by plundering the neighbourhood, cheerfully anticipating a further decade of extortion before Henry III came of age. The one case in which William took action was Newark. Too minor for the *History*, the episode provides a low-key epilogue to a military career reaching back over five decades. Newark Castle belonged to the Bishop of Lincoln, but was held for the Crown during the civil war. King John died there. Its castellan Robert of Gaugi, not to be confused with William's jousting partner of the 1170s, refused to return it when the war moved away following Lincoln. Robert's flagrant defiance combined with the bishop's offer of 100 marks to stiffen William's determination. He ordered thirty miners to muster at Stamford, and left London on 8 July 1218 with the king and what Roger of Wendover styled a large army. Government records list just twenty-four knights, although some of them, such as John Marshal, were themselves magnates with their own retinues. There was also the bishop's own following, perhaps thirty knights. One of the latter was killed and others wounded as they charged into town to stop the defenders firing the houses to deprive besiegers of cover. William waited four days (10–22 July) while siege engines were set up around the castle, presumably on the south-eastern side away from the River Trent, and then withdrew to Nottingham. Meanwhile Robert's friends negotiated the castle's surrender in return for £100 compensation for its warlike stores, and everyone went home.

Newark was unusual. William generally left the problem of evicting John's castellans to his successors. Not until 1224 would Hubert de Burgh feel strong enough to tackle Fawkes of Bréauté, the greatest alien castellan of them all, demolishing his stronghold at Bedford, hanging its garrison, and driving its owner into exile. William's administration was a work in progress. It takes more than a few months to heal the scars of a civil war that has been decades in the making. Fiscal recovery depended on economic revival, which only began in the 1220s. Nevertheless, William built a measure of acceptance of royal government through patronage and consultation. His numerous daughters were employed building bridges to ex-rebels, dissident royalists, and fellow Marchers. Isabel married Gilbert of Clare, Earl of Gloucester, a Marshal prisoner from Lincoln. Her sister Sybil married a son of Earl Ferrars, one of Chester's associates. Eve married a grandson of the same William of Braose that King John had destroyed.

The restraint that inhibited eviction of John's castellans saved the bitterness that characterised the Second Barons' War in the 1260s. As usual William was lucky. The Dauphin's supporters had never fought the king in person, mitigating the severity of their treason. Later in his reign, Henry III was much beaten with swords and maces at the battle of Lewes, a provocation not unrelated to the subsequent slaughter of 200 rebel knights at Evesham, a grim contrast to the bloodless pursuit following Lincoln. The Treaty of Kingston's clause reinstating the territorial *status quo* forestalled the emergence of a dispossessed faction intent on fomenting disorder like that which marked the reign of King Stephen. Direct evidence of William's personal responsibility for these positive aspects of his rule is inevitably hard to find. When his men occupied a manor claimed by Fawkes of Bréauté in June 1217, however, the latter swallowed what he would not have taken from anyone else: 'Against William Marshal,' he wrote, 'I should hate to do or start anything by which the accusation of greed or shame might be laid against me'. William's chairmanship saw none of the factional violence that disfigured Henry III's later minority, with the exile of Fawkes and the enforced departure of Peter des Roches on Crusade.

THE LAST BATTLE

William celebrated his last New Year at Marlborough, the scene of his childhood. Returning to Westminster in January 1219, he fell ill towards Candlemas (2 February). Doctors came from various quarters, to no avail. William rode through his pain to the Tower, staying there until Lent attended by the countess, while his condition worsened. He discussed his will, comforted his entourage, and began to make confession weekly – suggesting that he had been less assiduous before. In mid-March, William decided to leave town. London was too shut in, aggravating his symptoms. If he had to die, he preferred to do so at home. He was placed in a boat, the countess in another, and rowed gently upstream to his manor at Caversham, across the Thames from Reading. King and administration followed, lodging in Reading Abbey, while William ran the government from his sickbed.

The *History* devotes more than a tenth of its lines to the passing of its hero. A step-by-step evocation of how a medieval layman should face death, it provides unique insights into the Marshal's surrender of power. The chronology is sometimes confused, but the sequence of events is logical, its accuracy vouched for by the presence of John of Earley, the younger William, and John Marshal. As befitted the rearguard commander of Fréteval, there would be a phased withdrawal from government, world, and family. There would be no disgraceful scenes of last-minute despair or repentance such as had disfigured the death of the Old and Young Kings. Everything would be dignified and according to plan.

The regent's flow of instructions faltered the week before Easter, a royal council assembling at William's bedside on Easter Monday (8 April). The king was present, as were Hubert de Burgh and Pandulf the new legate. An experienced papal diplomat, Pandulf had won King John's gratitude by ending the Interdict in 1213, and replaced Guala in September 1218. William started by rendering an account of his record in office. Chosen *baillie* on John's death, he had served the new king loyally, defending his land when it was difficult to do so. He would serve him still, had God granted him strength, but that was not His will. It was necessary to choose someone else to defend Henry and his realm. When Peter des Roches pushed forward, claiming that the king's person had been entrusted to him, William cut him short. Peter was forgetting how the bishop and Earl of Chester had begged him with tears in their eyes to be guardian and master of both king and realm. It was well known that William had received both king and kingdom. If he had placed Henry in Peter's hands, it was because a child could not travel. Racked with pain, William asked the company to withdraw while he sought advice from his son and family. The restricted electorate reflects the individual nature of the Marshal's authority. He alone could hand it on.

Early next morning William spoke with 'those in whom he had most trust', his son and wife, John Marshal and others. There was no people like the English, he said, with such a variety of opinions, echoing the Barnwell annalist's comments on English inconstancy. If William entrusted the king to any one of them, the others would all resent it. In his perplexity William turned to an external actor, the Pope as represented by the legate: 'If the land is not defended by the Apostolic See ... then I do not know who will defend it.' Later commentators, from Matthew Paris to Protestant Victorians, lamented England's subjection to papal authority, but in the circumstances the Marshal's choice was sound. Nobody else stood above the hurly-burly as the Pope did. The only magnate of comparable stature to William, the Earl of Chester, had departed on Crusade the previous summer. Lacking a suitable replacement, William abolished himself, displaying a self-denial rare in politics. Defying the medieval predilection for making every office hereditary, there was no suggestion of the younger Marshal replacing his father.

When king and legate returned, William raised himself on his side, and taking the boy's hand, announced his decision to place him in the keeping of God, the Pope, and the legate. He prayed that Henry would grow up a worthy ruler, hoping that God would cut his life short if he took after any *felon ancestre*. If the admonition does more than reflect the *History*'s uncompromising antipathy towards King John, it was the nearest William ever came to revealing his true feelings about his late sovereign. When the poem referred to the Massacre of the Innocents in Bethlehem, *felon roi* was the epithet it saved for King Herod. Only a few were present in William's sickroom to witness the transfer of authority. Most of the magnates were assembled at Reading Abbey. Surprised by fresh pains, William sent John Marshal to ensure that the younger Marshal carried out his intentions correctly. When Bishop Peter laid hands on the boy king's head, seeking to assert his own pre-eminence, the younger William faced him down. Taking Henry's hand in the sight of everyone, he presented him to the legate, who received public charge of the king as he had already done in private. Rarely can a peaceful transfer of power have taken so physical a form, with competing factions laying hands on the king's sacred person. If Peter was disappointed of supreme power, his effective position was unaltered. Pandulf assumed Guala's overall directing role. The bishop retained his guardianship of the king, suggesting that the *History*'s squabbling owed more to the conflicts of the 1220s than the supposed differences of the 1210s. Administration reverted to Hubert de Burgh. The regent would have no single successor.

William summoned his people again next day. Live or die, the passage of power was a great relief. It was time to complete his will and take care of his soul, for his body was once more *en aventure*. Feudal custom determined the division of William's lands. After Isabel's death, William the younger would have all her inheritance of Leinster, Pembroke, and Striguil; Richard received the estates either side of the Channel granted by his royal namesake; Walter received Goodrich, a royal castle acquired as compensation for losses in Normandy. Gilbert was in holy orders, but Ansel, the youngest son and not yet a knight, had no great prospects. The old Marshal thought that Ansel might prosper through his own efforts, as he himself had done, but John of Earley spoke up for the lad, ensuring him £140 a year – enough to keep him in horse shoes. Four of the Marshal's daughters were safely married, but William was concerned for Joan, the youngest and still single. She should have land worth £30 plus 200 marks a year to keep her until her elder brother found her a husband. As was usual with great families, the distribution avoided patrimonial fragmentation, compensating middle sons from lands acquired in the testator's lifetime, but casting younger sons adrift. William observed the custom while taking care of his youngest, for whom he expressed more affection than his father ever did for him.

Relieved of family responsibilities, William took thought for his vassals on the Marches, sending John of Earley, or the latter's son and namesake, to check any rash enterprises there. William's mind was still on his own departure, however. While at Chepstow, John was to recover two silk cloths kept there, and hasten back, as his lord's condition was worsening. William had brought the cloths from Outremer, thirty years before, to cover his coffin. Faded without, they were fine within, a luxurious reminder of the exotic world beyond the Mediterranean. When his son asked where William should be laid, the Marshal sprung another surprise. While in Outremer he had vowed his body to the Knights Templar. It was time to make that promise good. In return for burial in the Temple Church in London, William granted the order his manor of Upledon in Herefordshire. Aimery of St Maur, Master of the Temple, a witness to Magna Carta, and an old friend from another Wiltshire family, was summoned to William's bedside. Before the countess and their daughters, William sent for a white Templar cloak made secretly the previous year, perhaps when the first signs of illness had appeared. Once he put it on, William would become a monk, divorced from the secular world and female company. For the last time he kissed his *bel'amie*, the countess, who had to be helped from the room with her weeping daughters. As William spread the cloak around him, Aimery assured him that he had done well to relinquish the earthly ties dividing him from God. No other knight had received such honour in this world, for his prowess, good sense, and loyalty. Now he could be certain of God's grace: 'Worthy you have been; and worthily you will depart.' Aimery himself departed for London to make the necessary arrangements.

William was now as secure as he might be from material and spiritual danger. He had been under constant guard for some time. Troubled by his father's suffering, William the younger had instituted a round-the-clock vigil by three knights. Medical understanding was rudimentary, but care unstinting. The young Marshal shared nights with John of Earley and Thomas Basset. Women were excluded. The burden of nursing the Marshal fell upon his closest male associates. William hung on grimly after Brother Aimery's departure, scarcely able to eat or drink, his heart failing and natural functions stopped for want of nourishment. For the last fortnight, his carers fed him white bread crumbled between their hands, and *moisserons*, thin gruel or perhaps mushrooms. His constant pain unrelieved by opiates, William's mind remained clear. When the knight, in whose arms he rested, sought his opinion of the ecclesiastical view that restitution must precede forgiveness, William rejected any such notion. The clergy would shave the laity too closely. He himself had captured 500 knights. He could hardly return their arms, destriers, and harness. He could only surrender himself to God, repenting the things he had done. Either the clerical argument was false, or no-one could be saved. A chaplain who proposed selling eighty scarlet fur-lined robes for charity received short shrift. They were for William's knights at

Pentecost. He would see them receive their livery one last time, as once he had received his.

Even the Marshal could not indefinitely resist 'greedy death who devours everything'. Death had no truck with ransoms: 'she takes no account of kings, nor dukes, nor earls … rich and poor are all hers'. The day before he died, William hardly slept. He hallucinated, seeing two men in white on either hand. John of Earley suggested that they were heavenly companions sent to put William on the right road. He long regretted not asking who the Marshal thought they were. That night William was worse. Next morning, Tuesday 14 May, he appeared to be sleeping quietly. Disturbed around midday, he spoke to John of Earley and tried to turn over, when he was seized by his death agony. 'Quick, John,' he cried, 'open the doors and windows; call my son here and the countess and knights, for I am surely dying; I can bide no longer.' Fainting, William recovered enough to scold John for not sprinkling his face with rose-water to rouse him to say farewell. 'Never,' he said to the man who once held his horses and prisoners in battle, 'have I seen you at such a loss.'

When the countess and young Marshal approached, William spoke for the last time, pale from his final struggle: 'I am dying. I commend you to God. I can stay with you no longer. I cannot defend myself from death.' The younger William took his father from John of Earley, a crucifix held before them. A succession of high-ranking ecclesiastics appeared with impeccable timing: the Abbot of Notley in Buckinghamshire, who had granted William the spiritual privileges of his order, and the Abbot of Reading bearing news that the legate had seen the Marshal in a vision. Greatly alarmed, Pandulf absolved William of all his confessed sins, by virtue of the powers delegated to him. Unable to speak, William joined his hands and bowed while the abbots pronounced the absolution. And so at last the Marshal died, still adoring the cross, his weeping followers consoled by the thought that he was surely with God and his friends in Paradise, for his death had been as exemplary as his life. He certainly made a better end than his royal masters, dying in bed not on an ash-strewn chapel floor; not cursing his sons, but in the bosom of his family and friends.

William's last journey down the Thames Valley, sewn up inside his coffin within a bull's hide packed with salt, lasted nearly a week. Even in death he provided a symbol of national reconciliation, the four earls who joined the cortège representing both sides of the civil war. After lying at Westminster Abbey, William reached his final resting place on 20 May, the second anniversary of Lincoln. The Temple in William's day occupied a pleasant suburb between the Cities of London and Westminster. The nave was circular, like the Holy Sepulchre Church he had seen in Jerusalem on the site of Christ's death and resurrection. Burial in such a place was a rare privilege. Nearby rested the entrails of St Hugh of Avalon, Bishop of Lincoln, whom William and his friend Baldwin of Béthune once sought to protect from the wrath of Richard the Lionheart.

Stephen Langton, with whom William had ridden between King John and his rebellious barons, delivered the eulogy. The best knight of their day was the mirror of our common fate, just so much earth. After the funeral, celebrated by a throng of lay and ecclesiastical notables, William's executors put more distance between the Marshal and his erstwhile lords, distributing the alms that Henry II and John had signally failed to provide: meat and drink, robes and shoes. So numerous were the poor, the wake was held at Westminster for want of space in the city. Afterwards, there were no more pence or loaves, and just three robes.

The Marshal's final eulogy came, not from an English source, but from his French opponents, the arbiters of chivalric excellence. Unlike the *History*'s previous anecdotes of French courtly life, there is a potential witness: William's second son, Richard Marshal. Absent from the deathbed, he is known to have been attending

Philip Augustus in July 1219. Receiving news of William's death during dinner, the king kept silence, waiting until Richard had finished eating. After the tablecloths had been removed, Philip asked William des Barres whether he had heard of the interment of the Marshal, who was so loyal a *prud'homme*, so valiant and wise. It was a great pity, thought William, himself one of the great exponents of chivalry, for in our time there was never a better knight anywhere, who better knew how to bear himself in arms, or did so to better effect. Not to be outdone in praise, Philip thought the Marshal the most loyal man he had ever known. A Norman knight, perhaps a veteran of Bouvines, added that William was the wisest knight of the age, wisdom joining prowess and loyalty to complete the moral trinity that had featured in Aimery of St Maur's bedside tribute.

Legacy

William has been accused of leaving only a semblance of peace. Is his personal reputation, founded largely on the *History's* biased testimony, any more solid? 'Finest knight' was a popular cliché, applied to Richard I and Saer of Quincy among others. The *History* plays with the image continually. One of the Lusignan cut-throats who dragged William across Poitou in the 1160s confided to a sympathetic lady witness that there was *nul meillor chevalier* – no better knight. After William broke with the Young King at Christmas 1182, a witness to the Ressons tournament told Baldwin de Béthune his friend was 'one of the worthiest knights to be found in the whole world'. William's final eulogy was pronounced by William des Barres, himself another 'finest knight'.

The positive view that *History* promotes of its hero proves little, but more than one independent witness conveys a similar appreciation. Eleanor of Aquitaine, an excellent judge of men, ransomed her protector and set him on the road to greatness. Henry II chose him, the younger son of a disreputable baronial backwoodsman, as tutor-in-arms to the crown prince. William's leading role at Richard I's coronation confirms the esteem in which that chivalric monarch held him. On John's accession, the Marshal was among those sent to England to hold the kingdom. From the late 1160s to the rupture of 1205, William was almost continuously in royal employment. Ecclesiastical sources noted his passing with little comment, although the barest notice from them indicates considerable celebrity. Thomas Wykes was an exception. A civil servant writing half a century after William's death, Thomas remembered him as 'a most valiant knight, renowned throughout the whole world'. Nearly a century after his death, the Marshal features alongside King Arthur in the chivalric *Song of Caerlaverock*, written for Sir Robert Clifford, a descendant of William's Marcher neighbours. Perhaps most telling, William's colleague Guala described him spontaneously as 'like gold tested in a furnace'.

Negative comments come mainly from Henry III and his echo Matthew Paris. The king preferred music and architecture to tournaments, and may have grown tired of an inexhaustible succession of troublesome Earls Marshal. Disenchanted with his foreign policy inheritance, Henry turned against the man who preserved his throne, complaining to William's third son Walter of the easy terms granted to the Dauphin. Paris went further, magnifying hearsay anecdotes from the French court into a full-blown accusation of treason. Written years after the event, the allegation says more about Matthew's character than that of his victim. When William's body was relocated in 1240, it was natural for Paris to ascribe its decayed condition to moral corruption rather than inefficient embalming.

Modern assessments reflect the ambiguities of their subject. Some critics have swallowed the chivalric legend in its crudest form. Georges Duby dismissed William's thoughts as few and brief, his brain too small to restrain the natural vigour of his tireless physique. King John's biographer, Ralph V. Turner, viewed William as an illiterate with no interest in administration. Even the admiring Sidney Painter thought William's strategy non-existent and his tactics simplistic. Any battle was better than none, as long as he could get at his enemy and hew him down. Such caricatures are contradicted by the evidence. David Carpenter, the most recent historian of Henry III's minority, sees William as the ideal choice in 1216, blending calculation with knightly vigour. The resolute exploitation of the Dauphin's division of his forces in May 1217 was no isolated flash of genius, as the earlier stroke at Rye suggests. William was more than just a man of action, however. The repository of half a century of Angevin tradition, he knew more about royal courts and feudal custom than anybody. He had picked his way through the quagmire of courtly politics for decades, inevitably coming to resemble the courtly dissembler Matthew Paris condemned.

The *History*'s account of William's actions in 1194 illustrates his potential for deviousness. Caught with a foot in both camps when Richard returned from Germany, William faced accusations of 'planting vines', hedging his bets by reserving homage for his Irish estates to the rebellious Prince John, titular Lord of Ireland. The Marshal claimed that he was bound to defend John's position in Ireland, just as he had defended Richard's in England. Richard accepted William's feudal logic-chopping; John was less forbearing in similar circumstances in 1205. Nevertheless, the Marshal's trimming achieved its objective, the preservation of a territorial conglomerate spanning Ireland, Normandy and the Welsh Marches, a microcosm of the Angevin Empire itself.

William's unswerving pursuit of personal advantage is well attested, from his refusal to pay increased taxes demanded from his shrievalty of Gloucester in 1199, to the secretive acquisition of the de la Perche estates, an abuse of office that Painter found inexcusable. The *History* confirms a shrewdness verging on disregard for other people's property, on and off the tournament field. It was a huge joke to trick the anxious people of Rouen out of a slap-up dinner in exchange for protection against a non-existent French army. Intercepting a runaway monk eloping with the daughter of friends, William thought nothing of confiscating the money which the couple meant to lend out at interest. In his defence, William could blame a savagely competitive society. Cast adrift by his family he had to make his own way. Initially naïve, he had learnt his lesson at Drincourt, and ruthlessly gathered the fruits of success. The Marshal's acquisitiveness, however, never excited the same hostility as office-holders in later reigns, the Despensers under Edward II, John of Gaunt under Richard II, or the Duke of Somerset under Henry VI.

On the military front, William is frequently accused of excessive caution. His restraining hand may have prevented King John taking decisive action against his enemies in Normandy or before Magna Carta, and was seen as contributing to John's paralysis at Stonar in May 1216. He failed to stem Llewelyn's advance, and drifted through the winter of 1216–17. Contemporary and modern critics have condemned William's failure to assault London after Lincoln. Similar prudence appears at a personal level in William's deliberate response to the Young King's urgent summons in 1183, when he carefully obtained safe-conducts from both French and Angevin courts before answering his lord's appeal. We should assume, however, that William had a more informed view of the odds than we do. He spent most of his career fighting superior numbers, from Drincourt via Le Mans to Lincoln. Royalist forces were insufficient to besiege a great city like London. The Marshal expelled the invaders and preserved the dynasty, but lacked the resources to recover Normandy or end the war. His successors were no more successful. The Angevin-Capetian feud dragged on ingloriously until 1259 and the Treaty of Paris.

Lincoln and Sandwich had wider consequences than simply ensuring that the Angevins not the Capetians would rule England. Dynastic separation from the continent reinforced a burgeoning sense of national unity that forms one of the *History's* recurrent themes. William de Tancarville's jibe that England was a poor country for knights errant reflected a Norman arrogance that was increasingly resented beyond the Channel. The *History's* English sources readily attributed William's unpopularity at the Young King's court to Anglo-Norman rivalry, the plotters resenting their being over-shadowed by an Englishman. The Marshal's household got their own back, mocking the Normans' decline: once they were grain, now they were chaff. No lord had done them any good since Richard's death. If William tolerated Norman pretensions to strike the first blow at Lincoln, his younger associates probably rejoiced when that honour was accorded to the Earl of Chester. The *History's* stories of French *ribauds*, boasting in their cups of English inferiority, reflect a rising tide of xenophobia revealed by monastic chroniclers less insular than Matthew Paris.

William's victory was no foregone conclusion. The battle of Muret in 1213 confirmed French predominance in the Languedoc until today. It suggests what might have happened had Lincoln gone the other way, forcing William to carry out his promise to retreat from one island to another bearing Henry III on his shoulders. The River Loire was as significant a political and linguistic boundary in the twelfth century as the English Channel. This did not prevent northern French Crusaders, among them the Dauphin as Louis VIII, stamping out Languedoc's legal autonomy and distinctive culture. French invasion plans in 1213 had the stated aim of uniting the French and English thrones. Philip Augustus and his successors had both the appetite and the capacity for game-changing conquest.

The comparison with Languedoc may be misleading. Southern France was less united than England. Its leaders were excommunicated heretics, ripe for dispossession. The Anglo-Norman nobility, on the other hand, were thoroughly entrenched. A new language, Middle English, was emerging from the mixture of Norman French and Anglo-Saxon or Old English. Among themselves, however, the elite spoke French well into the fourteenth century, especially at court. Baronial calls for English self-government and the expulsion of aliens co-existed with repeated appeals to foreign leaders, first the Dauphin, later the younger Simon de Montfort. Had the Dauphin won in 1217, he would have needed to reward significant numbers of his French followers with English estates, with unpredictable consequences for England's emergent cultural unity. The Scots and Welsh would have expected their reward. Could Louis have resisted the permanent transfer of Northumberland, Westmorland, and Cumberland to his Scottish ally, moving the border south from the Tweed to the Tyne and Morecambe Bay?

Increased isolation from the continent following Louis's defeat clearly reinforced English insularity after 1217. Politics continued down the well-established track of opposition to the Crown, unlike France where a weaker monarchy was perceived as the guardian of the poor against over-powerful magnates. The myth of St Louis, the Dauphin's pious successor, dispensing justice under a tree provides a stark contrast to the erratic despotism of King John that had made Magna Carta necessary. The Dauphin confirmed the charter, but the royalists under William's leadership made it their own, reflecting a common thirst for the liberties it embodied. Reissued twice by the Marshal, a definitive version was forced upon Henry III in 1225 in exchange for cash to defend Poitou against the French.

Magna Carta remains one of three iconic English historical documents, alongside Domesday Book and the Bayeux Tapestry. Several of its provisions remain on the Statute Book. Most notable are chapter 39 which forbids the imprisonment, dispossession, outlawry, or exile of any free man, except by 'lawful judgement of his peers or by the law of the land', and chapter 40 which forbids the denial, delay, or sale of justice. As the thirteenth century continued, the charter gathered authority to become the touchstone of good governance. Copies were kept in the counties for ready reference. No king ever dared sell justice again. The final reissue was sealed by that most assertive monarch Edward I in 1297. Magna Carta by then was inextricably linked with ideas of representative government and trial by jury, as 'parliament' acquired a broader context than the *History*'s simple meaning of a 'parley', and juries started assessing evidence for themselves. The sixteenth-century humanist Polydore Vergil saw 1297 as the moment the English achieved the ultimate liberty of not being taxed without consultation. A century later, Magna Carta began a new career as opponents of Stuart absolutism used it to attack royal monopolies, prerogative courts, and forced loans.

Puritan emigrants took Magna Carta's ideas to North America, where chapter 39 of the 1216 charter found its way into the Fifth Amendment of the United States constitution. Victorian historians saw the charter as England's first national event uniting all free men, a symbol of thirteenth-century social and cultural progress. Despite modern attempts to debunk it as a barons' charter, a good thing for everyone except the common people, Magna Carta remains a talisman of liberty. The US Supreme Court has referred to it when considering the plight of Guantanamo Bay detainees. Activists in orange boiler suits have brandished copies of chapters 39 and 40 outside Parliament when protesting the same issue. The British Prime Minister, David Cameron, cited Magna Carta at Strasbourg in January 2012 as evidence of Great Britain's long-standing commitment to human rights (*sic*), and has proposed that key quotations should appear in the Citizenship Test. A New York auctioneer has described a copy of the 1297 reissue as 'the birth certificate of freedom'.

Magna Carta's celebrity has outlived that of its guardian; others have usurped his central role. Stephen Langton is credited with framing the charter; Peter des Roches with masterminding victory at Lincoln; Guala with clinching the deal at Kingston. Langton, however, spent the crucial years in exile, having failed to impose the charter on either king or rebels. Des Roches found the chink in Lincoln's defences, but it was the Marshal who led the decisive charge. As for the decision to march on Lincoln, Roger of Wendover confirms William's leadership. Monastic accounts like the *Merton Chronicle* name Guala rather than William at Kingston, but the *History* and Anonymous of Béthune demonstrate the latter's control of the negotiations. Three months earlier, Guala's intransigence had wrecked the June peace talks, exposing the country to a third summer of civil war. As Paul Meyer commented, William was the enemy of unnecessary rigour. If he deprived the eloping couple of their usurious capital, he also prevented his companions despoiling them of their horses and other goods. The Marshal's peace of reconciliation, accompanied by positive steps to re-establish legal and financial order, steered a careful course between a relapse into the anarchy of his childhood, and the ultra-royalist reaction that Bishop Peter might have preferred.

Ecclesiastical obfuscation of the laity's political role is common in medieval narratives. Preservation of William's memory was the task of his descendants, whose efforts gave us the *History*. The fruit of William and Isabel's union, however, withered on the bough. Not one of their five sons left an heir. Baronial lineages typically lasted six generations; the Marshals managed only three. Matthew Paris ascribed this to an ancient quarrel between the Marshal and the Irish Bishop of Fearns, whose curse hung over William's deathbed. Today we might seek medical or social causes. Restriction of marriage to the elder sons of aristocratic families was a dangerous strategy, preserving their patrimony at the risk of physical extinction.

William the Younger was betrothed to Baldwin of Béthune's daughter, but the lady fell an early victim to gluttonous death. He did not remarry until 1224, dying without issue in 1231. Besides marrying late, aristocratic youth diced with death in tournaments, revolts, and border disputes. All Henry II's adult sons died violently or on campaign. The fifteen years following the younger Marshal's death swept away his male siblings. Richard died of wounds suffered during a battle with Peter des Roches's Poitevins, deserted by his own knights. Gilbert forsook holy orders to claim his inheritance, and was dragged to death by an unmanageable horse at Hertford, its reins allegedly cut through. The last two Marshals died within weeks of each other late in 1245; Ansel not yet forty. The husbands of William's daughters divided his estates: the modern Dukes of Norfolk inherit the title of Earl Marshal through Matilda, the eldest, named after the queen empress for whom the first John Marshal fought and bled. Memories of William's part in the stirring events of King John's reign had faded by Tudor times. Shakespeare's play *King John* makes no mention of Magna Carta or Lincoln. The Earl of Pembroke plays a minor role, eclipsed by Hubert de Burgh and the fictional Bastard Faulconbridge. Grant's *British Battles by Land and Sea*, a monument of Victorian popular military history, ignores Lincoln entirely and credits 'Dover' to the justiciar.

King John's short action-packed reign dominates the early thirteenth-century narrative. The loss of Normandy, the Interdict, above all his outsize wickedness make far better material for tragedy or for morality play than the interminable reign of his bumbling successor. William's brief regency falls between the two. Regents are rarely memorable. Few recall the Duke of Bedford's seventeen-year stewardship after Henry V's premature death, or the Lords Protector of Edward VI's brief reign. The regnal focus of standard historiography does not help. Volume III of the *Oxford History of England* ends with John's death, leaving volume IV – like William – to pick up the pieces. The issue, abrogation, and multiple reissue of Magna Carta does not help, entangling the casual reader in a plethora of dates and renumbered clauses.

A civil war in which the reactionary defenders of English liberties called on the ancestral enemy for assistance sits uncomfortably within a national myth that presents English history as a triumphant progress towards constitutional government and imperial greatness. The conflict's moral ambiguity permeates William's career. Committed by his knightly calling to defending the Church and the disarmed population, he consorted with despoilers of cathedrals like the Young King and Fawkes of Bréauté. No wonder William jumped at Guala's offer of remission and forgiveness of his sins. A longing for the clear-cut choices of the tournament field may have inspired William's repeated appeals to trial by combat. Alternatively, he may have calculated upon the networks of interest and friendship he had built up to keep him safe. The supreme decision to march on Lincoln may have stemmed from an overwhelming urge to end the uncertainties of civil war, or from deeper strategic calculation. William lived long enough to play and reprise a variety of roles. He was at one level the finest knight– *li proz, li franz e li lealz* as Philip Augustus described him – defending his lord in tournament and war, doing great deeds and undertaking great journeys. He was also the subtle *prud'homme*, combining the simplicity and deviousness of all great commanders. Able to appeal to the humble sergeants and crossbowmen who led the way at Lincoln, he could also weave a wide flung net of naval, land, and guerrilla forces to ensnare the Dauphin at Winchelsea.

Lincoln presents a similar combination of knightly audacity with strategic subtlety, first with the turning movement via Torksey, then with the double break-in through the castle and West Gate. A small-scale military masterpiece, Lincoln's dynastic and constitutional consequences make it England's most important battle between

Hastings and the Armada's defeat in 1588. Simon de Montfort's triumph at Lewes in 1264 was reversed a year later at Evesham. Better known encounters at Towton and Bosworth merely set a new military adventurer on the throne. After Lincoln William faced the very modern challenge of restoring peace to a war-torn country with a shattered economy, a task effected with none of the bloody purges that terminated England's later medieval conflicts. The 6,000 lines that the *History* devotes to William's tournament career were the distant reflection of a celebrity that was just a memory, a distraction from his true achievement.

Older than Winston Churchill was when he became Prime Minister in 1940, William rallied a country on the brink of defeat at an age when most men of his day had difficulty walking, let alone leading a cavalry charge. Other national heroes appear hollow by comparison: Drake was a slave trader; Lords Nelson and Montgomery lacked political sense. Cromwell, who won greater victories than William and restored peace after a longer civil war, remains tainted by the smouldering antagonisms of his day and the falsehoods of his enemies. Where Churchill liked to pose as a soldier, William was the real thing. He better resembles the Duke of Wellington, another military leader turned politician, a man whom even his enemies might respect. The closest comparison might be 'Honest George Monck', the Parliamentarian general who bloodlessly restored the monarchy after Cromwell's death, reconciled veterans of both sides, and oversaw royal government until his death.

William's physical memorial lies off the beaten track, just south of Fleet Street down Inner Temple Lane in London's legal quarter. The exact site of his burial is lost, but his effigy lies to the left of the Temple Church's modern entrance in the south face of the nave, flanked by those of his sons and five other knights. His feet rest on a dog – the symbol of loyalty. Nearly destroyed by German incendiary bombs, the effigy lacks its nose, the chain mail hood and clipped moustache suggesting a British soldier of the Great War, in a balaclava helmet. Unlike more celebrated rivals, William is safe indoors, spared the indignities of London weather and bird life. Surrounded by the quiet beauty of the Temple, the earl lies where he chose, within earshot of a liturgy sung in the vernacular whose birth he witnessed – a worthy setting for the knight who saved England.

GLOSSARY

arbalestrier	user of an arbalest or crossbow
avoué	hereditary title of secular representative of ecclesiastical institution
bachelier	unmarried household knight
bataille	squadron of mounted knights/sergeants 100–120 strong, cf. *eschiele*
Brabançon	mercenary soldier originally from Brabant in Flanders
Boulonnais	appertaining to Boulogne
chevauchée	mounted raiding expedition
Cinque Ports	confederacy of Channel ports, originally five in number
cog	large sailing ship, cf. *nef*
commençailles	opening stages of a tournament
conroi	troop of mounted knights/sergeants twelve to twenty-four strong
curialis	member of the court
demesne	land exploited directly by a feudal lord
denier	silver penny; the standard unit of currency
destrier	war horse
eschiele	squadron of mounted knights/sergeants 100–120 strong, cf. *bataille*
fee	landed estate held in exchange for military service; also *feodum* or fief
gambeson	padded protective jacket used by mounted or foot troops, cf. *pourpoint*

haubergeon	short mail shirt, sometimes hooded, used by foot troops
hauberk	long mail shirt with hood, used by mounted troops
Hospitaller	knightly monk, member of the religious order of the Hospital of St John
knot	nautical measure of speed = 1 sea mile per hour (2025yd/1.8km)
losengier	deceitful flatterer
Marcher	Anglo-Norman lord or knight resident on the Welsh border
mesnie	band of knights maintained in a lord's household
Michaelmas	29 September
nef	large sailing ship, cf. cog
Outremer	Frankish overseas possessions in the East, e.g. Kingdom of Jerusalem
palfrey	gentleman's riding horse
perrière	small counter-weight stone-thrower or *petraria*
pourpoint	padded linen jacket, cf. gambeson
Poitevin	someone from Poitou, south of the Loire
prud'homme	counsellor of repute
recet	palisaded refuge at tournament
rouncey	poor-quality riding horse or pack horse
routier	member of a band of mercenary soldiers or *ruta*
scutage	tax levied on knights in lieu of personal service
seneschal	originally steward of a great house, hence deputy for its absent lord
sergeant	mounted or foot soldier of non-noble origin
snecca	fast longship powered by oars, from *snekkjur* or 'snake'
tallage	tax levied on towns and the royal demesne
Templar	knightly monk, member of the religious order of the Temple
Tourangeau	someone from Touraine, near Tours on the Loire
trébuchet	large counter-weight stone-thrower
trovère	troubadour or poet
vavassour	knightly warrior living on his own estate

SELECT
BIBLIOGRAPHY

Primary sources are identified by name used in text, followed by published title, editor, volume(s) if relevant, publisher, and date; secondary works by author, title, publisher, and date; entries for articles also specify the publishing journal, volume, and page numbers. Abbreviations used are as below:

CUP	Cambridge University Press
EHR	English Historical Review
MM	Mariner's Mirror
OUP	Oxford University Press
RS	Rolls Series
TRHS	Transactions of the Royal Historical Society
W&N	Weidenfeld and Nicolson
Yale	Yale University Press

All publishers are London unless otherwise specified.

Primary Sources

Anglo-Saxon Chronicle: *The Anglo-Saxon Chronicles*, ed. M. Swanton (Phoenix, 2000)

Anonymous of Béthune: *Histoire des Ducs de Normandie et des Rois d'Angleterre*, ed. F. Michel (Societé de l'Histoire de France, Paris, 1840)

Barnwell Chronicle: *Memoriale fratris Walteri de Coventria*, ed. W. Stubbs, vol. ii (RS 58, 1872–73)

Chronicle of the Princes: *Brut Tywysogion or the Chronicle of the Princes*, ed. T. Jones (RS 17, 1860)

Crusades:

- *The Third Crusade (Itinerarium Peregrinorum et Gesta Regis Ricardi)*, ed. K Fenwick (Folio, 1958)

- *Joinville and Villehardouin: Chronicles of the Crusades*, ed. M.R.B. Shaw (Penguin 1963)

- *Chronicles of the First Crusade*, ed. C. Tyerman (Penguin, 2012)

Gervase of Canterbury: *The Historical Works of Gervase of Canterbury*, ed. W. Stubbs, vol. ii (RS 66, 1879–80)

Gesta Abbiatum Monasterii Sancti Albani, ed. H.T. Riley (three vols, RS 28, 1867–69)

Gesta Stephani, ed. R. Howlett in *Chronicles of the Reigns of Stephen, Henry II and Richard I*, iii (RS 82, 1884)

Henry of Huntingdon: *The History of the English People* 1000–1154, tr. D. Greenaway (OUP, 1996 & 2002)

History of William Marshal:

- *L'Histoire de Guillaume le Maréchal*, ed. P. Meyer (three vols, Societé de l'Histoire de France, 1891–1901)

- *The History of William the Marshal*, ed. A.J. Holden, D. Gregory and D. Crouch (three vols, Anglo–Norman Texts Society 2002–07)

Jocelin of Brakelond: *The Chronicle of Jocelin of Brakelond*, ed. Sir E. Clarke (John Murray, 1907)

John of Worcester (originally known as Florence): *A History of the Kings of England*, ed. J. Stevenson (Llanerch, Dyfed, n.d.)

Jordan of Fantôme: *Contemporary Chronicles of the Middle Ages*, ed. J. Stevenson (Llanerch, Dyfed, 1988)

Loch Cé: *Annals of Loch Cé – A Chronicle of Irish Affairs AD1014–AD1590*, tr. W. Hennessy, vol. i (RS 54, 1871)

Matthew Paris: *Chronica Maiora Matthaei Parisiensis*, ed. H.R. Luard, vols ii & iii (RS 57, 1884–89)

Melsa Chronicle: *Chronica Monasterii de Melsa*, ed. E.A. Bond, vol. i (RS 43, 1866–68)

Monastic Annals: *Annales Monastici*, ed. H.R. Luard (four vols, RS 36, 1865–69):
i) Margan, Tewkesbury, Burton
ii) Winchester, Waverley
iii) Dunstable, Bermondsey
iv) Wykes, Worcester

Ousama: Un prince syrien face aus croisés, ed. A. Miquel (Tallandier, Paris 1986)

Ralph of Coggeshall: *Radulphi de Coggeshall Chronicon Anglicanum*, ed. J. Stevenson (RS 66, 1875)

Ralph of Diceto: *The Historical Works of Master Ralph de Diceto*, ed. W. Stubbs (two vols, RS 68, 1876)

Robert of Torigni: *The Chronicle of Robert of Torigni*, ed. R. Howlett in *Chronicles of the Reigns of Stephen, Henry II and Richard I*, vol. iv (RS 82, 1889)

Roger of Howden: *Chronica Magistri Rogeri de Hoveden*, ed. W. Stubbs (four vols, RS 51, 1868)

Roger of Wendover's Flowers of History, tr. J.A. Giles (Llanerch, Dyfed, 1996)

- *Flores Historiarum of Roger of Wendover*, ed. H.R. Luard, vol. ii (RS, 1890)

Walter of Guisborough: *The Chronicle of Walter of Guisborough*, ed. H. Rothwell (Camden Soc, 1957)

Welsh Annals: *Annales Cambriae*, ed. J. Williams ab Ithel (RS 20, 1860)

William of Malmesbury: *Contemporary Chronicles of the Middle Ages*, ed. J. Stevenson (Llanerch, Dyfed, 1988)

William of Newburgh: *Historia Rerum Anglicarum*, ed. R. Howlett in *Chronicles of the Reigns of Stephen, Henry II and Richard I* (two vols, RS 82, 1884)

Secondary Sources

Baldwin, J., *The Government of Philip Augustus: Foundations of French Royal Power in the Middle Ages* (University of California, CA, 1986)

Barlow, F., *The Feudal Kingdom of England 1042–1216* (Longman, 1998)

Bartlett, R., *England under the Norman and Angevin Kings 1075–1225* (OUP, 2000)

Beeler, J., *Warfare in Feudal Europe 730–1200* (Cornell University, NY, 1971)

Beeler, J., *Warfare in England 1066–1189* (Ithaca, NY, 1966)

Beffeyte, R., *Les Machines de Guerre au Moyen Age* (Ouest France, 2008)

Brindle, S., *Dover Castle* (English Heritage, 2012)

Brooks, F.W., *The English Naval Forces 1199–1272* (no pub., 1933)

Brooks, F.W., 'The Battle of Damme', *MM* xvi (1930) 263–71

Brooks, F.W., 'Naval Administration and the Raising of Fleets under John and Henry', *MM* xv (1929) 351–90

Brooks, F.W., 'The King's Ships and Galleys, under John and Henry III', *MM* xv (1929) 15–48

Brooks, F.W., 'Naval Armament in the Thirteenth Century', *MM* xiv (1928) 115–31

Brooks, F.W. and Oakley, F., 'The Campaign and Battle of Lincoln 1217', *Associated Architectural Societies Reports & Papers* xxxvi 2 (1922) 295–312

Brooks, R., *Cassell's Battlefields of Britain and Ireland* (W&N, 2005)

Brown, R.A., *Rochester Castle, Kent* (English Heritage, 1989)

Burgess, G.S., *Two Medieval Outlaws: The Romances of Eustace the Monk & Fauke Fitzwaryn* (Boydell, Woodbridge, Suffolk, 1997)

Cannon, H.L., 'The Battle of Sandwich and Eustace the Monk', *EHR* xxvi (1912) 649–70

Carpenter, D.A., *The Struggle for Mastery* (Allen Lane, 2003)

Carpenter, D.A., *The Minority of Henry III* (Methuen, 1990)

Church, S.D. (ed.), *King John New Interpretations* (Boydell, Woodbridge Suffolk, 2007)

Contamine, P. (tr. M. Jones), *War in the Middle Ages* (Blackwell, Oxford, 1984)

Crouch, D., *William the Marshal: Knighthood, War and Chivalry 1147–1219* (Longman, 2002)

Danziger, D. and J. Gillingham, *1215 The Year of Magna Carta* (Hodder & Stoughton, 2003)

Davies, R.R., *Conquest, Coexistence and Change – Wales 1063–1415* (OUP, 1987)

Delbruck H. (tr. W.J. Renfroe), *History of the Art of War*, vol. iii (University of Nebraska, 1990)

Duby, G., *France in the Middle Ages* (Blackwell, Oxford, 1984)

Duby, G., *Guillaume le Marechal ou le meilleure chevalier du monde* (Fayard, Paris, 1984) tr. as *The Flower of Chivalry* (1986)

Duby, G., *Le dimanche de Bouvines* (Gallimard, Pais, 1973) tr. C. Tihanyi as *The Legend of Bouvines, Religion and Culture in the Middle Ages* (CUP, 1990)

Duggan, A., *Leopards and Lilies* (Chatto & Windus, 1954)

Edbury, P.W., *Crusade and Settlement, Papers read at the First Conference of the Society for the Study of the Crusades,* etc (Cardiff University, 1985)

Edgar, J.G., *Runnymede and Lincoln Fair* (JM Dent, 1908)

Flori, J., *Chevaliers et chevalerie au Moyen Âge* (Hachette, Paris, 2008)

France, J., *Western Warfare in the Age of the Crusades 1000–1300* (Routledge, 2007)

Gillingham, J., *The Angevin Empire* (Edward Arnold, 1984)

Gillingham, J., *Richard I* (Yale, 1999)

Gillingham, J., 'Richard I and the Art of War in the Middle Ages' (in Strickland, *Anglo-Norman Warfare*)

Gillingham, J., 'War and Chivalry in the History of William the Marshal' (Strickland *op. cit.*)

Grainge, G., *The Roman Invasions of Britain* (Tempus, 2005)

Grant, J., *British Battles by Land and Sea,* vol. i (Cassell, undated)

Harding, A., *England in the Thirteenth Century* (CUP, 1993)

Hattendorf, J.B. and Knight, R.J.B., *British Naval Documents 1216–1961* (Navy Records Society, 1993)

Hill, J.W.F., *Medieval Lincoln* (CUP, 1948)

Hill, R., *The Battle of Stockbridge 1141* (1989) in C. Harper Bill, *Studies in Medieval History Presented to R Allen Brown* pp.173–38 (Boydell, Woodbridge, 1989)

Holt, J.C., *Magna Carta and Medieval Government* (Hambledon, 1985)

Holt, J.C., *Magna Carta* (CUP, 1965)

Holt, J.C., *King John* (Historical Association, 1963)

Jones, M.J., *Lincoln: History and Guide* (History Press, Stroud, 2011)

Keen, M. (ed.), *Medieval Warfare: A History* (OUP, 1999)

Keen, M., *Chivalry* (Yale, 1984)

King, E., 'Mountsorrel and its Region in King Stephen's Reign', *Huntingdon Library Quarterly* xliv (1980) 1–10

Lindley, P. (ed.), *The Early History of Lincoln Castle* (Society for Lincolnshire History & Archeology 2004)

Lloyd, S.D., '"Political Crusades" in England c.1215–17 and c.1263–5' (in Edbury, *Crusade and Settlement*)

McLynn, S., *Blood Cries Afar: the Forgotten Invasion of England 1216* (Spellmount, 2011)

McLynn, S., *By Sword and Fire* (W&N, 2008)

Morris, J.E., *The Welsh Wars of Edward I* (OUP, 1901)

Mortimer, R., *Angevin England 1154–1258* (Blackwell, Oxford 1994)

Nicolas, Sir N.H., *A History of the Royal Navy from the Earliest Times to the Wars of the French Revolution*, vol. i (London, 1847)

Norgate, K., *The Minority of Henry III* (MacMillan, 1912)

Oman, Sir C., *The History of the Art of War in the Middle Ages*, vol. i (Methuen, 1924)

Painter, S., *William Marshal: Knight Errant, Baron and Regent of England* (Baltimore, 1933, reprinted 1971)

Petit-Dutaillis, C., *Etude sur le regne de Louis VIII 1187–1226* (Bovillar, Paris, 1894)

Poole, A.L., *From Domesday Book to Magna Carta 1087–1216* (OUP, 1955)

Portal, M., *The Great Hall at Winchester Castle* (Warren, Winchester, 1899)

Powicke, Sir M., *The Thirteenth Century 1216–1307* (OUP, 1962)

Powicke, Sir M., *The Loss of Normandy 1189–1204* (Manchester University Press, 1961)

Prestwich, M., *Armies and Warfare in the Middle Ages, the English Experience* (Yale, 1996)

Rodger, N.A.M., *The Safeguard of the Sea: A Naval History of Britain 660–1649* (Harper Collins, 1997)

Rodgers, Vice Admiral W.L. USN, *Naval Warfare under Oars 4th to 16th Centuries* (US Naval Institute MD, 1939)

Rose, S., *Medieval Naval Warfare 1000–1500* (Routledge, 2002)

Rothwell, H. (ed.), *English Historical Documents 1189–1327* (OUP, 1975)

Smail, R.C., *Crusading Warfare 1097–1193* (CUP, 1978)

Stephens, G.R., 'A Note on William of Cassingham', *Speculum* 16 (1941) 216–23

Strayer, J.R., *The Albigensian Crusades* (University of Michigan, 1992)

Strickland, M. (ed.), *Anglo-Norman Warfare* (Boydell, Woodbridge, 1997)

Strickland, M., *Against the Lord's Anointed: Aspects of War and Baronial Rebellion in England and Normandy 1066–1265* (CUP, 1994)

Stringer, K.J., *The Reign of Stephen: Kingship, Warfare and Government in Twelfth Century England* (Routledge, 1993)

Stubbs, W. (ed.), *Select Charters* (OUP, 1966)

Thomas, H.M., *The English and the Normans Ethnic Hostility, Assimilation and Identity 1066–1220* (OUP, 2003)

Tout, T.F., 'The Fair of Lincoln and the "Histoire de Guillaume le Marechal"', *EHR* xviii (1903) 240–65

Turner, G.J., 'The Minority of Henry III, part 1', *TRHS* (New Series) xviii (1904) 245–95

Turner, R., *Chepstow Castle* (CADW, 2006)

Turner, R.V., *King John* (Longman, 1994)

Verbruggen, J.F., *The Art of Warfare in Western Europe during the Middle Ages* (Boydell, Woodbridge Suffolk, 1997)

Vincent, N., *Peter des Roches: An Alien in English Politics 1205–1238* (CUP, 1996)

War Office, *Field Service Pocket Book* (HMSO, 1914)

War Office, *Field Service Regulations Vol. II Operations 1924* (HMSO, 1924)

Warren, W.L., *King John* (Eyre & Methuen, 1978)

Wright, T. (ed.), *The Political Songs of England* (Camden Society, 1839) rep. 1996

INDEX